THE LIFE OF ROBERT, LORD CLIVE (VOLUME II)

First published 1863
This edition published by Lector House in 2024

ISBN: 978-93-6138-381-6

Lector House LLP
Registered Office: H. No. 96, Block C, Tomar Colony,
Burari, Delhi – 110084, India
info@lectorhouse.com
www.lectorhouse.com

THE LIFE OF ROBERT, LORD CLIVE (VOLUME II)

JOHN MALCOLM

2024

LECTOR HOUSE LLP

THE LIFE OF ROBERT, LORD CLIVE
(VOLUME II)

COLLECTED FROM THE FAMILY PAPERS COMMUNICATED BY THE EARL OF POWIS.

BY

MAJOR-GENERAL
SIR JOHN MALCOLM, G.C.B. F.R.S. &C.

IN THREE VOLUMES,
VOL. II.

WITH A PORTRAIT AND MAP.

CONTENTS

VOLUME II.

MEMOIRS OF LORD CLIVE.

CHAPTER IX.

Success of the Expedition sent to the Northern Circars under Colonel Forde, 1758.—Transactions at Madras.—Siege of that Place by Lally

In the commencement of the last chapter mention was made of the sailing of the expedition which Clive detached to the Northern Circars under Colonel Forde, in September, 1758. Before narrating the operations of that force, it will be necessary to take a short retrospect of the affairs of the Deckan.

We have already seen[1] the success of Bussy in defeating the combination formed against him at the Court of Salabut Jung. When he was surrounded in the post he had taken at Hyderabad, Ibrahim Khan, to whom he had intrusted the management of the Northern Circars, threw off his allegiance. Bussy, sensible of the great value of the newly acquired possessions, obtained the Subah's permission to march with the greater part of his force to punish Ibrahim Khan, and settle the countries ceded to him. He proceeded by the route of Bezoara to Rajahmundry. Ibrahim Khan fled at his approach; but Vizeram Raz, the Hindu zemindar, or ruler, of the country of Chicacole, joined him from his capital of Vizianagur with a considerable body of men. Bussy thought it politic to give Vizeram Raz every support; and the French troops were employed in compelling the submission of his refractory chiefs, each of whom had his petty fastness, and, relying on its natural or artificial strength, and the devoted attachment and valour of his followers, yielded but an imperfect obedience to his acknowledged lord, and seldom paid his tribute until compelled by superior force.

The French arms were first directed by Vizeram Raz to the attack of Rangarow, Rajah of Boobilee, against whom he cherished a deadly hatred. The fort of this chief could not resist European artillery; but its defenders scorned to yield. They fought to the last; and the Rajah, with all those capable of bearing arms, except four who reserved their lives for a deed of vengeance, fell during the siege or on the breach. A more appalling spectacle than that of the carnage of these brave men awaited the successful assailants. In the interior of this stronghold, they found only the smoking ruins of houses, and the mangled and burnt bodies of all who were its late inhabitants; neither age nor sex was spared in the dreadful sacrifice: not a human being seemed to be left over whom his enemies could triumph. As

[1] Vide Vol. I. p. 73.

the horror-struck victors were contemplating this scene of desolation and of death, an old man rushed from the smoking ruins with a child in his arms. He was conducted to M. Law, who commanded the party: "This is the son of Rangarow," said the old man, "whom I have preserved against his father's will." The safety of this boy was felt as some alleviation of the horrid catastrophe. He was carried to Bussy, who received and treated him with that humanity and generosity which belonged to his character[2], constituting himself his guardian, and securing to him the terms offered to his father, before his fort was attacked.

Three nights after this event the camp was surprised by a tumult, and Bussy soon learned that two[3] of the four followers of Rangarow before mentioned had made their way to the tent of Vizeram Raz, and stabbed the inveterate enemy of their race[4] in thirty-two places. They might have escaped, but they disdained flight. "Look here," they said to the guards by whom they were attacked, "we are satisfied." Bussy, happy to leave such a scene of horror and bloodshed, continued his march north to Ganjam, where he received letters from his countrymen in Bengal, and from the Nabob Suraj-u-Dowlah, urging his march to that country to destroy the English. While waiting in expectation of persons from Moorshedabad to arrange for his advance through Cuttack, he heard of the fall of Chandernagore; on which he appears to have abandoned all thoughts of proceeding to Bengal, though he no doubt contrived to feed Meer Jaffier with hopes which might stimulate him to acts of hostility against the enemies of France.

Bussy's next effort was against Vizagapatam, which was compelled to surrender. His treatment of the English, whom he made prisoners, was more than humane; it was kind[5] and liberal. From thence he went to Rajahmundry, where he heard of a change at the court of the Subah very unfavourable to the views and interests of the French in the Deckan.

In consequence of an intrigue between Shahnavaze Khan, the prime minister, and the Subah's brothers, Nizam Ali Khan and Basalut Jung, the latter two princes had come into power; and, having compelled the weak Salabut Jung to intrust them with his great seal, had reduced him to a cipher in his own dominions. The French officer left in charge of the body of men which remained in the Subah's camp, had neither the talent nor the influence to counteract these intrigues, and limited himself to the guarding of Salabut Jung's person, and reporting to Bussy events as they occurred. That experienced commander saw that no time was to be

[2] The particulars of the storm of Boobilee are narrated, by Orme (vol. ii. p. 254.), with the clearness and a feeling which do honoured to that historian. Such scenes as are here described are but too common in the history of India; where Hindus, of a high tribe, often take the heroic, but barbarous, resolution of not leaving a living being for their enemies to triumph over.

[3] The other two remained concealed; but they were bound, by a vow, to murder Vizeram Raz if the first attempt failed.

[4] Rangarow, and his tribe, considered themselves of much higher race than the Rajahs of Vizianagur; and their contempt of his family was one cause of the inveteracy of Vizeram Raz.

[5] "Bussy promised the English their property; and all they claimed as such was resigned to them, without question or discussion."—Orme, vol. ii. p. 263.

lost. He immediately left Rajahmundry, and accomplished the march to Aurungabad, a distance of more than four hundred miles, in twenty-one days. He found on his arrival three separate armies; for Nizam Ali Khan and Basalut Jung had each his own encampment, and the Paishwah Ballajee Bajerow was in the vicinity; that ruler being, it was believed, concerned in the plot laid to deprive the Subah of his power.

The force of Bussy, which consisted of nine hundred Europeans (two hundred of which were cavalry) and five thousand five hundred sepoys, with ten field-pieces, was more than equal to any of the armies, or indeed to any two combined. All waited, therefore, to see the part he would take. He was aided by Hyder Jung, who, having some claims[6] upon the French, and being a man of ability, was raised in consequence by Bussy, who obtained him a title from the Emperor of Delhi. This person was consulted on all occasions, and displayed both talent and address: but his influence made him many enemies, and these were increased by his success in their own arts of intrigue, particularly in corrupting the Governor of Dowlatabad, and gaining that impregnable fortress[7] for the French, by whom it was kept as a place of security for Salabut Jung, instead of being his prison, the purpose for which it is believed to have been destined by the conspirators against his liberty, if not his life.

The Nizam's brothers were compelled to give up the great seal of the Deckan, which was not surrendered without undisguised marks of their indignation, and loud protestations against the European influence which now swayed the councils of their elder brother. Nizam Ali Khan, who showed at this period both ability and boldness, was directed to proceed to his government of Berar, and Basalut Jung to the charge of Adoni. Before his departure Nizam Ali received the ceremonious visits of all the chiefs and nobles in camp. Among others, Hyder Jung paid his respects. When that Omrah was seated, Nizam Ali arose; but made a signal for the former not to move, as he would immediately return. The moment, however, that he left the apartment, his visitor was stabbed to the heart. Letters, which had been previously prepared, were sent to Salabut Jung, Ballajee Row, Basalut Jung, and Bussy; ascribing the death of the French dewan or minister (for such Hyder Jung was termed) to accident; but the truth could not long be concealed, and Nizam Ali fled with some of his best horse to the city of Burhampore[8] in Berar.

[6] The father of Hyder Jung was governor of Masulipatam when Dupleix made himself master of that important fortress, and is believed to have betrayed his trust.

[7] The small fortress of Dowlatabad stands at the distance of eight miles to the north-west of Aurungabad. It is defended by walls and bastions: but what renders it impregnable is the solid rock being scarped perpendicular all round; and in no place is the scarp less than one hundred and eighty feet. The entrance is by a long tunnel, in which there are several traverses cut out of the rock. Shahnavaze Khan had obtained possession of this fortress. The manner in which it was seized by Bussy is minutely described by Orme, vol. ii. p. 345. Bussy himself, attended by a number of officers and three hundred men, went on the pretext of seeing the fort and paying a visit to the Killadar (or Governor); and when the garrison were so stationed by the Killadar, through respect for their guest, that they could make no resistance, he was made a willing prisoner by the French general, and such of his followers as made opposition expelled from the fort.

[8] The rapidity of his flight was great: he is said to have reached Burhampore in twen-

Bussy directed a party to seize Shahnavaze Khan, who was believed to be concerned in the murder; and that minister, with one of his sons, was killed in an affray which took place from his followers opposing the troops of Salabut Jung and the French, that were sent to make him prisoner.

All was for some time in confusion. The principal chiefs in the army hastened to disown any participation in the crime that had been committed; and the Paishwah Ballajee Bajerow sent to Bussy to assure him that he viewed the murder of Hyder Jung with detestation.

Salabut Jung was so greatly enraged with his brother, that Bussy could not prevent his making some marches towards Burhampore; but he soon succeeded in convincing him that the pursuit of Nizam Ali was as impolitic as it would be useless. The fact was, that Bussy did not wish that his nation should appear as the cause of discord in the Subah's family; and he had, also, some anticipation, from the accounts which he had received from Pondicherry, of the changes about to occur in the councils of that settlement. With these impressions, his object was to lead Salabut Jung to Golconda, where he would be conveniently situated for any event which might occur. During this march, M. Conflans arrived in camp with a letter from M. Lally, appointing him second in command to Bussy, and announcing to the latter his intended recall. Bussy, on receiving this intelligence, adopted measures to secure the garrison he had left in Dowlatabad reaching him in safety. This accomplished, he proceeded with the Subah to Hyderabad, where the commands of Lally were received, directing him to abandon all his projects in the Deckan, and to hasten with part of his troops to Pondicherry, leaving the remainder under Conflans to protect the Northern Circars, and to garrison Masulipatam, the able chief of which (Moracin) was also recalled.

The enemies of the French in the Deckan, and those who dreaded their rise, saw Bussy's preparations to depart with surprise and delight. None, however, could account for this sudden abandonment of an influence and strength which had been established with such labour and ability.

Salabut Jung had very different feelings; he viewed the departure of Bussy with deep despondency. It was the loss, as he said, to him, of his friend and preserver; and his mind presented sad forebodings of his future fate. These he communicated to Bussy, who supported him by an assurance that he would return; and in that expectation he was no doubt sincere; for, notwithstanding what he had heard of the character of Lally, he could not have anticipated that any individual in M. Lally's situation could have been so blinded by prejudice, and so misled by his passions, as to abandon the advantages which a commanding influence in the councils of the Deckan must have given to the French, at a period so critical to their interests in India.

When Bussy had been compelled to march to Aurungabad, he left but a small body of men in the Northern Circars; and Anunderauze, the successor of Vizeram Raz, no longer overawed by the presence of a French force, and desiring to throw off his dependence upon that nation, courted the alliance of the British Govern-

ty-four hours. The distance is one hundred and fifty miles.

ment.[9] Clive appears at this period to have been well-informed of the situation of parties at the court of the Subah of the Deckan. He had received an overture from Nizam Ali Khan, who, prompted by his hostility to Bussy, solicited the aid of the English. In his answer to this letter[10], Clive gives that Prince every assurance of friendship; and about two months[11] afterwards, he informs him of his having sent Colonel Forde into the Circars, to retake settlements in the Subah's dominions from which the English had been expelled by the French; and requests Nizam Ali to aid him, and to obtain the assistance of his brother the Subah in accomplishing that just object.

To Anunderauze, Clive wrote[12] in terms calculated to conciliate his continued friendship: he congratulated him on the advantages he had gained over the French, and desired him to consult with Colonel Forde on the operations necessary to expel that nation from the Northern Circars. He also stated his expectation of the Rajah's benefiting so much by the aid of this force, that he would contribute to defray its expenses. It was a serious error[13] to repose such confidence on this source of supply. It failed; and its failure caused great delays, and had nearly defeated the whole object of the expedition.

Colonel Forde, after retaking Vizagapatam, marched towards Rajahmundry, near which he engaged and completely defeated M. Conflans, who retired rapidly towards Masulipatam, leaving his guns and camp equipage in the hands of the English. Anunderauze, who remained in the rear, and either from caution or fear took no part in this contest, appeared averse to proceed any further south; nor was it until Colonel Forde had signed an engagement which secured him great advantages, that he consented to give him a small sum of money to relieve the urgent distresses of the English troops, and to accompany him in his march. Fifty days were thus lost; and the French had not only recovered from their panic, but their ally Salabut Jung was advancing, and a small French corps of observation had begun to plunder the countries in the rear of the English; while M. Conflans, with his main body, prepared to defend Masulipatam, scarcely expecting, however, that the English would attempt to attack a fortress the garrison of which outnumbered the troops of the assailants. But the result proved he was unacquainted with the bold character of the British commander.

To increase the embarrassments of Colonel Forde, the treasure sent from Bengal being prevented from reaching him by the operations of the French corps of observation, the distress for want of money, added to other grievances, caused the European part of his force to mutiny and leave their lines, threatening to march away. Being desired to state specifically their complaints, they demanded, through

[9] A correspondence, between this petty prince and Clive, was opened through the medium of an English merchant named Bristow.

[10] Clive's answer to Nizam Ali Khan is dated 27th July, 1758.

[11] 17th September, 1758.

[12] 7th July, and 17th September.

[13] Clive appears to have despatched treasure for this corps the moment he learned that none was likely to be recovered either from Anunderauze or the revenues of the country: but the activity of the French corps of observation prevented, for some period, Colonel Forde from receiving the benefit of this supply.

deputies, the immediate payment of the prize-money due to them, and an assurance that, if Masulipatam fell, they should have the whole of the prize-money, and not half, as was the usage with the Company's troops, the other half being reserved as the right of Government. The commander promised that the prize-money due should be paid from the first treasure received; and added, that he would recommend the full prize-money to be given them should their valour be crowned with success. Satisfied with these assurances, they returned to their duty, and the siege was prosecuted with vigour.

Salabut Jung, with a large army, was now within forty miles; and his mandates were issued to all Zemindars and others, to aid the French and to act against the English. The alarmed Anunderauze, on hearing this order, struck his tents, and marched sixteen miles towards his own country. Colonel Forde sent after him, to represent the extreme folly of his conduct: he could not (he directed his agent to explain to the Rajah) expect to escape the numerous parties of horse of the Subah; and, if he did, he had to encounter the French corps of observation, which was in the neighbourhood of Rajahmundry: the capture of Masulipatam, therefore, was the only chance he had for safety. The good sense of this remonstrance had its effect: the Rajah returned; and Colonel Forde, in order to inspire him and other natives with confidence, solicited and obtained leave to send a person to the camp of the Subah to explain the cause of the expedition, and its limited object of recovering the English factories, and taking those of the French upon the sea-coast. Mr. John Johnstone of the Civil Service, who had been the active co-adjutor of Colonel Forde throughout this expedition, was deputed to Salabut Jung; and the delay of a few days, which it was expected his mission would create, was deemed of ultimate importance to the success of the siege.

The situation of Colonel Forde was at this moment truly critical. Though the principal breach appeared practicable, the advance to the attack was over a deep morass, and the ditch of the fort could only be passed at ebb tide: a garrison superior to the besiegers was within the walls; and the army of the Subah was near Masulipatam, and on the point of forming a junction with the French corps of observation. To add to these difficulties, the ammunition for the heavy guns was nearly expended. Under these circumstances, and having no hope of being able to effect a retreat by land, Colonel Forde had only the choice between saving his troops by embarking them, or immediately storming the fort. He determined on the latter; and made a disposition for three attacks, one of which was a false one, for the purpose of distracting the attention of the enemy from the main attack on the north-east angle of the fort.

In addition to this disposition of his own force, the troops of Anunderauze were directed to move along the causeway that crossed the morass, and, by their skirmishing, to alarm the enemy at the principal gateway, and to keep a part of the garrison employed in the ravelin and outworks near it. To the Rajah's people was also entrusted the care of the camp; for every man of the English force was engaged in the storm.

The attack commenced at midnight; and though a great proportion of the troops soon forced their way into the interior of the place, a straggling fire was kept up for some hours, when M. Conflans surrendered, and the English found, in the morning, that their prisoners amounted to five hundred Europeans, and two thousand five hundred and thirty-seven Caffres, Topasses[14], and sepoys; being, altogether, far more numerous than those by whom they were captured. The loss of the French was small: the assailants had twenty-two Europeans killed, and sixty-two wounded; fifty sepoys were killed, and a hundred and fifty wounded.[15]

The French commander and his garrison had, from the first, treated too slightingly the efforts of their besiegers. Their confidence, which was increased by an expected re-enforcement from Pondicherry, was one of the chief causes of the loss of the place. Few precautionary measures appear to have been taken to give combination to the points of defence; and the attack being made at night, and on so many quarters, distracted those in the different works[16], whose contradictory and exaggerated reports so embarrassed M. Conflans, that he remained in the centre of the fort with his most select men, undecided where to direct relief, till he was so surrounded as to be obliged to surrender at discretion.

Though these circumstances promoted the success of the English, they only reflected higher honour upon the British commander and his gallant soldiers. The irregularity and extent of the fortifications made Colonel Forde foresee the confusion that must result from dividing his troops both before and after they entered the place. He also calculated upon that confidence with which the enemy's superior numbers were likely to inspire their commander; and he anticipated the success which so frequently crowns those daring attempts, which are made in contempt of all the ordinary maxims of war.

The able and bold plans of their commander were admirably carried into execution by his brave troops. The English soldiers, by their conduct, well redeemed the crime of their recent mutiny; and we are informed, by a contemporary historian[17], that "the sepoys behaved with equal gallantry to the Europeans!"

M. Moracin, with a re-enforcement of three hundred men from Pondicherry, arrived a few days after the place had fallen. On discovering what had occurred, he sailed to the northward, where the attempt he made to injure the English interests in the Vizagapatam and Ganjam districts altogether failed, though he continued, for some period, to excite considerable alarm.

Salabut Jung was encamped within fifteen miles of Masulipatam when the fort was taken. He and his ministers were alike astonished at the unexpected result of the siege; and, reproaching themselves as in part the cause of the misfortune to their ally, they refused to negotiate with Colonel Forde while there appeared a

[14] Native Christians, generally the descendants of Portuguese and Indian parents; called Topasses, from their wearing hats (topees) like Europeans, instead of turbans.

[15] The killed and wounded were nearly one third of the whole; so that the assailants, probably, hardly exceeded nine hundred, while the prisoners were three thousand and thirty-seven. Arunderauze, with his irregular native forces, was, indeed, at hand.

[16] The troops in the ravelin, beyond the main gate, were kept at their post by alarm at the false attack of the Rajah's troops, till the assailants, who entered at the breach, shut the gate on them.

[17] Orme, vol. iii. p. 489.

hope of their being joined by the corps under Moracin; but finding that he had proceeded north, the Subah evinced a wish to contract an alliance with the English. To this he was induced by another and more powerful motive. Nizam Ali Khan had, on the receipt of Clive's letters regarding Colonel Forde's expedition, not only written to Clive[18] expressing his desire to co-operate against the French, and his wish that Colonel Forde's force should join him; but had also addressed Colonel Forde to the same purport, in answer to a letter received from that officer. This correspondence with a brother whom he had just cause to dread, combined with the movement of Nizam Ali in the direction of Hyderabad, turned the scale of the Subah's court in favour of the English; and, notwithstanding the remonstrances of the leader of the French corps of observation, Salabut Jung concluded a treaty with Colonel Forde, by which he ceded Masulipatam and eight districts in its vicinity. The second article of this engagement stipulated, not only that he was to have no French troops in his service, but that he was not to allow that nation any settlement in his dominions; the third article was in favour of Anunderauze; and by the fourth Salabut Jung engaged never to give aid or protection to the enemies of the English; who, on their part, stipulated not to aid or protect those who were hostile to his person or government.

I have entered more minutely upon the progress and results of this expedition, from its being solely and exclusively the measure of Clive. Its consequences were very important, as tending to distract the enemy at the period of the siege of Madras[19], and materially to weaken his actual strength for subsequent operations[20]; but more so as they destroyed (Clive's great object) the French connection with Salabut Jung, and raised the military reputation of the English in the Deckan above that of their European rivals. Besides all these advantages, the occupation of the fort and dependent districts of Masulipatam was of itself a valuable object. This possession was annexed to the presidency of Fort St. George.

The government of Madras, anxious to add to the army in the field against the French, desired that Colonel Forde should leave Masulipatam with a garrison of five hundred sepoys, and send his remaining Europeans (about two hundred) to Madras. This he objected to, upon the ground of its exposing this important acquisition to recapture by the French fleet. Clive approved of this, as of every part of Colonel Forde's conduct throughout the late service. Besides those public thanks which, as head of the government, he gave to this able officer and his gallant troops, we meet, in Clive's private letters, with frequent and strong expressions of his sense of the importance of the defeat of Conflans near Rajahmundry, and the capture of Masulipatam. He justly concluded that these achievements,

[18] Letter received at Calcutta, 17th July, 1759.

[19] Mr. Call, the chief engineer at Madras, writing to Clive, under date the 11th October, 1758, observes, "I cannot but say you have added much to your reputation by the detachment (Colonel Forde's) which you have sent to our assistance on the coast. No sooner were your apprehensions for the safety of Bengal somewhat lessened, than you determined to support us."

[20] Including prisoners, and the corps under Moracin, at least one thousand Europeans, and nearly three thousand native troops, were subtracted from Lally's force by the effects of Colonel Forde's success.

independent of their immediate consequences, were calculated to promote our permanent interests in the Deckan; a point to which he always gave great importance, and to which he upbraids his friends in the government of Madras for being too inattentive.

In a private letter to Mr. Pigot of the 21st of August, in which he congratulates him on the raising of the siege of Madras, he observes, "I know there are many in England, especially the envious, who have endeavoured to persuade others, as well as themselves, that our wars in India are trifling and insignificant; but our late exploits will, I believe, induce another way of thinking, and add lustre to our quondam victories.

"Colonel Forde may, I think, step forth, and very justly claim his share of the laurels gained. His defeat of Conflans, with a great inferiority of numbers, was an important stroke; but his taking by storm such a place as Masulipatam, with a garrison within superior to the force which attacked it, is what we seldom hear of in these our modern times.

"I cannot add much to what has been represented to you in our general letter; only let me beg of you not to neglect the affairs of the Deckan; they are of great importance, and I know the gentlemen at home think them so. Besides, we never could be safe in Bengal, while the enemy is so near at hand, and a strong squadron, which may give ours the slip, and co-operate with them. If Colonel Forde had left Masulipatam with only a garrison of five hundred sepoys, and it had been afterwards lost (which I really believe would have been the case), what a load of disgrace would have fallen upon us, for putting the Company to so great an expense, and for losing all the fruits of our eminent successes in these parts."

In another letter[21] upon the same subject to his friend Mr. Vansittart, who was a member of council at Fort St. George, Clive expresses similar sentiments. "The news from the coast," he observes, "this year has been very important and interesting. The defence of Madras will do much honour to our arms in India, and greatly heighten our reputation as soldiers in these parts. I would gladly have given some of my riches to share some of your reputation. I know it has been a conceived opinion among the old soldiers in England, that our exploits in India have been much of the same nature as those of Ferdinando Cortez; but your foiling such a man as M. Lally, and two of the oldest regiments of France, will induce another way of thinking, and add a fresh lustre to all our former victories. Neither do I think Colonel Forde's successes fall short of those of Madras. His victory over the Marquis de Conflans was but one of the many we have gained over our enemies in the like circumstances; but his taking such a place as Masulipatam, with a garrison within superior to the force which attacked it, is, I think, one of those extraordinary actions which we seldom hear of in these modern times, and must gain him great honour when it comes to be known at home. And now I have said thus much, I cannot help thinking there has not been quite that attention bestowed on the affairs of the Deckan their importance deserves. Much has been risked in not sending Colonel Forde even a small assistance of money, which I think might have been done without greatly distressing yourselves; and still much more in not

[21] 26th August.

providing sea conveyances, or timely and sufficient land escorts for the French prisoners.

"This expedition was undertaken more with a view to benefit the coast than Bengal; and most of the Deckan forces would certainly have been at the siege of Madras, if not prevented by the diversion given from hence. Much I fear all our successes in the Deckan would have come to nothing, if Colonel Forde had complied with the late order sent him, of leaving only five hundred sepoys in Masulipatam, and coming, with the rest of the forces, to Madras. Excuse me in thinking the gentlemen in council have had too much at heart the securing to themselves Colonel Forde's detachment, without sufficiently considering the consequences; for I can never be persuaded that the addition of two hundred infantry would either have lost or gained us a battle over M. Lally; but the withdrawing them from the Deckan would certainly have rendered fruitless all that has been done. You will be surprised at hearing the French have landed upwards of five hundred Europeans at Ganjam with M. Moracin; but it is really matter of fact, and has been confirmed to us by no less than forty-seven deserters from thence, most of them English taken at St. David's, and forced into the service. By the latest advices, they were reduced, by death and desertion, to four hundred. I need say no more on this subject, as the board will write very fully on this and other matters of importance."

I shall now shortly refer to the occurrences at Madras, subsequent to the great effort made to restore the British interests in Bengal. It would be as unnecessary as it is foreign to my object to enter into a detail of events which have been minutely described by several able writers; but a general notice of them is required, not only to elucidate the grounds of Clive's conduct, as far as relates to the aid he gave or refused to Fort St. George, but as it is calculated to exhibit the character of his mind, which, amid all those critical and important events in which he was engaged in Bengal, appears to have dwelt with an earnest fondness upon the scenes of his first efforts, and to have retained the most anxious solicitude for the continued success of those who were the friends of his youth, and his early associates in danger. Absence appears, indeed, to have increased the interest he took in the affairs of the coast of Coromandel; and from the period of his proceeding to Calcutta till his departure for England, no occurrence of any magnitude took place in the Madras Presidency, on which we do not find numerous letters from Clive, which convey his opinion with equal freedom upon the measures of the government, and upon the conduct of individuals.

In 1757, the events of most magnitude on the coast were the capture of Madura by Captain Caillaud[22], who commanded the British troops south of the Coleroon; and the defeat of a party[23] which attacked Nellore, where the brother[24] of the Nabob Mahommed Ali Khan continued in rebellion. The fortress of Chittaput

[22] Captain Caillaud suffered two repulses before he succeeded in his attack on Madura.

[23] This party was commanded by Colonel Forde, then belonging to Adlercron's regiment. The circumstances attending the repulse were such as reflected no imputation on his character.

[24] Neazballa.

was taken by the French, owing to aid being refused to Nazir Mahommed[25], the killadar (or governor) who, holding this fortress independent of the Nabob, was an object of jealousy, and he succeeded in instilling into the minds of the English government a belief that the gallant defender of this important post was in league with the French. Succour was delayed till too late. The brave killadar resisted to the last; and, by his death on the breach, silenced his calumniators, and left the rulers of Madras to regret their unfortunate credulity and prejudice.

The capture of Chittaput was followed by the reduction of a number of small fortresses in the Carnatic. The successes of the French in this province balanced those of the English to the southward, where the gallantry and judgment of Captain Caillaud, and the indefatigable activity of Mahommed Esoof[26], the celebrated commandant of sepoys, supported the cause of the English, and of the Nabob Mahommed Ali, against the French and the rebel Maphuze Khan. The latter were aided by several polygars, or petty Hindu chiefs, who possess the wild mountainous tracts of this part of India; and who, from the attachment and habits of their rude followers, are the most troublesome of all enemies to the internal peace of the country.

These indecisive operations had no effect beyond keeping up the flame of war between the French and English, through whom every native power in India that they could influence became engaged in hostilities, in which their interests were deemed subordinate to the primary object which the two rival European nations alike cherished, of expelling each other from the eastern hemisphere.

The French government in Europe appear, at this period, to have determined on an effort to reduce the British settlements on the coast of Coromandel; and the armament they prepared seemed adequate to the object. Fortunately for the English, those who presided in the councils of Louis 15th were either so completely ignorant of Indian policy, or so inveterately prejudiced against their East India Company and its servants, as not only to overlook the advantages that these had gained, but to put aside as useless all who were acquainted with the scene, and to substitute a commander and officers, who, whatever experience they might have had in other quarters of the world, were profoundly ignorant of that to which they were sent, with the expressed hope that, while they reformed the gross abuses of the local government, they would restore the tarnished lustre of the French arms.

The bold and extensive, though, perhaps, premature, schemes of Dupleix had, at first, excited great expectations in France; but when, instead of those successes which his sanguine mind had led his government to anticipate, every despatch brought accounts of some failure or disaster, national vanity, combined with prejudice and ignorance, induced the ministers of that country to throw the whole blame on the Company and on the individuals whom they had employed to manage their affairs abroad. Their political and military conduct underwent equal condemnation; their operations in the field were deemed unskilful, and their connec-

[25] Nazir Mahommed held Chittaput, and a small surrounding district, by a sunnud, or grant, from the Subadar of the Deckan.

[26] Mahommed Esoof was best known, in the early part of his career, by the name of "the Nellore Commandant."

tions with native princes, particularly that with the Subah of the Deckan, were pronounced altogether chimerical, and calculated for no object but that of feeding the ambition, or adding to the wealth, of those by whom they were planned or conducted.

Though the form of the local government was not changed, controlling powers were vested in Lieutenant-General Count Lally, who was sent in command of this force, aided by a large staff of officers of high rank and reputation.

The character of Lally, from former services, stood high as a gallant soldier. He was, perhaps, skilled in European warfare, but he was wholly ignorant of the different modes and usages of that science in India; added to which, he was not of a temper to benefit by the experience of others; and his mind appears, before he left France, to have been imbued with the deepest prejudices against his own countrymen in India, as well as the most sovereign contempt for the natives of that country. He was, in consequence, alike indisposed to receive aid from the experience and knowledge of the one, or from the alliance of the other; and evidently expected to subdue all obstacles at the point of the bayonet.

Such was the man whom the French government sent to India. How different was the conduct of the great Chatham! When the troops of his sovereign were ordered to that country to support the national interests, he at once decided[27] that neither Lawrence nor Clive should be superseded in their command. Had the ministers of France been endowed with his wisdom, and the troops they so judiciously sent to India been placed under Bussy, there is every ground to conclude that the result of the ensuing campaigns would have been very different. But such was the infatuation or prejudice of the French ministers, that Bussy, slighted in the new arrangements, was left, unnoticed and unhonoured, to submit to the commands and bear the insults of an arrogant superior, whose jealousy of his fame and popularity was increased into perfect fury at the attentions shown him by all ranks, and by a memorial from the six colonels[28] who had accompanied him from France, praying he would nominate Bussy, yet only a Lieutenant-Colonel, a Brigadier General, that he might command them, and that their sovereign might derive those benefits which were to be expected from his name and experience.

Lally could not refuse compliance with such a request; but he endeavoured, by bitter sarcasms as to their motives, to detract from the just merits of those by whom it was made.

On the same evening that Lally landed with his troops from the fleet of M. D'Aché, he ordered one thousand Europeans and as many sepoys to move towards Fort St. David. They were led astray by their guides, and arrived at the end of their first march, harassed, and without provisions. To supply them, and to enable the remainder of his force to follow, Lally resorted to means which filled the natives with alarm and indignation. He pressed men of all castes and descriptions

[27] Vide Vol. I. p. 402.

[28] The six colonels who signed this memorial were, D'Estaing, De Landivisan, De la Fuère, Breteuil, Verdière, and Crillon. Their names merit to be recorded. They belonged to the noblest families of their country; and this act shows their patriotic feeling to have been as honourable as their birth.

to carry baggage, and derided the remonstrances of the Company's Governor, M. Deleyrit, who was forced to submit; for, though he and his councils retained their stations, they were placed completely under the control of the Lieutenant-General.

Cuddalore could make no resistance. But a very different result from what occurred was expected from Fort St. David. Its fortifications had been greatly improved, and its garrison was efficient: if it did not repel the assailants, no doubt was entertained but it would, for a considerable period, employ all their means and arrest their operations. But this hope was disappointed, and the place was surrendered before the enemy's works were so advanced as to enable them to storm it. Mr. Call, the chief engineer at Madras, in a letter[29] to Clive says, that he considers "the place to have been lost rather through want of conduct and proper management, than of bravery or the means of defending it."

Clive, as has been shown in the case of Colonel Forde and others, was warm and even enthusiastic in his encomiums of those who were distinguished in the service of their country. They not only became entitled to his notice in his official capacity, but received every mark of his private regard; and his utmost efforts were used to promote their advancement. But, on the other hand, he held no terms with any man whom he considered to have failed in this duty. His condemnation of such was undisguised and unqualified. Neither the ties of friendship, the suggestion of self-interest, nor the fear of resentment, had the slightest effect in preventing the open expression of his opinions, when there appeared a dereliction of those principles which he thought should actuate every individual in the public employ.

Many examples will occur to illustrate this part of his character; but none are stronger than we find in the letters he wrote to Madras, upon hearing of the capture of Fort St. David. The thought of the easy triumph of the French on a spot which had been ennobled by so many gallant achievements of the English, pained him (as he states[30]) to the soul, and he gives full vent to his indignation at those by whom this feeling had been produced. Whatever justice there may be in the sentence he passes on their conduct, the tone of elevated sentiment, and the excellence of the military maxims which we find in these letters, render them very valuable.

In a private letter[31] to Mr. Pigot, which expresses the deep interest he takes in the affairs of the coast, Clive states concisely, but strongly, his opinion upon the fall of Fort St. David.

"After waiting," he observes, "with much impatience, I have at last received your favour of the 10th of July. Let me request of my friend, if he has too much business upon his hands, that he will order one of his secretaries to write me a few lines, for I am always doubtful of the news I may receive from any other quarter.

"I cannot express to you my resentment and concern at the infamous surrender of St. David. Had there been no powder at all left but for the musketry, where was the excuse for giving up the place till a breach was made, the covered way

[29] 1st September, 1758.

[30] Letter to Mr. Pigot, 14th August.

[31] Ibid.

stormed, and the ditch filled? Were our enemies supplied with wings, that they could fly into the place? I am fully persuaded that, had M. Lally been obliged to make approaches to the top of the glacis, the climate would have done him more injury than all the powder and ball in the East Indies. I could wish, for the honour and welfare of our nation, that a court-martial would make the severest examples of the guilty in these cases. For the future, I would not leave it in the power of a commanding officer to forfeit his trust, but give him positive orders not to surrender any fort till a breach was made in the body of the place, and one assault at least sustained."

In a letter to Mr. Orme of a similar date[32], he enters upon the same subject.

"The advices," he observes, "you received of the bad condition of St. David was nothing less than an introduction to the infamous surrender of the place. I know not in what light you gentlemen of Madras may look upon that inglorious transaction: for my part, I have seen the council of war, and, from that only, think the severest example ought to be made of those who have set their hands to that base capitulation.

"They say they had not above three days' powder! Where was the necessity of throwing it so idly away? Had they no bayonets? Or, had they not powder sufficient for small arms? I fondly flattered myself that the hero[33] at Chittaput would, in some measure, have been an example for us at St. David.

"I must drop this disagreeable subject with the melancholy reflection, that Fort St. David so lost has given us cause to lament the departure of the English reputation on the coast of Coromandel. May our future actions retrieve all!"

In a subsequent part of this letter, Clive gives his opinion, that the enemy should be met in the field; and, if not, he suggests the measures that should be taken to promote the success of defensive operations.

"I do not flatter you," he adds, "in saying, I always had the highest opinion of the strength and activity of your abilities. Let them be exerted in pursuing vigorous measures; for you may depend upon it, Orme, if these cautious maxims, which seemed to possess the majority of our committee when I was with you, still prevail, we shall entail disgrace upon disgrace on the nation, until we are become the scorn of Hindustan, and have nothing left us without the walls of Madras. I insist upon it, victory will not depend upon the trifling odds of a few; good conduct in the commander, and a determined resolution in the officer and soldier, will make up for the deficiency, and insure victory to the English over M. Lally and his rabble—for I can call them by no other name, since I am well assured the major part of his forces are not much better, being composed chiefly of foreigners and deserters, raised by subscription: possibly, the King may have spared the Company some good officers to head them.

"The China and Bengal ships will bring you a reinforcement of twelve hundred men, which, added to the garrisons of Madras and Trichinopoly, will enable you to take the field with two thousand five hundred men. Our superiority at sea,

[32] 14th August.

[33] Nazir Mahommed. I have before adverted to his gallant conduct: vide p. 11.

by the arrival of two seventy-gun ships, and one fifty, will be beyond dispute. Of consequence, we shall have more resources than the French: we may remedy the ill consequences of a check, by having the sea open to us, and the assistance of our squadron. Our enemies cannot say so much, for, if they should be defeated, they must be confined within the walls of Pondicherry, and then their distress for want of money will ruin them, if supplies are not soon received, which cannot be effected without a superior force at sea, of which I see but little probability. In the mean time, we can supply you from hence with every thing you can possibly want. In short, if we look upon ourselves in any shape a match for our enemies in the field, I am fully of opinion a battle should be risked: a victory will be of more consequence than the loss of ten Fort St. Davids. If the old gentleman[34] take the field, Caillaud should be sent for at all events, and a commission of Major given him that he may act as second.

"Should an offensive war not be thought prudent, I think methods may be pursued which will near ruin the enemy without it. A body of Mahrattas may be taken into pay, which will ravage the country in such a manner as to prevent the French receiving any revenue from it. This will occasion them to disband their blacks, and their whites will soon disband themselves.

"You are acquainted with the disturbances in Golconda, and the insurrection of the rajahs. I have sent agents there; and you may be assured, if we remain at peace here (as at present there is the greatest prospect) I shall send into these parts as large a force as can possibly be spared, under the command of Colonel Forde. If the country be only thrown into such confusion as to prevent our enemies collecting the revenue, the expense and design of the expedition will be answered.

"I have wrote long letters both to Mr. Pocock and Mr. Pigot to enforce vigorous measures. To the former, I have proposed the destruction of the French squadron, even if they should be lying under the walls of Pondicherry."

This letter, probably from the delay of the vessel[35] by which it was to be forwarded, appears not to have been despatched for twelve days after it was written; and there is a postscript of the 26th of August added to it, which is peculiarly illustrative of the uncompromising character of Clive's mind on those points that related to the duty which he conceived every individual in the public service owed to the state. Mr. Orme was his most intimate friend, and, from what he knew him to have already written, Clive must have viewed him as the person to whose pen he was to be indebted for his fame with posterity. That he did so, is proved, indeed, by a letter to Mr. Orme[36] immediately after the enthronement of Meer Jaffier; in which we find the following paragraph:

"I am possessed of volumes of materials for the continuance of your History, in which will appear fighting, tricks, chicanery, intrigues, politics, and the Lord knows what;—in short, there will be a fine field for you to display your genius in.

[34] Colonel Lawrence.

[35] Almost all communications between Madras and Bengal, at this period, were by sea, which often occasioned a considerable interval between the writing and despatch of a letter.

[36] 21st August, 1759.

I shall certainly call at the coast on my way to England: I have many particulars to explain to you relating to this said History which must be published." Neither the ties of friendship, however, nor the expectations of increased fame from the partial pen of the historian, had sufficient influence to restrain his free and severe opinion of one of the Council at Madras quitting his post at such a moment.

"I have learned," Clive states in the postscript, "with great surprise, from yourself, of your resolution of going home. I suppose it is never to return. Your leaving the settlement at this juncture of time, when the service of every individual is wanted, will justly expose you to the censure and resentment of the Court of Directors."[37]

During these operations on shore, Sir George Pocock had made several efforts to bring the French fleet to a decisive action; but their superior sailing, the bad condition of several of the English ships, and on one occasion the conduct of some of his captains, had always enabled them to escape. Clive warmly sympathised with his gallant friend, in his feelings upon these fruitless attempts against the enemy: at the same time he could not refrain from associating in infamy and disgrace those who had not supported the Admiral, with those who had surrendered Fort St. David.

"You may be assured," Clive writes[38], "I felt much for you, when I heard of the unequal fight between the two squadrons, for want of your not being better supported by two or three of His Majesty's ships. The unthinking world, who never bestow applause but where there is success, would have been ready enough to have laid the censure at your door, if you had not called the authors of the late miscarriage to a public account. It is really a cruel case, after the eminent examples of bravery and conduct shown by you personally, that a certain victory should be snatched out of your hands by the misbehaviour of others. May infamy and disgrace attend all those who are backward in their country's cause; and may the worst of punishment attend those who so shamefully gave up Saint David's to the French! I cannot think of that transaction with common patience; every reflection about it pains me to the very soul; and the more I inquire into facts, the more reason I have to lament the lost reputation of the English on the coast of Coromandel. I do not mean that St. David's would not have been taken at last; but it certainly might have been made to cost M. Lally so dear, as to have rendered his future attempts much more uncertain and precarious."

Lally found among the prisoners at Fort St. David a pretender[39] to the throne of Tanjore; and, by threatening to support this man's claims, he expected to obtain, through the fears of the Prince of that country, a supply of treasure, of which he

[37] Mr. Orme appears to have embarked for England about six months after the date of this letter, but was obliged to leave the ship at the Cape, being unable, from serious indisposition, to proceed further until his strength was recruited.—(Letters from Mr. Vansittart to Clive, 28th June, and 3d July, 1759.)

[38] Letter to Sir G. Pocock, 14th August, 1759. A postscript is added to this letter, of the 26th August; the same date as that to Mr. Orme.

[39] This man's name was Gotica; he was uncle to the deposed King of Tanjore, whom the English had supported in 1749.

was in great want. To enforce compliance with the large demand he made as the price of his forbearance, he moved towards Tanjore. His march was the cause of equal distress to his own troops, and to the natives of the country through which he passed. The latter, alarmed by his indiscriminate violence and the licence he admitted, particularly in seizing their cattle, fled the country; and we may judge how general the desertion of their homes must have been, when we are informed that the French army was almost starving in the midst of plenty; for, while it found great stores of paddy, which is the name given to rice before the grain is separated from the husk, there were literally no persons to beat it out, as it requires before it can be used as food. The troops had neither tents nor baggage; for, in the common alarm at the violent measures of the French General, not even bullock drivers could be persuaded to remain in the camp.

Some days after the arrival of the army at Tanjore, a treaty was concluded, by which the King agreed to pay five lacs of rupees, and to furnish some aid in Lally's intended attack of Trichinopoly. Fifty thousand rupees of this amount were paid, and hostages interchanged for the fulfilment of the engagement; but recurring points of irritation soon broke this agreement. Lally charged the King with insincerity, and with having no design but to gain time; while the other accused the French General of many outrages, and particularly of having confined, on groundless suspicion, forty of the contingent of horse with which he had furnished him. Lally, seeing no prospect of an amicable termination to these disputes and recriminations, determined, with the advice of his officers, to attack the town; and he not only sent to the King to denounce vengeance upon his city and dominions, but expressly directed Colonel Kennedy[40], through whom this threat was conveyed, to state, that it was the French General's intention to carry the Prince and all his family as slaves to the Mauritius.

The counsels of the King of Tanjore had hitherto been fluctuating; they were decided, however, by Lally's conduct, and every preparation was made for defence. Captain Caillaud, who commanded in Trichinopoly, had before sent five hundred sepoys; and, being now convinced of the King's intention to oppose the French, sent a reinforcement of an equal number, with a small party of gunners. The day of their arrival, Lally had determined to retreat[41]; to which he was induced from want of ammunition, distress for provisions, and alarm at the British fleet, which was reported to be off Karical, a sea-port in the vicinity.

The Tanjore General Monack-jee, on receiving certain information of the intended movement of the French, determined upon attacking them. He made some impression from coming upon the camp by surprise[42], but was compelled to retire: when, however, the army marched towards the Carnatic, his harassing oper-

[40] Col. Kennedy was one of the hostages sent to Tanjore.

[41] A breach had been made, but it was not deemed practicable. Two of the principal French officers, General Saubinet and Count D'Estaing, strongly advised a storm; deeming the breach, though imperfect, to be assailable.

[42] A considerable body, cavalry and infantry, of Tanjore troops, with fifty Europeans, and one thousand English sepoys, were engaged in this attack; which is chiefly remarkable for the attempt made upon the person of the French General. A body of fifty horsemen advanced, at daylight, to the French outposts: they inquired for Lally, saying they wished

ations aggravated what they suffered from fatigue and want of food; and we learn from authentic sources[43], that the whole of the French force was obliged to live for several days upon gram[44] and cocoa-nuts.

The natural violence and acrimony of Lally's disposition were greatly increased by the bad success of this expedition. Instead of attributing its failure to the real causes, his own want of local knowledge, his obstinacy and presumption, he imputed it, and the privations the troops had suffered, to the corrupt practices of the Company's servants, to the general laxity of discipline and subordination in all departments of their government, and to the dread which M. D'Aché and his squadron appeared to have of the British fleet. These violent attacks produced abuse and recrimination, and nothing could exceed the discord and faction which at this period pervaded the settlement of Pondicherry.

Lally, after his return from Tanjore, found no difficulty in occupying almost all the towns in the Carnatic, and, amongst others, Arcot, the capital of the Nabob. Chingliput was the only place which the English preserved; but, its consequence being fully appreciated, every measure was adopted to strengthen its garrison and improve its defences. The government of Madras were not induced by Clive's advice to try their fortune in the field. They reserved their force unbroken for the defence of Fort St. George, the siege of which it was evidently Lally's intention to undertake, as soon as the season[45] permitted him to move. In deliberating on the course they ought to pursue, they possessed more correct information than Clive had procured regarding the actual composition of Lally's force; from which it appeared, that though some of his soldiers were of an indifferent description, others were of the French line, and belonged to corps of high reputation. He had besides, well equipped and well mounted, a body of three hundred European cavalry, who, being the first of this branch seen in India, were likely, added to his superior numbers of infantry, to give him a great advantage in an action in the field; whereas they could be of comparatively little benefit in a siege.

Governed by these considerations, they determined to await, within the walls of Madras, the approach of the French army. The siege which took place has been minutely described by a cotemporary historian.[46] It continued for two months, the French having taken up their ground on the 14th of December, 1758, and retreated on the 15th of February, 1759.

The enemy's force consisted of two thousand seven hundred European infan-

to take service. They were conducted to the General, who, being informed of their request, came out from a choultry to speak to them: at this moment one of the Tanjore horsemen, supposed to be intoxicated, fired his pistol into a tumbril, which, by its explosion, gave a general alarm. The leader of the party, observing this, rode at Lally, who, however, defended himself with a stick, and the man was shot by an attendant, while the French guard succeeded in repelling a charge made by his comrades.

[43] Orme's History, and Clive's MSS.

[44] A species of pulse upon which horses are fed in India.

[45] The north-east monsoon commences, on the coast of Coromandel, in the end of October; and military operations are difficult, and in some parts almost impracticable, till towards the end of November.

[46] Orme, vol. iii. p. 385.

try, besides their cavalry, artillery, and sepoys. The garrison was not more than a third inferior in number; and when, to that circumstance, was joined the established character of the Governor, Mr. Pigot, and of Colonel Lawrence, the commander of the troops, who was aided by some of the most distinguished officers in India, there appeared, from the first, but little doubt of the result. The most remarkable event of the siege was a sally, soon after the enemy took up their ground, by Colonel Draper; which, though not altogether successful, was attended with a great loss to the French as well as to the English: and Lally had to regret, which he did deeply, the loss of two of his best officers, Major-General Saubinet and Count D'Estaing, the former of whom was killed and the latter taken prisoner.

During the siege a corps of observation was kept by the French, under the partisan Lambert; but this did not prevent their receiving almost as much annoyance from the activity of the English parties without the walls, as from the courage of those within. Two small corps, sometimes acting separately, but oftener co-operating, hung continually upon the outskirts of their camp, attacking and intercepting their supplies. One of these, which had come from the southern territories, was commanded by the celebrated Mahommed Esoof; the other by Captain Preston[47]: but Captain Caillaud, who had been summoned from Trichinopoly, took the command of both, and by his operations greatly increased the distresses of the enemy.

While Madras was well stored with provisions, and had abundance of money supplied from Bengal[48], the treasury of Pondicherry was completely exhausted, and the conduct of Lally had destroyed credit. The violent and irregular means adopted, to anticipate the revenues of the country, had left the districts which the French occupied without the means of furnishing either the money or the supplies that were necessary for the subsistence of the troops. Notwithstanding the privations to which they were subjected, the French European soldiers performed their arduous duty with spirit and alacrity; and Lally fully appreciated their merits. With the natives, however, his contempt and severity produced their natural effects: they were loud in their clamours for pay, and, actuated by discontent and resentment, deserted in bodies, and began to plunder the country, under the pretext of obtaining payment of their arrears.

These circumstances, and the despair of success,—for he had made little or no serious progress in the siege[49],—made Lally resolve upon retreat; and that measure was almost converted into a flight by the arrival of six ships with the re-

[47] Captain Preston's corps was from the garrison of Chingliput.

[48] Orme, vol. iii. p. 453.

[49] Mr. Vansittart, a member of the Council at Fort St. George, in a private letter to Clive, dated 2d March, 1759, gives a general account of Lally's operations, from which the following is an extract:—

> "I am very glad," he observes, "to begin with acquainting you that the siege of Madras is raised. Certainly it was an undertaking too great for M. Lally's force, and it was undoubtedly a want of men that obliged him to confine his approaches to so narrow a front. I will send you a plan of them as soon as I can find one of our engineers at leisure. The trenches are the weakest that ever were seen, and yet they pushed them up close under our nose. Three or four times small detachments sallied, and took

possession of the head of their sap almost without resistance. Our people retired after destroying a little of the work, and then the enemy returned and worked on. Their grand battery, the first that they opened, tore our works a good deal, but our men were active, and got them repaired in the night. This continued for a few days, but our fire was not decreased. The enemy then lost all patience, and advanced with all our defences in good order; when they got to the foot of the glacis, they erected a battery against the east face of the north ravelin, but they could never stand there for an hour together, as we had a heavy fire both on their flank and front. In three or four days they abandoned that, but still kept pushing on their sap, and presently got up to the crest of the glacis, where they erected another battery close to the north-east angle of the covered way. This cost them very dear, and they well deserved to suffer; for all our defences were yet perfect, nay, we had more guns than we had at first.

"For six mornings running they opened this battery at daybreak, and were obliged in an hour or two to shut up their embrasures. Their loss there must have been very great; for it was raked from one end to the other by the flank of the royal bastion, had a front fire from the north-east bastion, and was overlooked by the demi-bastion so with musketry, that it was absolutely impossible for a man to live. At the end of six days they gave it up, and at the same time, I believe, gave up all hopes of success. It is true they had opened a narrow passage through the counterscarp of the ditch by a mine, and had beat down so much clay from the face of the demi-bastion, that there was a slope which a nimble man might run up, and that is what M. Lally calls a breach; but his people were wiser than he, if he proposed to assault it, and they refused. That letter of M. Lally's is a most curious piece. I am glad it was intercepted, that he may not say the arrival of the ships obliged him to raise the siege, and that the officers and men of the garrison may have the honour they deserve. Their duty was really severe, and what was yet worse, they had not a safe place to rest in when off duty; for there is not a bomb-proof lodgement in garrison, except the grand magazine, and the casemates under the Nabob's bastion, where the sick and wounded lay. Nevertheless there was a universal cheerfulness from the beginning to the end; and (what M. Lally so much expected) a capitulation never entered, I believe, into the head of any one man in the garrison.

"The enemy retired by the way of Poonamallee, and, by our last advices, were at Arcot. Our army is just now moving after them. We had a difficulty to get coolies and bullocks for a camp, by which many days have been lost. A large body of Mahrattas are upon the borders of the province: we have made them handsome offers. If they join us, it will be difficult for the French army to get to Pondicherry, or if they only stand neuter, Colonel Lawrence will have no objection to a trial of skill with the Lieutenant-general.

"I should not forget to mention that your old friend the Nellow Subhadar was of great service during the siege. He brought a large body of country horse and sepoys from Tanjore and Trichinopoly; and being joined by Captain Preston with about fifty Europeans from Chingleput, and afterwards by Major Caillaud, they occasioned a powerful diversion. The French were obliged four times to send out considerable detach-

inforcements from Bombay. Not only his battering train and camp equipage were left, but the sick and wounded. The latter he recommended to the care and humanity of the government of Fort St. George, from whom they received as much kindness and attention as if they had belonged to the garrison.

Lally, before he left Madras, blew up the bastion and powder mill at Egmore, and destroyed the Governor's garden-house, and many private buildings. He had threatened to reduce the Black-Town of Madras to ashes; and nothing, probably, prevented this threat from being put into execution but the hurry of his retreat. This may be inferred from the numerous instances of wanton severity he showed in the prosecution of hostilities against the English. Among other acts, the seizure of the persons of some ladies[50] at Nagapatam, and their harsh treatment, was one of the least pardonable, as alike contrary to the usage of civilised nations, and the boasted habits and character of his country. The proceeding, as will be hereafter stated, forced the English to measures of retaliation.

Clive had, from the moment he heard of Lally's intention to attack Madras, anticipated his complete failure: he dreaded nothing but the arrival of more troops from France, and the want of support from England; but his alarm on these grounds was considerable, as we find from a letter which he wrote to Mr. Pitt, (under date the 21st of February, 1759,) informing him that accounts had been received of the arrival at Mauritius of a third armament from France, and of the expectation of a fourth.

"I presume," Clive observes, "it must have been in consequence of this intelligence, that M. Lally took post before Madras, as I cannot think he would have been so imprudent as to come there with a force not double that of the garrison, were he not in expectation of a reinforcement. Should that arrive upon the coast before our squadron from Bombay, or should the enemy's fleet, by the addition of this third division, prove unfortunately superior to ours, the event is to be feared. Much, very much indeed,—perhaps the fate of India,—now depends upon our squadron. Should it miscarry, our land forces, without some extraordinary occurrence, will be in danger of being obliged to yield to the great superiority of the enemy. Advice has been just received, that the French were still carrying on the siege of Madras on the 25th of January. They had been before it upwards of six weeks; but I have so

ments; but our people always kept their post, till a scarcity of provisions forced them to move further off. The enemy, however, lost many men in these different actions, besides the hinderance it gave to their work."

[50] Mr. Vansittart, in his letter to Clive of the 2d March, 1759 (quoted in the last note), observes, "I believe I shall be obliged to apply to you to lay hands upon some of the Chandernagore ladies, in order to exchange against Mrs. Morse, Mrs. Vansittart, and some others, whom we sent away in a boat for Sadras, just at the time that M. Lally borrowed that settlement from the Dutch. They were received by the French officer, and told they were prisoners. They have been kept there ever since; and two days after the siege was raised I wrote to M. Lally, desiring he would let me know his resolutions concerning my family: he sent back the peon without an answer; nor have I got one yet. All this I could excuse if they had but been treated with politeness; but it has been far otherwise, as you will see by a letter I lately received from Mrs. Vansittart, and which I send enclosed. I beg you will let Carnac explain it to the French ladies at Bengal, that they may see, with thankfulness, the different usage they have met with."

high an opinion of the gentlemen within, that I dare answer they will make such a defence as will do honour to our nation, and end in M. Lally's disgrace."

"The repeated supplies," Clive adds, "furnished the French from home, compared with the handful of men sent out to us, affords a melancholy proof, that our Company are not, of themselves, able to take the proper measures for the security of their settlements; and, unless they are assisted by the nation, they must at last fall a sacrifice to the superior efforts of the French Company, supported by their monarch. Within these eighteen months, have arrived at Pondicherry two thousand five hundred men, and the third division will probably bring half that number; whereas, we shall not have received, including Colonel Draper's battalion, more than one thousand. It looks as if the French Government were turning their arms this way, in hopes of an equivalent for the losses they have reason to apprehend in America, from the formidable force sent by us into that country. But I cannot bring myself to believe that so valuable a possession as the East Indies, and which may make a material difference in bringing about a peace, will be abandoned; and therefore trust that the French armament will have been followed so closely by one from us, as to get in time to prevent the designs of our enemies.

"A son of the Great Mogul (but at present at variance with his father) has approached the northern frontiers, where he has been joined by a few disaffected people. As he has no authority from his father, he can neither, I think, have wealth nor influence enough to make any considerable progress. However, I have got every thing ready, and, in case he advances further, I have determined to proceed myself to the northward, in order to assist the Nabob in driving him out of his dominions, which I make no doubt will be easily effected, even with the small force we have. Would to God we could as easily remove our European enemies from India!"

In a letter to Mr. Sulivan[51], of the same date[52], Clive anticipates the result of Lally's operations.

"To give you my own opinion," he observes, "I think Lally will fail in his attempt, so great is my confidence in the strength of the garrison, and the experience and valour of the officers. The arrival of Captain Caillaud with the sepoy and Tanjoreen horse, will distress our enemies greatly, if not oblige them to raise the siege; and if they continue till the arrival of our reinforcements, daily expected from Bombay, they run the risk of a total defeat. I can no otherwise account for this undertaking of the French general, than from his distressed situation for want of money. He is really risking the whole for the whole."

Clive had from youth been engaged in efforts to prevent the establishment of the French power in India, and his mind was constantly and intently fixed on that object. He viewed the period of which we are writing as a crisis: but he had no doubt of the result, except from overpowering reinforcements arriving from France, and the English settlement being left unsupported. From the moment he learned Lally's proceedings on his march to Fort St. David and Tanjore, he foretold, that if our resistance was protracted, that general must destroy himself. In a

[51] Mr. Sulivan was Chairman of the Court of Directors.

[52] 21st February, 1759.

private letter[53] to Mr. Pigot, he recommends him to employ native horse[54] in laying waste the French territories. "By ruining the country," he observes, "you will infallibly ruin M. Lally. Remember, that he and his forces were obliged to eat gram before Tanjore. May he be reduced to the same necessity in Pondicherry itself!"

Clive's letter to Colonel Lawrence, of the same date, exhibits, in an equally strong manner, his sentiments upon this subject, as well as the affectionate respect he continued to cherish for his friend and commander. It is as follows:—

> "My dear friend,
>
> "I have heard with some surprise, that M. Lally has set himself down before Madras, not with an intent, I believe, to besiege it in form, or carry on approaches; if he does, I think he must be either mad, or his situation desperate; at all events, I hope it will be the means of adding fresh laurels to those already gained by my dear friend.
>
> "Colonel Forde has orders to join you with his forces; and we are endeavouring to send you a complete company of one hundred rank and file from hence. In short, we have put every thing to risk here to enable you to engage Lally in the field. I hope Mr. Bouchier will spare you some men from Bombay. I enclose you a short sketch of our strength in these parts; and, considering how much depends upon keeping up our influence in Bengal, you will say there never was a smaller force to do it with.
>
> "God give you success, which will be an increase of honour to yourself, and of much joy to
>
> "Dear Colonel,
> "Your affectionate friend and servant,
> (Signed) "Robert Clive."

State of the European Force in Bengal, 6th Feb. 1759.

Doing duty.	Military	Artillery
Captains.	6	1
Lieuts.	6	8
Ensigns.	9	0
Serjeants.	36	
Corporals.	29	5
Drummers.	20	2
Privates.	314*	86
* Whereof 140 are recruits.		

The delight of Clive at the result of the siege was very great: it was heightened by his warm feelings of friendship towards those who had so nobly supported the

[53] 6th September, 1759.

[54] This advice, as appears from Mr. Vansittart's letter, (note, p. 20.) was adopted.

reputation of the service of Fort St. George, to which he had a pride in belonging. He congratulates Mr. Pigot[55] on the fame he had acquired; but his greatest joy, as he repeatedly expresses, was, that his venerated friend, Colonel Lawrence, should so brilliantly close his Indian career.

The events upon the coast subsequent to the siege of Madras do not relate to our subject. Suffice it to say, that, after some indecisive operations in 1759, Lally, next year, suffered a signal defeat at Wandewash, from an English army under the command of Colonel Coote. He was soon after compelled to shut himself up with the remains of his army in Pondicherry, which was immediately invested by the English. Before this period, the increased irritability of his temper had led to discontent in the local government, and among the inhabitants of that settlement, almost amounting to sedition. The troops had been in a state of serious mutiny from want of pay. They nevertheless did their duty upon this occasion; but Lally had neither money nor provisions, and was forced to surrender.[56] This unfortunate commander left Pondicherry amid the insults of his countrymen; and on his return to France, he was tried, condemned to death, and executed for crimes[57] of which he was not guilty: for though his prejudice, violence, and tyranny, had no doubt been one cause of the misfortunes of his country in India, his courage, his zeal, and his loyalty were unimpeachable. But the voice of his enemies was loud and vehement, and the ministers of France were glad to save themselves from the disgrace brought upon the country by their own want of foresight and judgment. The Count Lally was the victim they offered to an incensed public. The principles of justice and the feelings of humanity appear to have been alike violated by this

[55] "Your defence of Madras," Clive observes, in a letter to Mr. Pigot of the 21st August, 1759, "and your foiling a man of Lally's rank, will certainly gain you much honour at home; but what affords me most pleasure is, the principal part you have acted in this famous siege. I always said my friend would shine whenever an opportunity offered, by what I saw of his behaviour, some years ago, near Verdiachelum woods."

[56] Pondicherry surrendered to Colonel Coote in January, 1761. It had been blockaded four months before the active operations of the siege, and there were only two days' provisions for the fighting men when it surrendered. The gallant regiments of Lorraine and Lally were reduced to a small number, and these worn out with famine, disease, and fatigue.—(Orme, vol. iii. p. 722.)

[57] Mr. Orme justly remarks, that "if abuse of authority, vexations, and exactions, are not capital in the jurisprudence of France, they ought not to have been inserted, as efficacious, in the sentence of death." The same author informs us that Lally was charged with treason, which deprived him of the aid of counsel. Among other crimes, this unhappy commander was accused of selling Pondicherry to the English; and was believed (so credulous is national vanity) to have betrayed the interests of his country to promote those of a nation that he hated, and whom he treated (on all occasions when he had the power) with a severity hardly consistent with the usage of civilised nations. The haughty spirit of the veteran was unbroken by the persecution of his enemies. His conduct throughout his protracted trial was collected, but proud and indignant. When he heard his sentence he threw up his hands to heaven, and exclaimed, "Is this the reward of forty-five years' service?" and snatching a pair of compasses, which lay with maps on his table, struck it to his breast; but it did not pierce to his heart: he then gave loose to every execration against his judges and accusers. His scaffold was prepared, and his execution appointed for the same afternoon. To prevent him from speaking to the spectators a large gag was put into his mouth before

act, which a philosopher[58] of France truly denominated, at the period of its perpetration, "A murder committed with the sword of justice."

Bussy, with a zeal and temper that do him equal honour, continued to serve under Lally, and to offer his best advice, which was, however, seldom regarded. Basâlut Jung, the brother of the Subah of the Deckan, had evinced an anxiety to preserve the friendship of the French; and Bussy strongly recommended that he should be declared Nabob of the Carnatic, and invited to aid their operations. No measure could have been more likely to support them. But Lally had precipitately proclaimed the son of Chunda Sahib Nabob: a person who had neither influence nor character to be a useful ally; and he was not only reluctant to repeal his own measure, but disinclined to attend to any proposition of Bussy. Overcome, however, by a sense of the urgent necessity of the expedient, he detached that officer with a small body of troops to the camp of Basâlut Jung at Kurpah. The French commander was received with honour; but not being able to comply with the demands made by Basâlut Jung, one of which was the immediate advance of four lacs of rupees, he was compelled to return without being able to conclude an alliance with that prince. He brought back with him, however, a body of four hundred excellent horse, whom he had taken into service; and he was enabled, through the credit he had with some of the native chiefs of the Deckan army, not only to supply this party with money, but also the French detachment by whom he was accompanied, who, like all Lally's troops, were many months in arrear, and almost destitute of clothing, as well as the means of obtaining food.

Bussy was made prisoner at the battle of Wandewash, (January, 1760,) but was instantly released by Colonel Coote, from respect for his character, and as a return for that kindness and consideration which he had invariably shown to English prisoners.[59] Soon after this occurrence, he returned to France, leaving behind him a name as fondly cherished by the natives of India as by his countrymen. That further acquaintance with the true history of remarkable events, which often diminishes the fame of military commanders and statesmen, has hitherto tended only to increase the reputation of Bussy. His courage and conduct as a soldier stood high, before the genius of Dupleix, appreciating his character, sent him into the Deckan.

Acting in that extensive country with a force, which, before he obtained the cession of the northern circars, had only an uncertain and imperfect communication with the coast, he supported, for a series of years, the influence and interests

he was taken out of prison, whence he was carried in a common cart, and beheaded on the Grève. He perished in the sixty-fifth year of his age.—(Orme, vol. iii. p. 736.)

[58] Voltaire.

[59] So high did M. Bussy stand in the public opinion, that when the Nabob Mohammed Ali wrote Mr. Pigot, the governor of Madras, congratulating him on the recent victory, he added, that M. Bussy's being taken prisoner was of itself equal to any victory, and at the same time suggested the propriety of his being sent to him, when he would take good care of him!

Mohammed Ali even then, after some years' acquaintance with the English, was astonished that M. Bussy was allowed to go on his parole to Pondicherry; and as much afterwards, when he heard how well he was received at Madras by every body there, before his departure for Europe. D. H.

of his country, in a manner which reflects the highest honour on his qualities as a man, and on his talents as a statesman. He thoroughly understood and held in respect the usages of the people among whom he was placed. He united a kindness and consideration for their errors and weaknesses with such a good faith and firmness of purpose in the prosecution of his own objects, as to extort respect even from those to whom he was opposed. This testimony to his character is not wholly taken from the page of history, though all writers agree in doing justice to his memory. The facts stated have been confirmed to the writer of these pages, by many who acted with and against Bussy, whose reputation, though now deservedly high in France, is not, even at this period, so great in that country as it continues to be with natives of the Deckan!

Clive, unless where their conduct compelled him to acts of severity, was kind and liberal in his treatment of French prisoners. This appears from a very voluminous correspondence[60], both official and private, with individuals of that nation; but the wanton outrages of Lally made him deem acts of retaliation indispensably necessary.

In several of his letters from Patna, Clive urged the committee at Calcutta to destroy the buildings at Chandernagore, and transmitted to them letters from Mr. Pigot and Mr. Vansittart, in proof of the wanton outrages committed by Lally at Madras, particularly in levelling with the ground the Company's country-house, and in having, without any object, destroyed the country-houses of several private gentlemen, and among others, that of Colonel Lawrence at St. Thomas's Mount. The Committee could not deny these facts, nor the right of retaliating such injuries; but, hesitating between the desire of attending to Clive, and their alarm at the future consequences of the measure pressed upon their adoption, they proposed to throw the odium of its execution upon the Nabob. Of this Clive wholly disapproved, stating, at the same time, his resolution, when he returned to Calcutta, to take the responsibility of this act exclusively upon himself.

"As to your proposal," he observes in a letter[61] from Patna, "of effecting it through the Nabob, I do not see what end it will answer. Our known interest with him is such, that it will never be questioned we were the advisers; and should an opportunity of retaliation ever offer, (the apprehension of which I presume suggested the proposal to you,) it will avail us little to attribute the fate of Chandernagore to the Nabob. If the French should hereafter have it in their power to destroy Calcutta, it will be matter of small moment whether they do it immediately themselves, or make use of a like evasion, and employ some of the country powers to effect it. So far from endeavouring to conceal our being the authors of the destruction of Chandernagore, we ought to make a merit of publishing it, as a laudable national revenge for the unfortunate treatment we have received from the French. The rules of war established among all civilised nations authorise and

[60] The letters of Clive's agents, also, mention many sums which he appears to have given and sent to French officers. Mr. Vansittart, writing from Madras, notices several individuals who have received considerable aid (two captains one thousand rupees each); stating that they are grateful, and have every disposition to repay Clive, but no ability; and that he will lose his money.

[61] 27th May, 1759.

applaud reprisals in such cases. I shall, therefore, very readily on my return take the risk upon myself: and the more so, as (if I forget not) last year we received directions from our masters[62] to that purpose."

I shall proceed in the next chapter to detail events which occurred previously to Clive's leaving Calcutta. The material changes in those vested with authority at Madras took place before that period, except the resignation of Colonel Lawrence, who took the field on the siege of Fort St. George being raised, but finding that his age and infirmities disabled him from active service, retired to his native land, to enjoy that repose in private life, which he now required, and to which he was entitled by the active and able fulfilment, during more than twenty years, of the most arduous public duties.

Colonel Lawrence must ever stand high among those officers who have distinguished themselves in India. He neither was, nor pretended to be, a statesman, but he was an excellent officer. He possessed no dazzling qualities, and his acts never displayed that brilliancy which men admire as the accompaniment of genius; but he was, nevertheless, a rare and remarkable man. We trace in all his operations that sound practical knowledge of his profession, which, directed by a clear judgment and firm mind, secured to him an uninterrupted career of success, under circumstances of great difficulty and danger. As one of the chief causes of this success, we may notice the absence of that common but petty jealousy, which renders men afraid lest they should detract from their own fame by advancing that of others, and the influence of which is, consequently, most fatal to the rise of merit. Lawrence early discovered, and fully employed, the talents of those under his orders; and we find him on all occasions much more forward to proclaim their deeds than to blazon his own. To this quality, which is the truest test of a high and liberal spirit, England is principally indebted for all the benefit she has received from the services of Clive. It was the fostering care and the inspiring confidence of his commander that led to the early developement of those talents, which, by the opportunities afforded him, were matured at an age, when most men are only in the rudiments of their military education. Clive continued, through life, fully sensible of the magnitude of his obligations to Lawrence, towards whom he ever cherished the most affectionate gratitude.

When his venerated commander was on the point of retirement, with a very moderate fortune, Clive settled 500*l.* per annum on him during life.[63] "It gives me great pleasure," he observes to Lawrence on this occasion, "that I have an opportunity given me of showing my gratitude to the man to whom my reputation, and, of course, my fortune is owing." This liberal annuity must have added to the comfort of his old age; but its value was greatly enhanced by the warmth and delicacy of the sentiments which Clive expressed upon this occasion. These expressions of

[62] The instructions from the Court of France to Lally had been intercepted, in which he was directed to destroy such of the British settlements as fell into his power: in consequence of which the Court of Directors gave orders to retaliate the same measures upon the French settlements.—(Orme, vol. iii. p. 726.)

[63] Extract from Clive's letter to his agents in England, 25th December, 1758:—"Having granted Stringer Lawrence, Esq., an annuity of 500*l.* per annum during the term of his natural life, I desire you will pay the same yearly to him or his order."

grateful obligation gave the retired veteran a right to associate his own fame with that of the successful pupil to whose progress to fortune and renown he had, by his early notice and encouragement, so greatly contributed.

CHAPTER X.

Dutch Armament against Bengal, 1759, destroyed by Clive.—Proceedings in England regarding the Government of Bengal.—Clive's Letter to Pitt.—Clive returns to England, 1760

While Clive was exulting at the advantages gained over the French in the Deckan and at Madras, and congratulating himself on the success which had attended his personal efforts in Bengal, a new and alarming danger arose, from a quarter altogether unexpected. Accounts had been received that the Dutch were preparing a strong armament in Batavia: and it was further added, that its destination was Bengal. To this report Clive at first refused his belief. Mr. Hastings[64] had written him, that the Nabob was led from several reasons to suspect that the Dutch were in league with the Sovereign of Oude, and that the armament at Batavia was meant to strengthen their factory at Chinsura; but Clive, in his answer to this letter, did not give credit to the surmise. "Although it will be necessary," he states[65], "to be upon our guard against the Dutch, yet I have reason to think that the armament fitted out at Batavia is only intended to garrison their settlements in Ceylon. Some intelligence lately received confirms me in this opinion."

It was not easy for Clive, or for any person, to foresee such a course of measures as the Dutch Government in India adopted at this period of profound peace between the two nations in Europe. I shall, before narrating what occurred, take a short review of the conduct of those in charge of their factory at Chinsura, from the capture of Calcutta till the period at which we are arrived.

The Dutch at Chinsura had, like others, suffered from Suraj-u-Dowlah, who had compelled them to pay a fine of five lacs of rupees. This and other oppressive acts made them rejoice at his downfall, and they addressed to Clive a letter[66] of congratulation on his success in dethroning that prince. Nevertheless, they did not

[64] Letter to Clive, 29th July, 1759.

[65] 3d August, 1759.

[66] The following is a translation of this letter:—

"To Mr. Robert Clive.

"Sir,—As you have had the principal charge of the enterprise against the late Nabob Suraj-u-Dowlah, we cannot refrain from congratulating you upon your success. Wishing that the arms of His Britannic Majesty may every where prosper and be triumphant, and that your fame, Sir, may become more and more renowned, we have the honour to be, with much consideration, &c. &c.

"Chinsura, 30th June, 1757."

recognise Meer Jaffier as Subah of Bengal; and the consequence was, so hostile a feeling towards them in the mind of that prince, that it required the continual good offices[67] of Clive to preserve terms betwixt them. This was not easy; for their not recognising him was a cause of just and frequent irritation to Meer Jaffier. Clive notices the subject in a letter[68] to the Dutch Governor, written in answer to one full of complaints.

"I am well acquainted," he observes, "with your attachment to the English, and the service you have at all times been ready to show them; but give me leave to observe, Sir, that good offices have always been reciprocal between the two nations: and, indeed, this is no more than we mutually owe each other, considering the close alliance and union of interests that have so long subsisted between us. It gives me, therefore, much concern that you should do me the injustice to reproach me with being in any shape accessory to the obstruction which the Subah has thought proper to lay upon your trade. I have, indeed, heard him make frequent complaints of the ill behaviour of your government towards him; and was really much amazed at his patience, in putting up so long with indignities which you would not have ventured to offer either to Mohabit Jung[69] or Suraj-u-Dowlah. I shall not pretend to inquire into your reasons for not acknowledging Meer Jaffier, in the same manner as the preceding Subahs have always been, more especially as you cannot be ignorant that he has received his sunnud from the Mogul; but, for my own part, I cannot conceive how you and your Council will be able to exculpate yourselves to your superiors for the present stoppage of their trade, since it appears evident to me that you have brought it upon yourselves, by your disrespect to a person of his high station."

The act which gave rise to stopping the trade was one of public disrespect to the Nabob, to whom the Dutch factory did not even pay the compliment of a salute, when he passed Chinsura on his way to Calcutta. The mode in which he resented this insult had its full effect. The Governor and Council of Chinsura made a very humble apology, which was accepted, and the prohibition on their commerce removed.

The chief complaints of the Dutch against the English were, the latter having the monopoly of saltpetre at Patna, and their insisting that Dutch vessels, coming into the river, should take English pilots. To the first it was answered, that saltpetre had always been a monopoly, and that, since the English obtained it, the Dutch had even bought the article cheaper[70] than they had ever done before. With regard to the insisting upon no pilot being employed in the river but English, it was stated to be a measure forced on the Committee of Calcutta, by considerations of

[67] M. Bisdom, the Dutch Governor of Chinsura, applied to Clive on all occasions of embarrassment or difficulty; and his applications appear, from the correspondence, to have been always treated with respect and attention.

[68] 2d October, 1758.

[69] Aliverdi Khan, the predecessor of Suraj-u-Dowlah.

[70] We find in a letter from M. Bisdom to Colonel Clive, of the 25th July, 1759, the following passage:—"Referring to your last favour I cannot refrain from offering you my grateful thanks on the subject of the saltpetre." It appears, from a variety of documents, that Clive gave every facility to the Dutch commerce in this as well as in other articles.

their own safety; and that, until the danger was over, they could not allow those of any other nation to be employed. These facts should have been satisfactory to the Dutch, could the Superior Government at Batavia have been contented to abandon, without a struggle, to another European power the political pre-eminence in India: calculating, however, upon the encouragement given them at the court of Moorshedabad, previous to the expedition to Patna, they determined to make a bold effort to establish such a force at Chinsura as might enable them to balance the predominating power of the English in Bengal. I find among Clive's papers an account[71] of this transaction; and as it exhibits, in a very clear manner, the progress of this serious difference between the two nations, from its commencement to its conclusion, I shall insert it at length. It is entitled "A Narrative of the Disputes with the Dutch in Bengal," and is as follows:—

"About the month of November, 1758, a prevailing party at the Nabob Jaffier Aly Khan's Durbar, headed by Meeran his son, had prejudiced him to look with an evil and jealous eye on the power and influence of the English in the provinces, and taught him to think and look upon himself as a cipher, bearing the name of Subah only. From subsequent concurring circumstances, it must have been at that period, and from this cause, that, we imagine, a private negotiation was set on foot between the Nabob and the Dutch, that the latter should bring a military force into the provinces to join the former, and balance our power and sway. The Dutch, stimulated by envy at our very advantageous situation, and a sense of their own very small importance, readily embraced the overture, and hoped another Plassey affair for themselves.

Actuated by these golden dreams, and encouraged by the absence of our troops on the Golconda expedition, the Director and his Council at Chinsura forwarded remonstrances to Batavia, for this purpose, where, by the event, it appears they had the intended effect. Subsequent to this private negotiation was the advance of the Shah-Zada, and Governor Clive's march to Patna in support of the Nabob and his Government, which perfectly convinced him and his son of our faithfulness, affection, and attachment, and struck an iniquitous party at the Durbar dumb, who were ever insinuating to them that the English were aiming to be Subahs of the country in breach of their treaty.

"Early in August we received advice that a powerful armament was fitting out and embarking at Batavia, its destination not perfectly known, but rumoured to be for Bengal. The Governor sent early notice of this to Meer Jaffier, who immediately sent a Purwannah to the Dutch Governor, a copy of which he forwarded to Governor Clive, demanding withal, by virtue of the treaty subsisting with the English, that he should join his forces to oppose and prevent any foreign troops being brought into his country.

"About this time a Dutch ship arrived in the river with European troops and buggoses, of which the Governor advised the Nabob, who was much embarrassed at the news; he, however, despatched a second Purwannah to the Dutch, and or-

[71] This paper is not dated; but, from a correction in the rough copy, it appears to have been drawn up in November, 1759; and was, no doubt, transmitted to England at that period.

dered Omarbeg Khan Fouzdaar of Hooghley, immediately to join the Governor with a body of troops, and repeated his demand of our assistance, to prevent the Dutch troops or ships advancing up the river. To the Nabob's first Purwannah, the Dutch sent a reply and solemn promise of obedience to his orders; to the second, they as solemnly assured him, the ship which was arrived came in by accident for water and provisions; that she was drove from her destined port of Nagapatam by stress of weather, and that she and her troops should leave the river as soon as they were supplied.

"Notwithstanding these solemn assurances from the Dutch, it was judged expedient to send a detachment of troops, joined with one of the Subah's, under the command of the Fouzdaar's officer, to take possession of Tanna Fort and Charnoc's Battery opposite to it, with orders to stop and search all boats and vessels that passed, without giving them further molestation; and parties were likewise sent out on each side of the river to prevent any foreign troops advancing by land. In consequence of these orders, every Dutch boat and budgerow was brought to, and those that had no troops suffered to pass; amongst others, Mynheer Suydland, the Dutch master-attendant, not only refused for sometime being either brought to or searched, but struck the commanding officer at Charnoc's Battery. Himself and another Dutch gentleman with him were made prisoners for a few hours, until an order from the Governor went down for releasing them and the budgerow, on board of which were found concealed eighteen buggoses, which were conducted down under a guard by land, until within sight of their ship at Fulta, and released. On these transactions, we received very long remonstrances from the gentlemen at Chinsura, to which we replied, that, as principals, we had, by the custom and laws of nations, a right to search all vessels whatever, advancing up this river, not knowing but they might introduce French troops into the country; and that as auxiliaries to the Mogul, we were under a necessity, by solemn treaty, to join his Viceroy in opposing the introduction of any European or foreign troops whatever into Bengal; and that we should absolutely and religiously do our duty to the utmost of our strength and power in both capacities.

"Early in October, Jaffier Ally Khan arrived here on a visit to the Governor. During his stay with us, advice came from below, of the arrival of six or seven more Dutch capital ships, crammed with soldiers and buggoses. Now the Dutch mask fell off, and the Nabob (conscious of having given his assent to their coming, and at the same time of our attachment and his own unfaithful dealings with us,) was greatly confused and disconcerted. He, however, seemed to make light of it; told the Governor he was going to reside three or four days at his Fort of Hooghley, where he would chastise the insolence and disobedience of the Dutch, and drive them soon out of the river again.

"On the 19th of October he left Calcutta; and in place of his going to his Fort at Hooghley, he took up his residence at Cajah Wazeed's garden, about half way between that and Chinsura; a plain indication that he had no apprehensions from the Dutch, whom he received there in the most gracious manner he could, more like friends and allies than as enemies to him and his country. In three or four days after his departure from Calcutta, the Governor received a letter from him, wherein he informed him of 'some indulgence he had granted the Dutch in their trade, and that they had engaged to leave the river with their ships and troops as soon as the season would permit.' The season permitting their immediate departure with the greatest safety and propriety, the last condition in the Nabob's letter, joined to his whole behaviour, convinced us, that leaving the river was no part of their intention, but that, on the contrary, they had his assent to bring up their troops if they could; which Colonel Clive was determined they should not, as the Nabob had not withdrawn his orders to oppose them, and in this he was heartily joined by his Council. Ruin to the Company, if not to the country, must have been the inevitable consequences of their junction with the troops they had in garrison at Chinsura; which once accomplished, would have been beyond all doubt attended with a declaration from the Government in their favour, and as probably a union between them, which must have ended in our destruction. A very few days justified our suspicions and resolutions; for in place of the Dutch leaving the river, we received certain intelligence of their moving up, and that they were enlisting troops under every denomination, at Chinsura, Cossimbazar, and Patna, and this plainly with connivance of the Nabob.

"Whatever may have been the joint or separate views of the Dutch and Nabob against us, it is most certain they never could have had a more favourable conjuncture to carry them into execution; for what with the unforeseen and inevitable long stay of our troops on the Golconda expedition, the detention on the coast of Coromandel of the forces appointed for this settlement, and the necessity the Governor was under of leaving a considerable party at Patna, in May last, our garrison here was inconsiderable. Our Governor, with indefatigable despatch, made every necessary disposition to circumvent the designs of our enemies; the 'Calcutta,' 'Duke of Dorset,' and 'Hardwicke' (the only ships we had in the river), were ordered to proceed immediately to town; the detachments at Tanna and Charnoc's were strengthened, and heavy cannon mounted at each, as also on two faces of our new fort commanding the river. The Patna party was recalled, and the militia put under arms. The Governor wrote likewise to the Nabob in strong and peremptory terms, to send his son down with his army to invest Chinsura; but the politics of the Durbar at this period, we believe, ran counter, where we judge it was determined to let the English and Dutch weaken and destroy one another, when they would probably have attempted to reduce both, or join with the strongest.

"Soon as the Dutch thought their schemes ripe for action, they sent us an immense remonstrance, recapitulating the whole of all their former ones, and vowing vengeance and reprisals if we persisted in searching their boats, and obstructing the advance of their troops up the river. To this we replied, once for all, that we had given no insult to their colours, or attacked or touched their property, or infringed their privileges; that with respect to their bringing troops into Bengal, the Nabob knew best how far it was incumbent on him to preserve the peace and tranquillity of his country; that their boats had been stopped and searched, and the advance of their troops opposed, by orders from the Viceroy, and under the Emperor his master's colours, and by his troops; that they must apply therefore to him, and that we were ready to interpose our friendly offices to mitigate his resentment. This, it may be thought, savoured a little of audacity, but facts vindicated us; as the Fouzdaar had neither withdrawn his troops (which consisted of four or five hundred horse), nor the Nabob his orders; and all that was done below was under the Government's colours. Notwithstanding which, on receipt of the last Dutch remonstrance, we found our sentiments a good deal embarrassed, doubting whether we should stand justified to our country and employers, in commencing hostilities against an ally of England, supposing they should persist in passing the batteries below with their ships and troops. In this situation, we anxiously wished the next hour would bring us news of a declaration of war with Holland; which we had indeed some reason to expect by our last advices from England. Another strong reason which determined us to oppose them, and on which subject we had been guarded against by the Court of Directors, who had intimated that in all likelihood the Dutch would first commence hostilities against us in India.

"Thus circumstanced, the Dutch themselves removed all our difficulties by beginning hostilities below, attacking with shot, and seizing seven of our vessels, grain-boats, &c., tearing down our colours, disembarking our guns, military stores, &c., from our vessels to their own ships, making prisoners of the captains, officers, &c. They also began hostilities on shore in our Purgunnahs off Fulta and Riapore, where they tore down our colours, and burnt the houses and effects of the Company's tenants in those parts. Amongst the vessels they attacked and seized was the 'Leopard Snow,' Captain Barclay, whom we had despatched with expresses to Admiral Cornish, to hasten his coming to our succour, which we judged would meet him somewhere on the Arracan coast.

"On this event, we concluded, with the greatest probability, that the Dutch had received intelligence of a rupture between them and us in Europe, or that they were sure of the Nabob joining them, or of his standing neuter at least; and having the utmost reason to suspect the Nabob's whole conduct, Governor Clive apprised him of the acts of violence the Dutch had committed below, adding, that as they had commenced actual war against us, he should judge the quarrel now subsisted between them and us only, desiring he would leave chastising the Dutch to us, and desist from sending either his son or any part of his army to our assistance; but that, if he would convince us of his sincerity and attachment, he should directly surround their subordinates, and distress them in the country to the utmost.

"Hitherto we knew not whether the Dutch intended to pass the batteries with their ships and troops on board, or whether their intention was to land the latter as high up as they could, and march them over land. The Governor, however, made the necessary dispositions against both, as far as our small body of troops would permit, consisting, on the whole, of about two hundred and forty Europeans of the battalion, about eighty of the train, and one thousand two hundred sepoys. The best troops and largest proportion of these, with many volunteers draughted from the militia, and part of the independent company, formed into a troop of horse, were stationed at Charnoc's and Tannas under the command of Captain Knox. Colonel Forde, on account of his ill state of health and dismission from the service, had returned to us a few days before these troubles; and, notwithstanding both, most obligingly and readily, at the Governor's request, took upon him the command of the remaining troops in the garrison, which marched to the northward the 19th of November; on which day Mr. Holwell was ordered to take charge of Fort William with the militia, consisting of about two hundred and fifty Europeans, besides some of the Portuguese inhabitants; the Governor dividing his attention and presence between both divisions, those at Charnoc's and those in the field.

"The first stroke struck against the Dutch, was possessing ourselves of Barnagore, from whence Colonel Forde passed over the river with his troops and four field artillery to Serampore, the Danish factory, and marched towards Chandernagore; not only with a view of striking terror into Chinsura, but to be ready to intercept the Dutch troops, in case they should disembark, and attempt to gain that place by land.

"During this period, the Dutch ships kept advancing with their captures and prisoners, and our three ships in their rear, whose orders were peremptorily to pass them and station themselves above the batteries, where fire-boats and every other needful step was taken to destroy the Dutch ships if they attempted to pass. The Dutch commodore sent two orders to Commodore Wilson prohibiting his passing their ships, and that if he attempted it, he would fire upon him.

"On the 21st of November the Dutch armament came to an anchor in Sankeral Reach, whose point was within the range of our cannon from the batteries. On the 23d of November they landed on the opposite shore seven hundred Europeans, and about eight hundred Buggoses, and dropped down with their ships to Melancholy Point, the lower end of the reach being near where our three ships lay; of which advice was immediately despatched to Colonel Forde, with assurance that he should be reinforced with the utmost expedition by Captain Knox and the parties at the batteries, who were accordingly recalled. On the 23d, orders were sent to our commodore to demand immediate restitution of our ships, subjects, and property; or to fight, sink, burn, and destroy the Dutch ships on their refusal. The next day the demand was made and refused. True British spirit was manifested on this occasion. Notwithstanding the inequality (the Dutch having seven to three, and four of them capital ships,) we attacked them; and after about two hours' engagement, the Dutch commodore struck, and the rest followed the example, except his second, who cut and run down as low as Culpee, when she was stopped short by the 'Oxford' and 'Royal George,' who arrived two days before, and had our orders to join the other captains. The Dutch Commodore had about thirty men killed, and many wounded: she suffered the most amongst them, as did the 'Duke of Dorset' on our side, who was more immediately engaged with her.

"On the same day (the 24th) Colonel Forde marched from the French gardens to the northward, intending to encamp between Chandernagore and Chinsura. In his march through the former, he was attacked by the Dutch with four pieces of cannon, and the garrison from Chinsura, which had marched out and lodged themselves in the houses and ruins of Chandernagore, at the very time the Colonel entered with his troops at the southernmost end. However, he soon dislodged them from their ambush, took their cannon, and pursued them with some slaughter to the very barriers of Chinsura, which he prepared to invest, being now joined by Captain Knox and the troops from the batteries, and Charnoc's and Tannas.

"The next day Colonel Forde received certain intelligence of the near approach of the Dutch troops from the ships, who had been, in spite of his vigilance, joined by part of the garrison from Chinsura. He immediately marched with two field-pieces, and met them on the plains of Bedarra (about two coss from Chinsura), where they soon came to an action. The Dutch were commanded by Colonel Roussel, a French soldier of fortune. They consisted of near seven hundred Europeans, and as many buggoses, besides country troops: ours of two hundred and forty infantry, and eighty of the train, and fifty more Europeans composing the troops of horse, independents and volunteers, and about eight hundred sepoys. The engagement was short, bloody, and decisive. The Dutch were put to a total rout in less than half an hour: they had about one hundred and twenty Europeans, and two hundred buggoses killed, three hundred and fifty Europeans and about two hundred Buggoses taken prisoners, with M. Roussel and fourteen officers, and about one hundred and fifty wounded. Our loss was inconsiderable. After this action, Colonel Forde returned, sat down before Chinsura, and wrote for further orders. The Dutch were now as abject in their submission as they had been insolent in their supposed superiority. They wrote to Colonel Forde, and likewise to the Board here, requesting he would cease hostilities and propose terms of amity.

"We judged we had sufficiently chastised and humbled them, without taking their settlement (which must have surrendered on the first summons), and agreed to enter on a treaty with them. Deputies were appointed, and things brought to a speedy and amicable conclusion. They disavowed the proceedings of their ships below, acknowledged themselves the aggressors, and agreed to pay costs and damages; on which their ships were delivered up to them.

"Three days after the battle of Bedarra, the young Nabob, with about six or seven thousand horse, arrived and encamped within a coss of Chinsura: this struck the Dutch with the deepest terror. Governor Clive was wrote to, in the most supplicatory terms, to interpose, and not abandon them to the violence of the Moors. The Governor interposed, and went directly to the French gardens, that he might be a nearer check upon the young Nabob, and prevent his proceeding to extremities with them. His friendly interposition had its proper effect: the young Nabob received their deputies; and after severe altercation, forgave them, and promised ample protection in their trade and privileges, on the following terms:—That they shall never meditate war, introduce or enlist troops, or raise fortifications in the country; that they shall be allowed to keep up one hundred and twenty-five European soldiers, and no more, for the service of their several factories, of Chinsura, Cossimbazar and Patna; that they shall forthwith send their ships and remaining troops out of the country; and that a breach of any one of these articles shall be punished with utter expulsion. These terms, ratified by the council of Hooghley, and the Nabob (otherwise) satisfied for the trouble and expense of his march, he broke up his camp and returned to the city."

"Thus ended an affair which, had the event been different, threatened us in its consequence with utter destruction; for, had the Dutch gained the same advantage over us, we have now the most convincing proofs to conclude, that the remembrance of Amboyna would have been lost in their treatment of this colony. Mr. Bisdom was in a dying condition during these whole transactions, and opposed, jointly with Messrs. Zuyaland and Bachracht, the violence of their proceedings; but they were over-ruled by the rest of their council, led by Messrs. Vernet and Schevichaven, two men of desperate fortunes and violent and evil principles, who, we doubt not, will pay severely for their imprudence."

"There appears every reason to conclude from this narrative, as well as from other accounts, that Meer Jaffier had originally given countenance to an intrigue with the Dutch, carried on through Cajah Wazeed[72]; but there can be no doubt that the conduct of Clive, on the subsequent invasion of the Shah-Zada, had made a change in his sentiments. He readily, therefore, gave the requisite orders to the Dutch, forbidding them to land any troops. 'He declared to me,' Mr. Hastings[73] writes to Clive, 'that if they brought any armed force into his country, he would look upon them as enemies, and treat them accordingly.'"

Notwithstanding these professions, when the Dutch armament arrived with a European force superior to that of the English, the Nabob appeared to falter in his resolution. He had paid Clive a visit at Calcutta, and on his return (as stated in the narrative) saw the principal persons of the Dutch settlement at Chinsura; but instead of commanding them to send away their ships (as he had promised) he treated them with such marked favour and distinction, that Mr. Hastings, who accompanied him, wrote Clive[74], that every day's transactions confirmed him more and more in his opinion, that the Nabob was acting a treacherous part.

This communication, added to some suspicious circumstances, determined Clive to take the strongest measures, with the primary view of recalling the Nabob to a better understanding of his own interests; and, if that failed, of counteracting his evil designs. He wrote to Mr. Amyate[75] to acquaint Ram Narrain of the situation in which affairs stood, that he might be prepared to act, if occasion required. He also directed Mr. Sykes to seize the persons of Cajah Wazeed and his son before they reached Moorshedabad, to which they were proceeding; having had full proof of their combination with the enemies of the English. Cajah Wazeed has been before mentioned as the agent of the French. He had for a period transferred his allegiance to the English; but disappointed of the high reward he anticipated, had subsequently directed all his influence and ability (which were considerable) to their overthrow, through the means of their European rivals. When the French cause appeared hopeless, he had attached himself to the Dutch, and was no doubt the principal agent of all their intrigues at the Court of Moorshedabad. The strongest presumptive proof of Meer Jaffier's concern in this plot, was, the favour and distinction with which he had recently treated Cajah Wazeed. Though that person was employed by the Dutch, he was the subject of Meer Jaffier, who, both on that

[72] This person is styled Fakker-u-Toojar (a title signifying "Glory of Merchants") in the correspondence; but we continue to call him Cajah Wazeed, the name by which he is generally known.

[73] 4th August, 1759.

[74] This letter is dated "Hooghley, Thursday evening;" probably the 12th of November.

[75] 7th January, 1760.

account, and from his partiality to the man, was likely to resent his seizure as an indignity and insult. Clive was quite aware of this feeling, but he thought himself justified by the emergency of the case. He expected that one of the effects of this decided measure would be to alarm the Nabob in such a degree, as to arrest his progress in any plan hostile to the English, in which he might have engaged; and, to add to this effect, he wrote to Meer Jaffier, disclaiming all future connection with him, unless he changed his course of action. Clive's object, throughout this affair, was not to inculpate the Nabob, but to save him from the consequences of his weakness and want of faith. With a thorough knowledge of his character, he addressed himself to his fears, and the result proved the correctness of his judgment. Mr. Hastings writes from Moorshedabad on the 18th of November:—

"The particulars of my conversation with the old Nabob," he observes, "I will acquaint you with, after I have seen him again to-morrow. He appeared (and I am convinced was) extremely disturbed in mind, during the whole time I was with him. He changed colour upon the receipt of your letter; and when he had read it, he turned to me and told me, that you had broke off all connection with him. He declared himself innocent of any deceitful intention towards you, and offered to give every proof that you could require of his friendship and sincerity."

In his letter of the 21st of November, Mr. Hastings observes, "Every thing goes on in this quarter as it ought. The Nabob appears as zealous in the cause as he was before remiss in it, nor will, I hope, give you any further cause for complaining, at least in this affair. He has desired me to endeavour to accommodate the misunderstanding which has risen betwixt you and him, which office I cannot undertake more effectually than by assuring you, that I do believe him now to be sincere. I have already acquainted you fully with what has lately passed, nor need I trouble you with a repetition of it. The Chuta Nabob[76] has lately written to me upon the same subject, and has called upon Mr. Sykes and myself to declare how earnest he was, from the beginning of these troubles, to join you, which I know to be fact (so far as his word in that instance could be credited), and Mr. Sykes' letters to you will sufficiently testify the same.

"The firmness which you have shown, and your resentment of the Nabob's cold behaviour, have had every effect that could be wished for; and pardon me, Sir, if I offer it as my opinion, that it would be proper so far to change the style of your letters, as to show that you are satisfied with his present conduct. The Nabob really wants that encouragement: whenever you forsake him, his ruin will be inevitable; and he must shut his eyes against the most glaring conviction, if he does not perceive it himself."

The only subject of complaint Meer Jaffier had now left was the seizure of Cajah Wazeed, which he was too conscious indicated suspicion of himself. Mr. Hastings, referring to this feeling, writes to Clive[77]:—

"I had a long conversation with the Nabob yesterday morning; the particulars I need not acquaint you with, as it consisted of little more than a repetition of his complaint of the distrust you have shown him. He mentioned the affair of Cajah

[76] Meeran, son of Jaffier Aly Caun.

[77] Letter from Mr. Hastings, 23d November.

Wazeed yesterday, for the first time. I excused your proceedings therein, from the necessity there was of seizing him immediately, as he was the prime instigator of these troubles; and it appeared from the long consultation held between him and the Dutch, the evening before his departure, and their letter of defiance immediately following it, that he was going up to strengthen their cause at the city, where the Nabob was sensible he had many enemies. I added, that though it was no time to stand upon the strictness of ceremony, when the enemy were almost at our gates, yet that you had only given orders that Cajah Wazeed should be seized on the way; but that no attempt should be made upon him, if he was arrived within the districts of the city of Moorshedabad.

"I believe he was not satisfied with my reasons: he ascribed this event entirely to your suspicions of himself, which I did not attempt to deny.

"The enclosed letter is in answer to your last. This is the last letter the Nabob will write, till he hears what your present sentiments are with respect to himself."

Clive, on receiving these assurances, readily forgave what had passed; and the Nabob showed every disposition to give his aid. A few of his troops co-operated in the attack upon the Dutch, but the young Nabob did not arrive at Hooghley till after the armament had been destroyed.[78]

The strength of the small force which Clive had with him on this occasion is stated in the narrative. It was divided into parties; some of which were directed to stop and search the boats of the Dutch coming up the river, and others to intercept any small bodies of men that might attempt to reach Chinsura by land. Every line of orders or instructions on this delicate and alarming occasion appears to have been written by Clive himself. He, indeed, had at first no person of any distinction to aid him, till Colonel Forde arrived from Masulipatam. This officer was in bad health; and accounts had reached Bengal that the Directors had not confirmed his nomination to the service; but neither indisposition, nor disgust at this treatment, prevented him from offering his valuable services to his friend and patron, at a crisis when they were so much required. His skill and gallantry were alike conspicuous in attacking and defeating so superior a force. This is shown by the narrative. According to other accounts, his success was greatly to be attributed to the position of the enemy at the period of the attack. It is stated upon good authority, that foreseeing this advantage, but acting with the caution which the attack upon the troops of a European nation not in a state of war required, Colonel Forde wrote a note, stating, "that if he had the Order in Council, he could attack the Dutch, with a fair prospect of destroying them." Clive, to whom this note was addressed, received it when playing at cards. Without quitting the table, he wrote an answer in pencil, "Dear Forde, fight them immediately. I will send you the Order of Council to-morrow."

Clive appears to have been upon the best footing with several of the principal inhabitants of Chinsura, particularly their Governor, Mr. Adrian Bisdom, who, though his name (as he stated) was often and freely used, had been throughout hostile to the violent proceedings of his countrymen. We find, indeed, in his letters

[78] Clive states in his evidence before the House of Commons, that the Nabob's horse were useful in pursuing the fugitives, after Colonel Forde's victory.

during these differences, a tone of deep regret at the violent measures resorted to by both parties, mixed with the strongest expressions of personal regard for Clive, and gratitude for his kindness both in his private and official station.[79] We discovered, also, from his letters to Clive[80], that the large remittances the latter had made through Batavia or Holland were not settled, and that the Dutch East India Company were discontented, and had deferred the payment of the bills, expressing their displeasure at the terms their local government had granted. The conduct Clive pursued towards their armament was not likely to make them view any transaction in which he was concerned in a more favourable light; but the thoughts of himself, or his fortune, had no weight in a question where the interests of his country were so deeply involved.

A more critical situation than that in which Clive was placed by the arrival of the Dutch armament can hardly be conceived. The responsibility he took upon himself, in determining to oppose it, was great; but his mind never faltered when the public welfare was to be promoted by his personal hazard. When some of his friends remonstrated with him on the danger which he incurred, in opposing, during the existence of peace, the passage of the armament of a friendly power up the Ganges, he is said to have answered, that "a public man may occasionally be called upon to act with a halter round his neck." The inadequacy of his means was to him the most appalling circumstance; but this was remedied by the wisdom of his plans, and the vigour of their execution. The moderation he showed after victory was calculated to allay, as far as possible, that feeling of hostility which these proceedings must have excited. A very minute investigation of the whole subject took place in Europe: but the Dutch Local Government, in the treaty into which they entered with the English, had acknowledged themselves the aggressors, and Clive had been so cautious in every step he took, that his conduct could not be impugned; and he received, as he merited, unqualified approbation for this last act of his government, which terminated, as it was meant to do, all attempts of the Dutch

[79] When Clive wrote to M. Bisdom to warn him against the danger to be feared from the advance of the Nabob's army, he offered protection, in his own house, to Mrs. Bisdom, and any ladies she might bring with her. I extract the following remarks on this subject from a very minute official account of the whole transaction:—"This kind proposal of Colonel Clive was accepted in the manner it deserved; and M. Bisdom's sensible and polite answer manifests his having a suitable sense of the favour, and, at the same time, expresses what was very true, that though, from the rank he held, his name had been very freely used throughout the whole of this transaction, yet his sentiments never went along with it, but that he had always retained that respect for the English nation, and that affection for his friends at Calcutta, which a long acquaintance, and the exchange of reciprocal good offices, had rendered equally sincere on both sides."

[80] M. Bisdom, in a letter to Clive, under date the 26th of July, 1759, observes, "With regard to the money sent to Batavia, I have no doubt it will be credited; but, as no vessel has yet arrived, I can at present say no more. As to the remittances to Europe, I must not conceal from you that they are much displeased with the negotiation of the bills, which they think unfavourable to our Company. I can, nevertheless, assure you that your remittance will be paid after the Company's sale. This has been stated to me by an individual of power in the Company. This has been a great mortification to me. I had flattered myself that the transaction would have given equal satisfaction to both parties; and it proves exactly the reverse, which really grieves me. As soon as I hear from Batavia, I will write you."

to rival the political power of the English in Bengal. Their views in that country were thenceforward limited to objects of commerce.

By the events (A. D. 1759) narrated in the preceding chapter, Mahommed Ali Khan, whom the Government of Fort St. George had so long supported, became the undisputed Nabob of the Carnatic. Salabut Jung, the Soubahdar of the Deckan, had entered into an alliance with the Company; and his brother Nizam Ali, who was rising rapidly into power, was most favourably disposed to cultivate their friendship.

The affairs of the small but important settlement of Bombay appeared as prosperous as those of Madras. Surat, one of the principal sea-ports and richest towns on the western side of India, had fallen into decay, as the power of the Mogul government declined. This city, independent of its wealth, had great value with the Mahommedans, from being the port at which the pilgrims annually assembled on their way to the sacred tombs of their prophet or of his descendants. The Emperor furnished the vessel which conveyed to Jidda (a port in the Red Sea) those pilgrims who went to Mecca. The convoy of this vessel, as well as the protection of the commerce of Surat, had been for some time intrusted to the chief of Jinjeera, who was styled the Admiral of the Emperor, and had, in virtue of that office, an assignment on the revenues of Surat, amounting to the sum of three lacs of rupees per annum. On the ground of this amount not being regularly paid Seedee Massoud, the ruling chief of Jinjeera, had first seized the castle of Surat, and afterwards greatly encroached upon the other local authorities of that place. He died in 1756; and his son not only retained this usurpation, but demanded one third of the revenues of the city; another third was paid to the Mahrattas, as the price of their abstaining from hostilities, and the remaining third was divided among those officers who governed in the name of the Emperor of Delhi.

This division of authority, together with the intrigues and disputes to which it gave rise, was ruinous to the prosperity of the town, and attended with continual alarm and danger to the inhabitants. The English factory, which had been settled at Surat for a century and a half, suffered considerably during this distracted state of affairs, and the Government of Bombay, consequently, listened with approbation to an overture made by the principal officers and merchants of Surat, inviting them to take the castle, to expel the Seedee, and on receiving an assignment of two lacs of rupees, to become the future protectors of the commerce of the port. An expedition was sent, which, after a short opposition from the Seedee, completely succeeded; and the garrison of the castle were compelled to surrender to the English, who acted throughout with the sanction and aid of the officers of the Emperor.

An account of the events which had occurred was sent by Mr. Spencer (the chief of Surat) to Delhi; from whence he obtained sunnuds[81], or deeds, appointing the English Company governors of Surat Castle, and admirals of the Emperor's fleet, and granting them an assignment upon the revenues of the city for two lacs of rupees per annum.

[81] The sunnud, as admiral, is dated the 26th of August, 1759; that constituting them governors of the castle, 4th of September, and the assignment, the 18th of the same month.

These events added both to the strength and the fame of the settlement of Bombay, and rendered it better able to cope with its predatory neighbours the Mahrattas. The principal chiefs of that nation, however, were at this period more occupied with the affairs of the northern than of the western parts of India.

Alumgeer the Second was still the Emperor of Delhi; but he continued a prisoner in the hands of his ambitious minister, who, himself surrounded by Mahratta armies, and expecting another invasion of the Affghauns, exercised but a precarious authority. The Shah-Zada was still in a state of hostility; and having lately received countenance from the ruler of Oude, he again threatened with invasion the territories of Bahar. This danger would not appear to have been considered serious by Clive: but he was very uneasy regarding the internal state of Bengal; and the last months of his stay in India were devoted to arrangements for securing its tranquillity.

The treasury of the Nabob had been exhausted by the great sums he had paid as the price of his elevation. His extravagance, that of his son, and, above all, the maintenance of large bodies of useless troops, aggravated his distress. The slave of habit, and devoid of energy, Meer Jaffier was incapable of remedying his condition, which became daily more embarrassing. The conduct of his son, also, alarmed him; and from his communications to Mr. Hastings, it evidently appeared that he sometimes thought the impatient ambition of Meeran would lead him to accelerate, by an act of violence, the hour of his succession. Yet, notwithstanding the urgent advice of Clive[82], he would neither diminish the troops of his son, nor cease to employ him in situations which were calculated to increase his influence, and add to his power. The Nabob disliked the superiority and influence of Clive, but he certainly was personally attached to him.[83] He regarded him with the same dread and apprehension which a wayward scholar bears his preceptor. Though he feared his anger, he had complete reliance on his justice and good faith, and from habit looked to him with hopes of every consideration that was possible for his errors and weakness. With such sentiments, he was alarmed at the near prospect of Clive's departure; and his feeling affords strong presumptive proof, that, into whatever intrigues or plots Jaffier had been hurried or led, he could not, at this period, have deliberately contemplated any plan of hostility against the English power. If he had harboured any such scheme, it is quite evident that Clive's quit-

[82] Clive had, on many occasions, stated his sentiments very freely to the Nabob, both in regard to the character of his son, and the persons by whom that Prince was surrounded, particularly his Dewan Rajah Bullub. The following extract from a letter to Mr. Hastings, dated 21st of September, 1759, will show how decided he was in his opinions upon this subject:—"What you write me," he observes, "about the young Nabob, does not at all surprise me; it was what I always expected. Meer Jaffier's days of folly are without number, and he had, long before this, slept with his ancestors, if the dread of our power and resentment had not been his only security. Sooner or later, I am persuaded, that worthless young dog will attempt his father's overthrow. How often have I advised the old fool against putting too much power into the hands of his nearest relations. Tell him, from me, that Rajah Bullub is an aspiring, ambitious villain; and, if he does not get him removed from his son's presence, he will push him to some violent and unnatural resolution."

[83] The letters of Scrafton, Hastings, and Sykes, afford abundant evidence to the truth of the fact, that Meer Jaffier was personally attached to Clive.

ting the scene was the only event that could give it the least prospect of success.

The chief cause which alarmed Meer Jaffier and other natives of rank at the intended departure of Clive was the fear of his successor not exercising the same authority in checking and controlling the subordinate officers of their government. They feared, and with reason, that spirit of contemptuous superiority, which the extraordinary and sudden rise of the English in Bengal had engendered among many of the Europeans in the service of the Company, and still more the assumed influence and power of the natives in their employment.

The Nabob and his chief managers had, notwithstanding Clive's efforts, too great reason to complain of the insolent pretensions and fraudulent practices of Gomastahs (or agents) employed by the gentlemen in office at Calcutta, and in different parts of the country. Many of Clive's public and private letters convey his sentiments very strongly upon this subject; and from one of them we learn, that he had punished most severely a native in his own service, for using his name as a sanction to some abuses. This afforded him an opportunity, of which he availed himself, of stating to the Committee of Fort William, the great importance of continued and vigilant attention to a point, upon which the temper and good feeling of their ally and his principal subjects must so much depend.

The alarm at Clive's return to England was not limited to the natives: all the first civil servants, Mr. Amyatt, Mr. Holwell, Mr. Sykes, Mr. Hastings, and many others, entreated him to remain some time longer. Their sentiments are nearly similar. I shall, therefore, content myself with stating those reasons which Mr. Hastings brought forward in support of his arguments on this subject.

"I own," Mr. Hastings observes[84], "with great concern I learnt that your resolution is fixed to return this season to Europe. The disinterested regard which, without fearing the imputation of flattery, I may declare you have ever shown for the Company's welfare, convinces me, that you would not have determined upon this step, were it in the least respect inconsistent with that principle. Yet permit me, Sir, upon this occasion, to lay before you such consequences as, from my little experience of the Durbar affairs, I apprehend may attend your absence.

"I am, and always have been, of opinion, that the Nabob is, both by interest and inclination, heartily attached to the English; but I think it as certain that the people about him, especially his Muttaseddies[85] and the Seits, who are evidently great sufferers by the large acquisitions of power which the English have obtained in this Government, would gladly use every possible means to alienate his affections from us. At present, the personal obligations which he confessedly lies under to you are sufficient to intimidate them from any open attempts against us; but as your absence will encourage these people to throw off the mask, and the Nabob is but of an irresolute and unsettled temper, I don't think it possible that he can hold out against the united influence of so many evil counsellors, as will be perpetually instilling into his mind the necessity of reducing the English power. I am the more apprehensive of their success, from the expressions which he has frequently made

[84] Letter from Mr. Hastings to Clive, 17th of August, 1759.

[85] Muttaseddie means a "clerk;" but the plural term, as here employed, describes all the subordinate civil officers of the government.

use of, before the late attempt of the Shah-Zada, intimating that he knew nobody amongst the English but yourself to whom he had any obligations, and that nothing but his friendship for you restrained him from retaliating the many insults which he pretended to have received from the English.

"As there is nobody to succeed you with the same influence, and other advantages which you possess, nothing but a large military force will secure our privileges from being encroached upon, as soon as you quit the country; not to mention the dangers we are threatened with from our natural enemies the French, which, by your resignation of the service, will be doubled upon us, and in which it is very probable the Nabob will stand neuter. I believe I mentioned to you already, that, in conversation with one of the Nabob's principal confidants, a day or two before I went down to Calcutta, he inadvertently dropped, that the French had made some overtures towards an accommodation with the Nabob through his means, and seemed, by his discourse, to wish that it might be brought about; but whether he spoke his own sentiments only, or the Nabob's, I could not judge, as he would not explain himself further upon the subject. This much, indeed, he added, that the proposal was at that time rejected. I do not advance this as an argument that the Nabob is inclinable to favour the French; but I think it would not be difficult to persuade him, that it would be for his interest to suffer the French to come into his country again, both for the increase of his revenues (a very prevailing argument) and to balance the power of the English; and with regard to his engagement by the treaty to succour the English against their enemies; I don't apprehend it will be any further binding, than as it is for his advantage to abide by it.

"Of the great consequence which a junction of the country forces would prove to us in case of an invasion from the French, I would not presume to say any thing in an address to you. If the French attempt any thing against Bengal before your departure, I think I can answer for the Nabob's readiness to assist you against them; but that he will exert himself as zealously in our favour when you are gone, I greatly doubt.

"I know not in what light you may regard the proposal lately made from Delhi, or whether the consideration of the further advantages that may result from a nearer connection with that Court (in which your intervention appears of indispensable necessity) deserve to be thrown into the scale; though I must own it is my opinion, that nothing can contribute so much to establish the power of the English in this country on the most solid and lasting foundation as an interest properly established at that Court.

"Such other arguments as might be produced for the necessity of your stay, till affairs are a little more settled in this country, not coming properly under my province, I shall pass over; nor should I have troubled you with so much on this subject, but that, as these reflections have been suggested to me by my particular employ at the Durbar, I thought they might not so readily occur to, or carry the same weight with, any other person; to which I may add, that, as I have in common with the whole settlement an interest in your stay amongst us, I have a particular one from the difficulties which I well foresee will attend me in my present situation, as soon as I lose your influence."

Clive's correspondence at this period contains the fullest evidence, that, independently of other motives, one great object of his return to England was the hope of being able, by his personal representations and influence, to obtain the adoption of measures which he thought calculated to preserve India. He desired to obtain for the Governors of the three Presidencies commissions from his Majesty as Major-Generals, in order that their superior rank might put an end to the pretensions and independent powers of his Majesty's officers, which had been found, on some occasions, seriously to impede and injure the public service. He was also anxious, as he stated in several letters, to arrive in England before peace was concluded with France.

Writing to Mr. Vansittart upon these subjects, he observes[86], "All things considered, my design is to get with the utmost expedition to England. Supposing I set out in January, I may arrive the beginning of May; and an answer to my proposals may come to hand the end of the same year. My intention is to get you fixt in this government, and to have Forde and Caillaud at the head of the military; and, if possible, to prevail on the Directors" (for it entirely depends upon them) "to apply to his Majesty for commissions of Major-Generals for the Governors, for the time being, of the three Presidencies. If my interest prevails, I flatter myself I shall have rendered the Company more service by my return to England than by my stay in Bengal. If a peace should be on the tapis, I may be of some use likewise; for convinced I am the Directors are not masters sufficiently of the subject, and will probably conclude a peace in Europe, which cannot possibly be abided by in the East Indies."

I shall, hereafter, have occasion to show the correctness of his conjectures, with respect to the benefit which might be derived from his presence in England on the expected occurrence of a peace with France.

To understand the causes of the contradictory orders from England, which weakened and distracted the governments in India, it will be necessary to take a short view of the actual state of the Court of Directors, and of that of the proprietors at this period.

Mr. Payne was Chairman, and at the head of the majority by whom the government of rotation was first appointed. To judge from the facts before us, and, indeed, from his published narratives, we should believe Mr. Holwell to have been the person who first suggested this expedient. He had proceeded to England soon after he was released by Suraj-u-Dowlah; and his claims and sufferings appear to have made a considerable impression upon many of the Directors. Still he was too young a servant to be nominated governor; but the plan of the rotation government gave him a share of that dignity which he could not hope to hold alone; and he himself informs us, that the Directors, after protracted discussions upon this subject, agreed unanimously[87] in the scheme of vesting the government of Bengal in four of their servants, Messrs. Watts, Manningham, Becher, and Holwell; but this resolution, as stated at the period, was only intended as a temporary measure.

[86] This letter is dated the 20th of August, 1759. Clive had written to Mr. Pigot a few days before upon the same subject.

[87] 11th of November, 1757.

A general reform of the settlement of Fort William was subsequently taken into consideration, and a plan was adjusted at various meetings, at which none were present but the two Chairmen, the Secretary, and Mr. Holwell.[88]

About this period, violent opposition arose to the Chairman and his friends, headed by his deputy Mr. Lawrence Sulivan, Mr. Stephen Law, and several men of talent. This party were indefatigable in their exertions; and, although they were a minority in the Court of Directors, they had great influence with the Proprietors. They early declared themselves decidedly hostile to the continuance of the rotation government; and when the accounts of Clive's successes led to his nomination, Mr. Sulivan proposed that a resolution should be added, to the following effect:—

"That the important changes in their affairs in Bengal, made the expedient of the rotation no longer needful, but that Mr. Watts should be appointed to succeed the Colonel."

After a debate on this question, in which the opposing parties were very violent, Colonel Clive was nominated, but to be succeeded, on leaving India, by the rotation government; and the proposed reforms in the government of Fort William were directed to be carried into execution. The minority, undismayed by their defeat, had recourse to the General Court, and carried by their influence the proposition,—

"That the rotation of four should be abolished, and the government of Bengal be conducted by a single Governor and Council as heretofore."

The Court of Proprietors, at the same time that it came to this resolution, declared it had no intention of interfering with the appointment of the Governor and Council, which belonged wholly to the Court of Directors; in which this subject gave rise to further discussions. The names of Mr. Watts and Mr. Holwell were brought forward as successors to Clive; and the majority being in favour of the latter, he was elected. This choice was no sooner made than the Chairman read a letter he had previously received from Mr. Holwell, requesting, should he be elected, to decline the station in favour of Mr. Manningham, who was (he stated) senior, and whose claims were so great, that, if he were superseded, he would in all likelihood retire; and his loss would be seriously injurious to the public service.

Those who opposed Mr. Holwell's elevation gave him little credit for this display of self-denial. It was certain, they alleged, that Mr. Manningham was on the eve of his return to England, and that Mr. Holwell, if appointed his successor, would have both the station, and the merit of having waived his own pretensions in favour of a much older and more deserving public servant. Whatever were his motives, his suggestion was attended to. Mr. Manningham was (in the event of Clive's leaving India) nominated Governor; and Mr. Holwell and Mr. Becher were appointed to be, in their turn, his successors. Affairs continued in this state until the general election of Directors in April, 1758, when the minority brought forward a list of Directors in opposition to that of the majority, or house-list. A violent contest arose, but the ballot terminated in favour of the late minority; whose friends in the new direction outnumbered their opponents. From this date, Mr.

[88] Holwell's Narrative, p. 156.

Sulivan, who became Chairman, acquired an influence and power in the India House which he long maintained. He was, at this period, greatly indebted to Clive, who gave him all his support, believing him, from his talents and his former residence in India, more fitted than any of his competitors for the management of the affairs of the Company.

Writing to Mr. S. Law[89] on this subject, he observes:—

"It has given me much pleasure to hear Mr. Sulivan is at the head of the Direction. Much more may be expected from one who has laid the foundation of his knowledge in India, than from those who have no experience but what they have pick't up in the city of London."

Clive, writing to Mr. Smyth King[90], ascribes the fall of Mr. Payne's party to their "endeavours to keep up that absurd system (as he justly terms it) of the rotation;" and in the same letter he says, "I have to request you will support Mr. Sulivan as far as your interest goes; he shall have all mine, because I am persuaded his endeavours are used for the good of the service."

In almost all his letters[91] of this period to his friends in England, he urges the same request, and upon the same grounds. He could, at this time, have little anticipation, that he was strengthening the man, who was hereafter to prove the most violent and powerful of all the assailants of his fame and fortune.

When Mr. Sulivan had gained the ascendancy, his first measure was to stop the vessels under despatch, and to change the commission of Government, and indeed to annul all the appointments of his predecessor. Colonel Clive was re-appointed Governor; Mr. Watts second and successor; after him, Major Kilpatrick and nine other members of Council, who were to succeed according to their seniority. Mr. Holwell was no more than fifth on this list; but, by death and the departure for England of those above him, he became, when Clive left India, the person to succeed him.

The Directors, in the contests and changes which have been described, were believed to be as much (if not more) governed by personal attachments and resentments, as by considerations of duty. The public clamour was loud against them; and when, after stopping the ships, they applied for convoy, Lord Anson (then at the head of the Admiralty) told them[92], "that in place of labouring for the interest of the Company and the nation, their sole aim seemed to be gratifying their private resentments, distressing His Majesty's service, and embroiling their constituents' affairs."

[89] 29th of December, 1758.

[90] Id.

[91] The grounds of Clive's strong support of Mr. Sulivan appear to have been entirely public. Among other friends, he wrote (29th of December, 1758) to his agent, Mr. Belchier, on this subject:—

> "As I have," he observes, "great designs in view for the advantage of the Company, I must request you will give all your interest, and that of your friends, in favour of Mr. Sulivan, who, I am persuaded, will pursue vigorous measures, now become absolutely necessary."

[92] Holwell's Narrative, p. 170.

The mind of Clive was naturally much occupied in devising the best means of preserving to his country the valuable possessions in India which he had been so greatly instrumental in acquiring. After what has been stated of the conduct of the Court of Directors, it is not surprising that he should have come to a conclusion, that the India Government in England, in its actual condition, was incompetent to the large and increasing duties which it had to perform. With regard to Bengal, while he saw no stability in the administration of Meer Jaffier, a vision of its future greatness was before him; and he submitted his thoughts upon this subject in a letter to Mr. Pitt, whom alone, among the Ministers of England, he considered competent to comprehend all the points and interests of this important question. The following is his letter to that great statesman:—

"To the Right Hon. William Pitt,
"One of His Majesty's Principal Secretaries of State.

"Sir,

"Suffer an admirer of yours at this distance to congratulate himself on the glory and advantage which are likely to accrue to the nation by your being at its head, and at the same to return his most grateful thanks for the distinguished manner you have been pleased to speak of his successes in these parts, far indeed beyond his deservings.

"The close attention you bestow on the affairs of the British nation in general has induced me to trouble you with a few particulars relative to India, and to lay before you an exact account of the revenues of this country, the genuineness whereof you may depend upon, as it has been faithfully extracted from the Minister's books.

"The great revolution that has been effected here by the success of the English arms, and the vast advantages gained to the Company by a treaty concluded in consequence thereof, have, I observe, in some measure, engaged the public attention; but much more may yet in time be done, if the Company will exert themselves in the manner the importance of their present possessions and future prospects deserves. I have represented to them in the strongest terms the expediency of sending out and keeping up constantly such a force as will enable them to embrace the first opportunity of further aggrandising themselves; and I dare pronounce, from a thorough knowledge of this country government[93], and of the genius of the people, acquired by two years' application and experience, that such an opportunity will soon offer. The reigning Subah, whom the victory at Plassey invested with the sovereignty of these provinces, still, it is true, retains his attachment to us, and probably, while he has no other support, will continue to do so; but Musselmans are so little influenced by

[93] The application is here limited to the government of Bengal.

gratitude, that should he ever think it his interest to break with us, the obligations he owes us would prove no restraint: and this is very evident from his having lately removed his Prime Minister, and cut off two or three principal officers, all attached to our interest, and who had a share in his elevation. Moreover, he is advanced in years; and his son is so cruel, worthless a young fellow, and so apparently an enemy to the English, that it will be almost unsafe trusting him with the succession. So small a body as two thousand Europeans will secure us against any apprehensions from either the one or the other; and, in case of their daring to be troublesome, enable the Company to take the sovereignty upon themselves.

"There will be the less difficulty in bringing about such an event, as the natives themselves have no attachment whatever to particular princes; and as, under the present Government, they have no security for their lives or properties, they would rejoice in so happy an exchange as that of a mild for a despotic Government: and there is little room to doubt our easily obtaining the Moghul's sunnud (or grant) in confirmation thereof, provided we agreed to pay him the stipulated allotment out of the revenues, viz. fifty lacs annually. This has, of late years, been very ill-paid, owing to the distractions in the heart of the Moghul Empire, which have disabled that court from attending to their concerns in the distant provinces: and the Vizier has actually wrote to me, desiring I would engage the Nabob to make the payments agreeable to the former usage; nay, further: application has been made to me from the Court of Delhi, to take charge of collecting this payment, the person entrusted with which is styled the King's Dewan, and is the next person both in dignity and power to the Subah. But this high office I have been obliged to decline for the present, as I am unwilling to occasion any jealousy on the part of the Subah; especially as I see no likelihood of the Company's providing us with a sufficient force to support properly so considerable an employ, and which would open a way for securing the Subahship to ourselves. That this would be agreeable to the Moghul can hardly be questioned, as it would be so much to his interest to have these countries under the dominion of a nation famed for their good faith, rather than in the hands of people who, a long experience has convinced him, never will pay him his proportion of the revenues, unless awed into it by the fear of the Imperial army marching to force them thereto.

"But so large a sovereignty may possibly be an object too extensive for a mercantile Company; and it is to be feared they are not of themselves able, without the nation's assistance, to maintain so wide a dominion. I have therefore presumed, Sir, to represent this matter to you, and submit it to your consideration, whether the execution of a design, that may hereafter be still carried to greater lengths, be worthy of the Government's taking it into hand. I flatter myself I have made it pretty clear to you, that there will be little or no difficulty in obtaining the absolute possession of these rich kingdoms; and that with the Moghul's own consent, on condition of paying him less than a fifth of the revenues thereof. Now I leave you to judge, whether an income yearly of upwards of two millions sterling, with the possession of three provinces abounding in the most valuable productions of nature and of art, be an object deserving the public attention; and whether it be worth the nation's while to take the proper measures to secure such an acquisition,—an acquisition which, under the management of so able and disinterested a minister, would prove a source of immense wealth to the kingdom, and might in time be appropriated in part as a fund towards diminishing the heavy load of debt under which we at present labour. Add to these advantages the influence we shall thereby acquire over the several European nations engaged in the commerce here, which these could no longer carry on but through our indulgence, and under such limitations as we should think fit to prescribe. It is well worthy consideration, that this project may be brought about without draining the mother country, as has been too much the case with our possessions in America. A small force from home will be sufficient, as we always make sure of any number we please of black troops, who, being both much better paid and treated by us than by the country powers, will very readily enter into our service. Mr. Walsh, who will have the honour of delivering you this, having been my Secretary during the late fortunate expedition, is a thorough master of the subject, and will be able to explain to you the whole design, and the facility with which it may be executed, much more to your satisfaction, and with greater perspicuity, than can possibly be done in a letter. I shall therefore only further remark, that I have communicated it to no other person but yourself; nor should I have troubled you, Sir, but from a conviction that you will give a favourable reception to any proposal intended for the public good.

"The greatest part of the troops belonging to this establishment are now employed in an expedition against the French in the Deckan; and, by the accounts lately received from thence, I have great hopes we shall succeed in extirpating them from the province of Golconda, where they have reigned lords paramount so long, and from whence they have drawn their principal resources during the troubles upon the coast.

"Notwithstanding the extraordinary effort made by the French in sending out M. Lally with a considerable force the last year, I am confident, before the end of this, they will be near their last gasp in the Carnatic[94], unless some very unforeseen event interpose in their favour. The superiority of our squadron, and the plenty of money and supplies of all kinds which our friends on the coast will be furnished with from this province, while the enemy are in total want of every thing, without any visible means of redress, are such advantages as, if properly attended to, cannot fail of wholly effecting their ruin in that as well as in every other part of India.

"May the zeal and the vigorous measures, projected for the service of the nation, which have so eminently distinguished your ministry, be crowned with all the success they deserve, is the most fervent wish of him who is, with the greatest respect,

"Sir,
"Your most devoted humble servant,
(Signed) "ROBT. CLIVE.

"Calcutta,
"7th January, 1759."

The reader will, no doubt, be curious to learn Mr. Pitt's sentiments on this very remarkable letter, and fortunately the means are preserved of gratifying so natural a curiosity. Mr. Walsh, by whom the letter was sent, on the 26th of November, 1759, gives Clive an account of his interview with Mr. Pitt. That great minister, while he acknowledged the practicability of the plan, was aware of the difficulties that attended its principle and details. "It was not till six days ago that I had admittance to Mr. Pitt. He had made one or two appointments, but was obliged by business to postpone them, for certainly he has an infinite deal on his hands. He received me with the utmost politeness, and we had a *tête-à-tête* for an hour and a quarter, of which I will endeavour to sum up the particulars. He began by mentioning how much he was obliged to you, for the marks you had given him of your friendship; and then began on the subject of your letter. I said I was apprehensive, from my not having had the honour to speak with him before, that he looked upon the affair as chimerical: he assured me, not at all, but very practicable; but that it was of a very nice nature. He mentioned the Company's charter not expiring these twenty years; that upon some late transactions it had been inquired into, whether the Company's conquests and acquisitions belonged to them or the Crown, and the Judges seemed to think to the Company. He spoke this matter a little darkly, and I cannot write upon it with precision: he said the Company were not proper to have it, nor the Crown, for such a revenue would endanger our liberties; and that you had shown your good sense by the application of it to the public. He said the difficulty of effecting the affair was not great, under such a genius as Colonel Clive; but the sustaining it was the point: it was not probable he would be succeeded by persons equal to the task. He asked how long you proposed continuing there; that by your letter he might conclude you intended to carry the business into

[94] Clive's prediction of the result of affairs in the Carnatic proved, as has been shown, true to the very letter.

execution. I answered that no one's zeal for the public service was greater than yours; but that I believed your ill health would oblige you to return shortly. I then mentioned Van's abilities, and that he was upon the point of being made Governor of Bengal. I observed to him that it was necessary for him to determine whether it was an object for the Company or the State; for I was persuaded, that, if the State neglected it, the Company, in process of time, would secure it; that they would even find themselves under a necessity to do it for their greater quiet and safety, exclusive of gain. He seemed to weigh that; but, as far as I could judge by what passed then, it will be left to the Company to do what they please.

"I took an opportunity of mentioning that the French seemed to direct their views greatly towards India; spoke of Dupleix's designs, Bussy's letter, and Lally's armament, which, happily for us, had melted away to nothing, but that in time of peace, if not somehow restrained, they would certainly pour men into India, and be formidable in after times. He asked me about Mauritius; whether the reduction of that would not be laying the axe to the root, and how far it was practicable. I gave him what information I was capable of on the subject, and referred him, for further, to Speke, who I said was a clever officer, and, I believed, had revolved the matter in his breast for some time past. Before parting, he hinted to me a supply for this season of four men-of-war, and a thousand men: these generally are granted pretty late, and we must imagine they will be so this season, as an invasion has been seriously thought of, and we are still doubtful as to the destination of Brest fleet. I don't recollect any thing further, of any consequence, that passed in our conversation. I might, indeed, acquaint you, that he asked very particularly if I had any thoughts of returning to India."

The line of policy which subsequently marked our progress in India, is strongly depicted in this conversation. Mr. Pitt saw, in their infancy, the difficulties which have so long prevented the final settlement of that country; and Mr. Walsh, tutored in the school of Clive, already clearly discovered the future inevitable extension of our dominions and power.

Clive's letter was written a twelvemonth before he left Calcutta. Neither the events in India, nor those in England, were calculated to alter the sentiments it contained, regarding the necessity for the interference of the legislature of Great Britain in the administration of the interests of the nation in India. The despatches received from the Directors immediately before he resigned the Government, appear to have excited equal disgust in his mind, and in the minds of his ablest colleagues; and in the concluding paragraphs of a general letter to the Directors, the Bengal Government expressed their sentiments with a freedom, which, though becoming their high sense of the duty which they owed to themselves and to their country, was but little suited to the temper or constitution of their superiors.

The following are the observations made in this letter upon the conduct of the Court of Directors.

> "Having fully spoken to every branch of your affairs at this Presidency, under their established heads, we cannot, consistently with the real anxiety we feel for the future welfare of that

respectable body, for whom you and we are in trust, close this address without expostulating with freedom on the unprovoked and general asperity of your letter per the Prince Henry Packet. Our sentiments on this head will, we doubt not, acquire additional weight, from the consideration of their being subscribed by a majority of your Council; who are at this very period quitting your service, and consequently independent and disinterested. Permit us to say, that the diction of your letter is most unworthy yourselves and us, in whatever relation considered, either as masters to servants, or gentlemen to gentlemen. Mere inadvertencies and casual neglects arising from an unavoidable and most complicated confusion in the state of your affairs, have been treated in such language and sentiments, as nothing but the most glaring and premeditated faults could warrant. Groundless informations have, without further scrutiny, borne with you the stamp of truth, though proceeding from those who had therein obviously their own purpose to serve, no matter at whose expense. These have received from you such countenance and encouragement, as must assuredly tend to cool the warmest zeal of your servants here, and every where else, as they will appear to have been only the source of general reflections thrown out at random against your faithful servants of this Presidency, in various parts of your letter now before us—faithful to little purpose, if the breath of scandal, joined to private pique or private and personal attachments, have power to blow away in one hour the merits of many years' services, and deprive them of that rank and those rising benefits which are justly a spur to their integrity and application. The little attention shown to these considerations, in the indiscriminate favours heaped on some individuals, and undeserved censures on others, will, we apprehend, lessen that spirit of zeal so very essential to the well-being of your affairs, and consequently, in the end, if continued, prove the destruction of them. Private views may, it is much to be feared, take the lead here, from examples at home, and no gentlemen hold your service longer, nor exert themselves further in it, than their own exigencies require. This being the real state of your service, it becomes strictly our duty to represent it in the strongest light."[95]

This despatch was signed by Clive, and by Messrs. Holwell, Playdell, Sumner, and M'Guire, Members of Council. I shall only so far anticipate the narrative as to state, that it excited the utmost indignation and violence at the India House.[96]

---

[95] Although, in point of composition, the despatches of the Indian authorities, both at home and abroad, at this early period of our political administration, will not bear comparison with those of a later date, they exhibit a degree of simplicity and plainness which is both interesting and amusing.

[96] In the first general letter to the Governor in Council, at Bengal, dated 21st of January, 1761, the Directors write, "We have taken under our most serious consideration the

The Directors had immediate recourse to the extreme measure of removing and commanding to be sent to England, the four gentlemen who had joined Clive in this strong remonstrance. This vindication of their authority, which they deemed necessary to prevent the further diffusion of the contagion of disrespect and insubordination among their servants, was attended with the most unhappy results. It deprived the public, at a critical period, of the aid of some of the most moderate and experienced of the civil servants in Bengal, and promoted to high stations others of a very opposite character: and there can be no doubt, the result of these changes was the massacre at Patna, one of the most shocking catastrophes to be found on the page of the History of British India.

Clive was at no pains to conceal the sentiments which the conduct of the Court of Directors had excited in his mind. In his answer to an address from the European inhabitants of Calcutta, he observes:—

"I am so thoroughly sensible, Gentlemen, of this testimony of your approbation of my conduct, that though the ill-treatment I received from the Court of Directors in their last general letter, has fully determined me in throwing up the service, yet I could waive all personal considerations, and without hesitation comply with your request, did the state of your affairs really require my making such a sacrifice to you. But the additional credit you have gained throughout the country by your late success over the Dutch, the arrival of Major Caillaud, with the reinforcement from Madras, and the approach of the detachment lately commanded by Colonel Forde, which you now shortly expect, ensure you from the least shadow of danger for some time to come. In the interim, proper measures may be taken at home for the better security of this valuable settlement, to promote which, you may depend upon my exerting my utmost interests; and I may perhaps be able to serve you more effectually than by my continuing here."

Mr. Amyatt, the Chief of Patna, had written to Clive, expressing his fear for the continued tranquillity of the country. Clive, in his answer[97], observes, "Your reflections on the situation of affairs in general are very just. I make no doubt but the troubles will begin again in the North. The Nabob will be here in a few days, and I shall advise him to take the field, the instant the weather will permit. He will have a party of our troops with him, and, if it should be necessary, I will accompany him myself. 'Venienti occurrite morbo,' is the advice given by all physicians; and if the Nabob settles the Purneah country, and then marches to the pass of Ter-

general letter from our late President and Council of Fort William, dated 29th of December, 1759, and many paragraphs therein contain gross insults upon, and indignities offered to, the Court of Directors, tending to the subversion of our authority over our servants, and a dissolution of all order and good government in the Company's affairs. To put an immediate stop, therefore, to this evil, we do positively order and direct that, immediately upon receipt of this letter, all those persons still remaining in the Company's service, who signed the said letter,—viz. Messrs. John Zephaniah Holwell, Charles Stafford Playdell, William Brightwell Sumner, and William M'Guire,—be dismissed from the Company's service; and you are to take care that they be not permitted, on any consideration, to remain in India, but that they are to be sent to England by the first ships which return home the same season you receive this letter."

[97] 7th of September, 1759.

riagully, the evil-minded will be overawed, and probably your province of Bahar may remain quiet and in peace."

The arrival of the Dutch armament, while it prevented the proposed march of the Nabob, gave encouragement to the Shah-Zada to repeat his invasion of Bahar. Clive received advices of his movement in January, 1760, when at Moorshedabad on a farewell visit to the Nabob; but he appears to have had no alarm for the result, as Major Caillaud (whom the Madras Government had at his request sent to command in Bengal) had arrived with a considerable reinforcement of troops, and Colonel Forde's detachment was daily expected. Besides being confident in the Commander, and in the number and quality of the troops, Clive had every reliance upon Ram Narrain; whose fidelity, however, he thought it proper on this occasion to fortify, by repeating his solemn assurances of protection.

"You will deliver the inclosed" (he writes[98] to Mr. Amyatt), "which is an encouraging letter to Ram Narrain; and at the same time assure him yourself from me, that he may depend upon my taking care of his interests; and that I will recommend him in so strong a manner to the protection of Major Caillaud, who has now the command of the English forces, that he may look upon himself as safe from any danger as if I myself were at their head.

"Our forces move to Ghyreebaug to-morrow; and in a few days, I hope, will proceed as far as Rajamahul at least, and further, should it be found necessary. There has been some dispute, between the father and son, who should go upon this expedition. I have thought it necessary to come to the city to adjust this affair amicably, and I believe the old man will make the campaign himself.

"The force with the Shah-Zada is so inconsiderable, that you can have nothing to fear from him in your parts; and Ram Narrain's troops with our detachment is an overmatch, I am well persuaded, for any number the unfortunate Prince can bring into the field."

Clive's instructions to Major Caillaud are short, but decisive, as to his opinion that no serious danger was to be apprehended. "I have this morning" (he writes[99]) "received advice by a letter of Ram Narrain to the Nabob; that Suraj-u-Dowlah was preparing to enter these provinces in support of the Shah-Zada. I have, therefore, ordered two hundred men, in addition to the reinforcement this day despatched to you, to be in readiness to proceed after you. When these have joined you, with the troops you already have, proceed with all expedition in conjunction with the Chŭta[100] Nabob, settle matters with the Purneah Nabob, and then endeavour to come up with the Shah-Zada before his party have gained head, and before Suraj-u-Dowlah, should he really have such intentions, can join him. If you meet with the Prince, I am persuaded you will give a good account of him; and that the check he will receive will deter others from making any incursions into the Nabob's dominions."

Clive returned from Moorshedabad, and after remaining a few weeks at Cal-

[98] 7th of January, 1760.
[99] 22d of January, 1760.
[100] Meeran.

cutta, he embarked for England. He was succeeded by Mr. Holwell, who, however, was soon superseded by Mr. Vansittart, (a member of the Council at Fort St. George,) with whom Clive had long been in terms of intimate friendship, and of whose integrity and abilities he had so high an opinion, that he earnestly recommended the Directors to appoint him to the government of Bengal. Mr. Vansittart states in several letters from Madras, that all his expectations of attaining that station rested on Clive, whose solicitude on this point appears to have been very great.

"I am preparing for you," (he observes in a letter to Mr. Vansittart[101],) "many papers and accounts, which will give you some insight into the affairs of this province, and of our great consequence at this juncture in Hindustan. As I have fixed upon you for this Government, it is necessary you should know how glorious a government it may prove for you and the Company. I hope to God, my interest in England will not fail me. I tremble when I think of the fatal consequences of such a mercenary man as * * *.

"The expected reinforcements," (Clive adds) "will in my opinion put Bengal out of all danger but that of venality and corruption."

I have before noticed Clive's exertions in favour of Mr. Sulivan. In one of his letters to that Gentleman, he congratulates him upon his becoming a Director, and assures him he will give him all his interest, "Because," (he observes) "I was always of opinion the Company's affairs could never be carried on to advantage, but under the management of one of those gentlemen who brought home with them a just knowledge of India, acquired by many years' experience."

In the same letter, Clive gives his opinion as to the future importance of Bengal, and the measures best calculated to secure the greatest benefits from that rich country. He also expresses his sentiments in the freest manner, as to the character of the public servants best qualified to fill high stations in India. I cannot refrain from quoting the concluding paragraphs of this able letter.

"As the Company's privileges," (he observes,) "have been greatly extended, so ought their views also; to conduct and carry on the affairs of Bengal to advantage, not only requires servants of ability, but many of them.

"Mr. Watts, I think, has not had that justice done to his merit which his services at Moorshedabad, and since, have deserved; therefore I cannot blame him for resigning. It was with much difficulty I prevailed upon Messrs. Manningham and Frankland to give me their assistance another year. They may, I believe, be prevailed upon to stay still longer.

"Mr. * * * * has talents, but I fear wants a heart, therefore unfit to preside where integrity as well as capacity are equally essential. Those who are more immediately to supply the vacant seats of this Board I dare not recommend to you, (Mr. Sumner excepted,) and I think it a duty I owe to my employers to call your remembrance to Messrs. Vansittart and Dupré, two gentlemen whose abilities and integrity would do credit to any employ. The merit of the former shines with so peculiar and bright a lustre, as must make his services coveted by every well-wish-

[101] 20th of October, 1759.

er to the Company; and they cannot shine in my opinion to greater advantage than at the Council Board of Calcutta. The Rev. Mr. Palk, without regard to his cloth, was deemed worthy of a seat in the Committee at Madras. Mr. Fullerton is not less so, and may be of equal utility in Bengal.

"There is not a gentleman on this side of the Cape so well qualified to be your Major as Captain Caillaud; it is hard to say, whether his abilities or zeal for your service be greater. I know not one so equal to the task of carrying on a part or the whole of my designs, under the direction of a President and Council, as that gentleman. If any accident should happen to him, or he should choose to remain on the coast, let me recommend as a fit person to succeed him Captain Carnac; I have had an opportunity of studying him, and can assure you he is master of an excellent heart, and of talents, in the military way, sufficient to do honour to his employers. I believe this gentleman will be recommended to you by Colonel Lawrence, and other hands, which will serve to illustrate my account of him.

"I can declare to you, Sir, with great truth and sincerity, I have no other attachment to particular persons than what their capacity of serving the Company entitles them to. As I am independent in my circumstances, so am I in my affections, where the good of the service calls upon me to be so; and I should never have given Mr. Sulivan the trouble of reading this letter, if I was not convinced he would look upon every syllable of it as proceeding from the dictates of a heart full of zeal and gratitude for the Company."

Mr. Sulivan had warmly congratulated Clive[102] upon his successes in Bengal; and I have great satisfaction in giving that gentleman's answer to Clive's letter just quoted; first, as it proves the congeniality of their views; and, secondly, as it conveys, in the most unqualified manner, a full approbation of Clive's conduct, as far as that was within the knowledge of Mr. Sulivan, and that gentleman could have been ignorant of no facts of any importance, except, perhaps, the grant of the Jaghire.

This letter is as follows:—

"Sir,

> "As there is a possibility you may still remain at Calcutta to cherish and protect your own offspring, which certainly had been sacrificed without your presence, I shall just confess the receipt of your friendly and confidential letter; and every essential part is, or will be, carried into execution. The many judicious reflections you have made coincide with my own sentiments; and Mr. Vansittart, so justly your favourite, will, I hope, firmly establish this great and noble settlement.

[102] The letter of congratulation, from Mr. Sulivan, is dated the 20th of February, 1758. The following are the concluding paragraphs:—"If your health would allow of a stay sufficient to fix the government of Calcutta (recovered and infinitely extended by Col. Clive) on a solid and lasting basis, the Company are deeply interested in their wishes that you would remain to cherish and establish this noble colony beyond the reach of danger. But should your own preservation determine a return to your native country, may you live to receive the personal thanks of your employers, together with higher honours intended you."

"By our last advices, your situation was critical indeed; but I trust the same Providence that has hitherto so wonderfully protected you, has extricated you from that new labyrinth of dangers.

"I cannot conclude without confessing myself much obliged for your good opinion of my disinterested intentions. The Company have certainly a grateful sense of their obligations to Colonel Clive, and I hope ever to be esteemed,

"Sir,
"Your most obedient servant,
(Signed) "LAW. SULIVAN.

"To Col. Clive.
"London, 7th Dec. 1759."

Clive, though he saw no immediate danger in the actual state of affairs at the period of his departure, indulged no hope of the continued tranquillity of the country. It was his decided opinion, that in India, peace could only be made and preserved by our maintaining a strong and commanding military force. All his sentiments on this subject are summed up in the following short paragraph of a private letter to Mr. Stephen Law, one of the leading Directors.

"Peace," (he observes[103],) "is the most valuable of all blessings; but it must be made sword in hand in this country, if we mean to preserve our possessions. There is no alternative; either every thing in India must be reduced to their first principles, or such a standing force kept up, as may oblige the Musselmans literally to execute their treaties."

Clive sailed from India on the 25th day of February, 1760, rich both in fortune and in fame, far beyond any European who had ever visited that country. His departure was viewed with regret by many, and with apprehension by all who were interested in the prosperity of the British nation. He left a blank that could not be filled up. "It appeared," (to use the strong and expressive language of a contemporary observer,) "as if the soul was departing from the body of the Government of Bengal."

[103] 29th of December, 1758.

CHAPTER XI.

Clive in England.—His private Life and Character

However important the public services of individuals may be, however entitled to the notice and gratitude of their country, their reputation will lose much of its lustre, or receive additional splendour, from the tenor of their conduct in the different relations of private life. Speculative men may argue, that, if a statesman by his wise counsels, or a general by his military talents, promote the interests and glory of his country, it is of little consequence whether he is moral and virtuous. But such a conclusion is unjust: for men who attain distinction, by becoming objects of imitation, do infinite good or harm in the community to which they belong, by the influence of their example. Few can hope to emulate their higher qualities; but their failings and imperfections are within the reach of every one, and are copied by the lowest, in the belief that they thereby approximate themselves to him whom the public voice has raised to such celebrity. This influence over society renders such persons far more responsible than ordinary men, for every action, and becomes therefore one test by which public characters must be tried. There is, indeed, no way in which we can more satisfactorily confirm our opinion of the superiority of an individual, than by accompanying him into the walks of private life; for we may be assured that no stronger proof of his just title to pre-eminence can be obtained, than his not being intoxicated with his own elevation, and its effecting no alteration in his personal habits, or in the ties of family or of friendship; while, on the other hand, we may pronounce, that he who does not contemplate unchanged and undisturbed his own fame and fortune, is deficient in that simplicity and strength of mind, which are the most essential of all attributes in the composition of a truly great character.

If there be justice in these remarks, the general historian even should not lightly pass over the incidents of the private life of those eminent men whose public deeds it is his duty to record; but with the biographer such facts are of essential importance, not only as they develope the character of the subject of his biography, but as they establish or contradict the sincerity and truth of the alleged motives and principles of his public acts. I am very anxious to do justice to this part of my task, which for the sake of perspicuity I have separated from those official details, which have hitherto occupied so much of our attention. I can only hope the reader will experience the same satisfaction that I have had, in escaping for a time from the description of battles, sieges, crimes, and intrigues, to the less brilliant, though more pleasing subject of domestic habits, and the formation and maintenance of those ties of love and friendship which form the bonds of human society.

I have already spoken of the youth of Clive. In the review of his private life in this chapter I shall limit myself to the period which elapsed from his leaving England in 1756, until his return to that country in 1760.

During his short visit to England in 1753, Clive appears not only to have revived all his family connections, but to have extended very considerably the circle of his personal friends; and on his return to India, we discover that he numbered amongst his correspondents men of the first rank in his native land. Many of his private letters are addressed to Lord Barrington, the Chancellor[104], the Archbishop of Canterbury, and Mr. Henry Fox.

To the first of these noblemen, who was Secretary at War, Clive, in a letter under date the 23d of February, 1757, acknowledges himself under obligations for many marks of friendship, and particularly for his aid "in the election of Mitchell." To Mr. Henry Fox he owns himself indebted for much kindness; and he emphatically addresses him as the "patron and protector of the East India Company." He writes[105] to the Archbishop of Canterbury and the Lord Chancellor in terms which show that he had been honoured with their particular notice and kindness during his short residence in England.

Clive was in Parliament, but only for a few months; during which period, though on friendly terms with some members of the administration, he appears, as far as he engaged in public affairs, to have been in opposition to the King's ministers.[106] It is very evident, from the letters of his father at this period, that though he was disappointed[107], he had established some political influence; for the Duke of Newcastle, before he resigned the situation of Prime Minister, expressed himself most anxious to give his father a situation; and though this promise was never performed, the solicitude the Minister showed on this and other occasions to conciliate Clive's friendship and support, could only have proceeded from an impression of his talent, as he had at this time nothing that could give him any influence on the ground of wealth.

Though Clive's fortune was not large when he returned to England, he had realised, from his prize-money, and from the emoluments of the civil and military

[104] Lord Northington.

[105] 23d of February, 1757.

[106] In a letter from Mr. Richard Clive, dated 18th of April, 1755, we find this subject mentioned. "I was glad," he writes to his son, "to hear from you last post; and though you banter me about the election at Dover, I think, as you are so near, and the electors so well disposed to oppose the ministry, you have a fair opportunity to disappoint the Duke of Newcastle; and after you are elected you can proceed on your voyage."

[107] Mr. Richard Clive, in a letter to his son on the 22d of December, 1756, expresses his sentiments on this subject with all the warmth and partiality of a father. "Before I left London," he observes, "the Duke of Newcastle repeated his promise to do for me; and the last time I saw him, he told me it must be something in my own way.[*] I have little expectation, especially at this time of life: but the great and solid satisfaction I enjoy is to think I have a son, who is a benefactor to the public, as well as his own private relations; and though you may not have met with what might have been expected from your countrymen, 't is no discredit to you, but a reflection on them never to be erased."

[*] The law.

stations he had filled, a competence which would have satisfied a less aspiring mind; but he never seems to have even contemplated retirement from public life. Such a step, indeed, was neither consistent with his ambition, nor the generosity of his disposition. His first use of his wealth was to place all his family (and above all, his parents,) in a state of comfortable independence. He greatly added to the joy of his father, by appropriating a part of his fortune to save the family estate of Styche, to relieve which, he probably advanced its full value, as we find that it was transferred to him.[108] His father was delighted at his son becoming the owner of this property. This we see from many letters; and in one[109], written after Clive had sailed for India, he informs him that he had been at "the old place, which," he adds, "I always loved, and have kept the walls from tumbling, in hopes of seeing the new landlord come and take possession."

Clive appears himself to have been quite alive to all those family and local feelings, which have great value as associated with the earliest and most vivid of our recollections and affections. To judge from his private correspondence, no man ever more cherished such ties; for during the busiest periods of his public life, his letters continually refer to his relations and to the scenes of his boyhood; but above all, he speaks of old Styche with a fond familiarity that conveys an idea of the pleasure he must have had in becoming its possessor. Many of his letters upon these subjects are addressed to his father, by whose answer to one of them we may judge of the tone in which they were written. "Your letter," he observes, alluding to himself, "made the *old man* drop tears of joy, that you still survive with honour and success. May you go on and prosper!"

Clive did not remain two years in England. When he returned to India, accompanied by his lady, they left two infant boys; the eldest, Edward, is the present Lord Powis; the second, Richard, died shortly after the departure of his parents.

The great generosity of Clive to every branch of his family during this short visit to his native country, together with the manner in which he lived, and the expenses of his election, greatly diminished his property[110]; and it would seem from his agent's letters, that he had not, when he returned to India, more than three thousand pounds of money[111]; the interest of which, together with a small annuity

[108] The transfer of the title-deeds of Styche is stated in his father's letter of the 22d of July, 1756.

[109] 22d of December, 1756.

[110] In a letter from his father, dated 22d of December, 1756, we find the following curious account of the sale of Clive's establishment:—

"The coach	£40	0	0
"Pair of horses	40	0	0
"A grey riding horse	12	12	0

"One horse broke his neck; another fell backwards; and one pair kept to go in a chaise."

From this statement of property, we infer that Clive, while in England, must have lived very expensively.

[111] This is independent of the sum he had paid for Styche.

he had purchased, he directed to be given to his father[112], whose letters are full of gratitude for the comfort given to his declining age by the liberality of his son.

"I am entirely obliged to you," he observes[113], in one of these now before me, "for the comfortable subsistence I may expect from your generosity, if I should live a few years longer. If among the dead, don't forget the old place of our nativity; but let Ned[114] reside there. If the Judge[115] does not take him, (as I think he will, if her Ladyship pleases,) he will soon be with us, and will divert me in the decline of life. I shall be desirous of living a little longer, in hopes of seeing the joyful day when you and my daughter return to England; but whatever events may happen before that time, God only knows, to whose pleasure I desire to submit."

The house of Styche had been given by Clive as a residence to his uncle, Mr. Robert Clive, who, with the other branches of the family, appears to have taken an interest in its being improved and beautified. I cannot refrain from making an extract from one of his letters on the subject.

"Things go on," he writes[116], "as usual at Styche, and I enjoy a very comfortable existence, under your roof. My income enables me to keep house while the family are in town; and when they come down, I am glad to see them. Aunt Fanny is with me this winter. I am in hopes of seeing you here again, and your most amiable lady, to whom I beg my most affectionate compliments. O that these next ships might bring you over! But I am well assured, your desire is towards your native country and your friends, and that you will be with us as soon as you can. Styche is now leased to a tenant; but as the term is expired within about two years, I think it will be better not to renew it but only from year to year, that you may be able to make such alterations as you please when you come to England. Mr. Mackworth has consented to our having a road over the meadows, and we have built a bridge for that purpose, which is a great convenience; many more might be thought of and had, were you here with one of Rajah Dowlah's millions. In the mean time, if you think of any thing that you would have done, I shall think myself honoured by a commission from you."

Clive's return to India in 1755, and the successes which attended him during the three following years, attracted more of the public notice from being contrasted with the reverses which had attended the British arms in Europe and America during this unpropitious period.

The success at Gheriah even, which (had the public mind not been full of disappointment) would probably not have been mentioned, was spoken of in all the newspapers of the day as an achievement of importance.

Mr. Smyth King, in a letter to Clive[117], observes, when alluding to this event; "The news of your success could not have reached England at a season more advantageous for the increase of your reputation; a season in which there was a gen-

[112] This appears, from Clive's letter to his agent, Mr. King, of 6th of October, 1756.

[113] 29th of April, 1755.

[114] Lord Powis.

[115] Sir Edward Clive, a near relation, who always acted as one of Clive's agents.

[116] 27th of December, 1757.

[117] 27th of December, 1756.

eral clamour and indignation for the ignominy that had been brought on our arms by the losses in the Mediterranean and North America, of which you will hear so much: I need not say any thing. The consequence has been driving out all the Ministry, Duke of Newcastle, Lord Chancellor, Mr. Fox, &c. &c. Mr. Pitt, and a new set in the Treasury and Admiralty, are now the steersmen: they have set out well at the opening of Parliament: how long they will continue in the good course, time will show. You will easily imagine how opportune and grateful the taking of Gheriah was, notwithstanding the distance of the place, and its not being so generally known. Colonel Clive was again in all the newspapers. I believe you have made a maxim of what I have somewhere read, that 'a man who has got himself a great name should every now and then strike some *coup d'éclat*, to keep up the admiration of the people.'"

The capture of Calcutta, the taking of Chandernagore, the battle of Plassey, and the dethronement and death of Suraj-u-Dowlah, with the elevation of Meer Jaffier, were events which, at any time, would have excited attention; but the impression they made was greatly increased by the depressed state of the public mind at the moment when intelligence of their occurrence reached England. They were hailed by all ranks, as redeeming, in some degree, the national reputation that had been lost in other quarters of the globe.

We meet, in a letter from his friend Mr. King, a concise and vivid description of the causes which combined at this period to raise Clive's fame in England.

"You are too well assured," that gentleman observes[118], "of the joy I must have felt at the news of your great actions, for me to profess it: they can add nothing to my admiration of your military capacity, which was at the height, with what you had achieved for several years. I can only tell you, what your love to your country will make you sorry for, that your conduct shines with a peculiar brightness, from the unglorious doings of our leaders of armies and admirals of fleets in Europe; and that the name of a Clive is made use of in the public papers to reproach and stimulate his superiors in rank, but not in fame. That you may judge how little we have to boast of at home, I will give you a compendium of our exploits since the beginning of the war.

"You already know Minorca is taken, for which Admiral Byng was shot, and Blakeney, who defended it, adorned with a title and a riband, though it is at this time undetermined whether his merit or demerit was the greater. Lord Loudon went to America last year, with a great number of troops and a strong fleet. All that we have heard from thence is, that the French have taken several of our forts, but that we have taken none of theirs, nor otherwise incommoded them.

"The Duke of Cumberland, in the beginning of the summer, put himself at the head of a German army, to defend the Electorate of Hanover; but after the loss of a battle, and being driven from post to post, was necessitated to capitulate with the French General, Duke de Richelieu, and signed a convention, whereby those favourite dominions are to be possessed by the French King till he shall think proper to evacuate them. His Royal Highness, a few days after his arrival in England,

[118] 2d of November, 1757.

resigned all his commissions. Ligonier is made Commander-in-chief of the army. Less than two months ago, a fleet of about thirty ships of the line, commanded by three admirals, attended with a number of transports, carrying ten thousand land forces and three general officers, a noble train of artillery, and every thing proportionable, sailed upon a secret expedition; so secret, that it was never divulged, till this pompous armada of near a hundred sail arrived at Spithead, then was it known that the design had been against Rochelle; but that, after holding councils of war for five days, in sight of the coast, it was judged proper to sail home again and attempt nothing, for the Isle of Aix may be called nothing. Thus has a million been expended to set the people in an uproar. The Parliament is to meet in a fortnight; when it is expected they will find out, as Shakspeare says,—

"'The cause of this effect,
Or rather say, the cause of this defect,
For this effect defective comes by cause!'"

The name of Clive was heard every where: we are assured the King himself spoke of the Indian hero in the most flattering terms. Lord Ligonier asked his Majesty, "Whether the young Lord Dunmore might go as a volunteer to the army of the King of Prussia?" Leave was refused. "May he not join the Duke of Brunswick?" was the next request. "Pshaw!" said the King, "what can he learn there? If he want to learn the art of war, let him go to Clive!"[119]

But a higher honour was reserved for Clive, and one he valued more than all others. His name was not only brought forward, but held forth as an example, by the celebrated William Pitt. That statesman, in his speech on the Mutiny Bill, after adverting to the late disgraces which had attended the British arms, said, "We had lost our glory, honour, and reputation every where but in India. There the country had a heaven-born general who had never learned the art of war, nor was his name enrolled among the great officers who had for many years received their country's pay. Yet was he not afraid to attack a numerous army with a handful of men." After this he drew a character of Clive, which excited the admiration of every one, but above all, of the father of the distinguished individual whose name was honoured by such praise. The above extract of Mr. Pitt's panegyric is from his letter to his son[120], which is written in the pride of his heart, and concludes in the following words: "Thus you are, with truth, honourably spoke of throughout this nation: may you continue to be so, till you return to your native country, and to the embraces of an aged father!"

Clive, in 1758, had written to his father to try whether he could not obtain the appointment of General Governor of India. I do not find among his manuscripts any copy of his letter on this subject, which is to be regretted, as the notice taken of the suggestion by his friends proves, that his clear and penetrating mind saw, and desired to avert, the evils which were likely to result from the three presidencies (extended as our connections with native states had become) continuing to be ruled by distinct and independent authorities.

Clive's friends in England, to whom his father referred for advice, were of

[119] Extract of Mr. R. Clive's letter to his son, 1st of January, 1758.

[120] 6th of December, 1757.

opinion that the proposition would never be entertained by the Court of Directors, and that regard for his interest should prevent its being made. There was another reason for not agitating this question. A motion[121] had some time before been brought forward in the Court of Proprietors, to give Clive a sum of 6000*l.*, which was opposed on the ground of his having sufficient opportunities of acquiring fortune in the course of the service. This had occurred before the news of the battle of Plassey reached England. The reputation which that and subsequent events gave Clive with the nation, and with his Majesty's ministers, excited a spirit of jealousy amongst some of the Directors. His father informs him that several leading men in the India House appeared offended at the recommendations they had received of him from persons of high rank and members of administration.

Clive knew the world, and was fully aware of the feelings which his success was likely to produce; and judged wisely that his prospects of future notice and reward might be impeded, instead of being promoted, by the imprudent zeal of his friends. He was particularly apprehensive of the effects of the natural feelings of his father, and wrote to Mr. Belchier, one of his agents, to endeavour to repress the old gentleman's desire to intrude the merits of his son upon all the great men of the land.

"As this good news," he observes[122], "may set my father upon exerting himself too much, and paying too many visits to the Duke of Newcastle, Mr. Fox, and other great men, I desire you will endeavour to moderate his expectations; for although I intend getting into Parliament, and have hopes of being taken some notice of by his Majesty, yet, you know, the merit of all actions is greatly lessened by being too much boasted of. I know my father's disposition leads this way, which proceeds from his affection for me."

It was not easy, however, to moderate either the language or the expectations of a father whose pride in the public services of his son, though great, was exceeded by the admiration and gratitude with which he viewed the conduct of one, whose ties of duty and of love for his parents and family appeared to gain additional strength as he advanced in riches and in fame, and who seemed to place his chief happiness in making those for whom he cherished regard or affection participators in his own good fortune.

The moment, indeed, Clive found himself, from unexpected events, abounding in wealth, his first object was to impart comfort to all who had claims upon him, either from kindred or friendship. His gifts, though liberal, had in them no spirit of prodigality. They were adapted with judgment to the wants and dispositions of those on whom they were bestowed: but it was the manner, even more than the substance, of his acts which gave them value with those who loved him. His correspondence with his family and friends will afford the best evidence of this fact.

---

[121] Mr. King, who highly disapproved of this attempt, informs Clive that the motion was made by a Proprietor at the suggestion of his father, but withdrawn on seeing it was not relished by the Directors.

[122] Letter to Mr. Belchier, 21st of August, 1757.

Clive, in a letter[123] to his father, written shortly after the battle of Plassey, giving him an account of the events which had occurred from the capture of Chandernagore till the enthronement of Meer Jaffier, informs him, that the Nabob's generosity will enable him to live in his native country, in a manner much beyond his most sanguine expectation.

"I have ordered," he states in this letter, "2000*l.* to each[124] of my sisters, and shall take care of my brothers in due time. I would advise the lasses to marry as soon as possible, for they have no time to lose. There is no occasion for you following the law any more: but more of this when I have the pleasure of seeing you, which, I hope, will be in twelve or fourteen months."

"You may order the Rector[125] to get every thing ready for the reparation of old Styche. I shall bring his brother home with 15,000*l.*, and also Mrs. Clive's brother. If I can get into Parliament, I shall be very glad; but no more struggles against ministry: I choose to be with them.

"Mrs. Clive will write my mother at large. My kind wishes attend her, not forgetting my brothers and sisters."

When Clive resolved, as has elsewhere been stated, to defer his departure for England, he directed his agents to add to the allowance before given to his father and mother the sum of 500*l.* per annum, and to keep a coach for them[126]: he also desired them to pay 25*l.* per annum to each of his four aunts, and to two of Mrs. Clive's, to whose other relations in England he gave liberal assistance. For her brother, Captain Maskelyne, who was on the Madras establishment, Clive cherished a very sincere regard; but I should conclude, from what appears in the manuscripts in my possession that, though a pleasant and respectable gentleman, Captain Maskelyne had little talent as an officer. His conduct to part of the Nabob's family, while commanding at Arcot, had been severely condemned by Mr. Pigot. We find amongst his letters to his brother-in-law an indignant remonstrance against the treatment he had met with from the Governor, who also wrote Clive fully upon the subject. The latter in his reply[127] to Mr. Pigot states the great uneasiness which the circumstance had caused him, but adds, that he derived consolation from the belief, that it entirely proceeded from an error of judgment. This instance, added to others, proves that, though the title to Clive's regard rested more upon the heart than the head of the individual by whom it was possessed, yet he was rigid in his principle of never nominating any one to public station whose qualities did not fit him to perform its duties. He regretted, as is shown by his letters, that Captain Maskelyne did not accompany him to Bengal, as a member of his family; but, instead of appointing him to one of the many high and lucrative

[123] 9th of August, 1757.

[124] In Clive's letter to his agents, of the 21st of August, 1757, he directs 2000*l.* to be paid to each of his five sisters, Rebecca, Sarah, Judith, Frances, and Anne: this amount to be given for their use for ever.

[125] The Reverend Mr. Clive, his cousin.

[126] This order is repeated as one some time before given in a letter to Sir Edward Clive, Bart., and his other agents, dated 9th of November, 1758.

[127] 25th of December, 1757.

stations he had in his gift, he recommended him to go to England, and added to his small means what he deemed necessary to place him in independence[128]: and we are amused with the following passage, in a letter[129] from Clive to his father:—"My brother-in-law, Captain Maskelyne, goes by this conveyance, and will bring you this: he is worth 10,000*l.* or 11,000*l.* I beg you will assist in settling him in the world, and in getting him a good wife."

In the same letter he observes, "Should you have occasion for money to purchase commissions for my brothers, or to answer any other purpose that may be for their advantage, you will apply to my attorneys, who I desire may supply you accordingly."

The letter[130] from Mr. Clive to his son, acknowledging the receipt of the accounts of his success, commences with one of those simple but natural bursts of paternal affection that mock all imitation.

"Your last letter," he says, "gave me joy beyond all possibility of expression. The whole kingdom is in transports for the glory and success their countryman has gained. Come away, and let us rejoice together!"

In a subsequent letter, he dwells with true paternal feeling upon the same subject.

"May Heaven," he writes[131], "preserve you safe to Old England, where not only your friends and relations, but strangers who never saw you, will congratulate you for the glorious actions you have done your country. With what joy shall I embrace you! Oh, may I live to see that day! Your mother and sisters are sitting with me round the fire, drinking to your health and safe voyage."

Mr. Clive appears, from his own statement, to have been involved in his circumstances, and to have felt much distress in becoming such a burden to his son. In his answer to the letter which informed him of Clive's agents being directed to give him the additional sum of 500*l.* per annum, and to keep a coach for him, he observes[132], "I have received your letter of the 9th of November, 1758, and am under the greatest obligations that ever father was to a son, especially in the unhappy circumstances my own imprudence and being bound for others hath rendered me. Mr. Woolaston, for whom I was surety, is now dead; and what he owed the government, together with what remained unpaid on my account, amount to no less than 9000*l.* more than we have to pay. The Treasury, by direction of the Duke of Newcastle, have postponed the payment to a future day; but I fear that day will come before you arrive in England; and when you come, what pretence have I to expect or desire you should set me free, when I have already had your benevolence in so extraordinary a manner? Thank God you have so much in your power! Let us live on a fifth part of what you have so generously allowed me. If I am free, I shall be content; and, while I live, bless Providence, and pray for the increase of

[128] I have not been able to ascertain the exact amount Clive gave Captain Maskelyne, but judge it must have been considerable from a passage in one of his letters.

[129] 29th of December, 1758.

[130] 23d of March, 1758.

[131] 23d of December, 1758.

[132] 29th of July, 1759.

your happiness, who have saved a distressed family from utter ruin."

The letters from Clive's mother breathe the truest maternal affection. Her warmest gratitude is expressed for that comfort which he has diffused throughout all his family, and above all, as the old lady states, for his great kindness to "her girls."

The greater part of the letters from Clive's mother and sisters, subsequent to his marriage, are addressed to Mrs. Clive, but docketed by himself, and placed among his own papers; a proof of the value he attached to the feelings which they expressed. They contain the common topics of such correspondence, marked with a feeling of the warmest affection for one who, amid all his public avocations, was continually affording them proofs of his love and attachment. Towards Mrs. Clive there appears to have been but one sentiment throughout the family: all speak of her constant attention and kindness with gratitude, and appear to rejoice as much in their brother's happiness in the married state, as in the other instances of his good fortune.

Besides occasional acts of generosity, Clive continued incessant in his endeavours to render happy, by his regard and attention, every branch of his family, however distant. In this he was wholly disinterested, for none of them (except, perhaps, Sir Edward Clive) were in a situation to afford him the slightest aid; but they gave him, what he more valued, their gratitude and affection.

The impressions produced by his conduct towards every one with whom he was connected cannot be better shown than by inserting some short extracts from the entertaining letters of one of his female cousins[133] to Mrs. Clive in India.

"I don't know what title I must give you now[134], but I am sure I may say, 'To the agreeable Mrs. Clive.' I have always wrote whenever I heard the ships sailed, and by Captain Tully and Mr. King. Ill fate for you and me, that so many fine thoughts should be sent to the bottom of the sea! Neptune will be quite entertained. As to the name of Clive above ground, the Colonel has made it so famous, that it is the only comfort I have in still being a Clive. * * * * * * * He is in the highest esteem in this part of the world, and does honour to all his relations. * * * * Your father, my cousin Clive, dined with us yesterday, and read, or tried to read, one of the Colonel's letters; but his joy, with tenderness at the thoughts of such a son, made him burst twice into tears before he could go on. Is it to be wondered at? for sure it must be a pleasure so great, the strongest mind must be greatly affected. Well, I sincerely wish you all safe on your native shore, with your bags of money, and bushels of diamonds; with the Eastern Prince the Colonel is so good as to say he will get for me. I can't possibly refuse him. I have a taste to be a princess. As to Captain Clack, you are so good to think of for me, if this Prince don't care to take so long a voyage, don't leave the Captain behind. The war makes men very scarce. He shall talk for ever, and I for ever have patience. I have been in town a fortnight, at two plays; one, a new tragedy somewhat resembling the story of The Children in the Wood. Did you ever read that old ballad? Garrick is in as much vogue as ever; operas at a low ebb. I suppose you are a complete mistress of harmony.

[133] Miss Sarah Clive.

[134] 26th of December, 1758.

"I hope you will never receive this letter: not that I don't think it very clever; but I wish the Colonel and all his family may be in a ship, the sails filled with most prosperous gales, that will, soon as possible, send you safe to your own country and friends; one of whom I hope ever to be styled, which will always be a pleasure to your sincere and affectionate cousin."

We meet the following passage in another letter from this lady, which appears to have been written about the same period (for, like many ladies' letters, it has no date.)

"I have a thousand things to say to you, and but a moment's time. I find the bearer of this is a painter; hope the Colonel and you will let him take your pictures. I should be glad of them in miniature. I begin to fear the Colonel will not bring me the Eastern Prince till it is too late: the bushel of diamonds runs strangely in my head. Fanny is going to enter into the happy state of matrimony. I have seen the lover: upon my word, a pretty, cherry-cheeked, agreeable young counsellor. I hear he is called to the bar, and will have 500*l.* a year. I wish I had been the Colonel's sister; not to detract from them; certainly he is a great advantage to his family; and I believe, after my aunts and myself, that horrid name of old maid will be extirpated out of the house of Clive.

"I have still a thousand things to say. Apelles is arrived, and must have this letter: I don't know, but it may be of service to him, his occasioning me to release you. Well, a little more. All diversions go on as usual; a gloomy town—general mourning for the Princess of Orange; the linen that is worn is crape, as yellow as saffron, and what they call Turkey gauze, that looks like sarcenet: a sketch that the world is as ridiculous as ever. A most elegant ball at Lord Sandwich's! I must not say any more, only beg my respects and most sincere love to the Colonel. I wish for your speedy return to England. Pray my love to cousin George, who I would write to had I a moment, but will in the next ship."

Clive had appointed several of his relations and friends joint agents in England; and he was very fortunate in having his near connexion, Sir Edward Clive, Bart. (a Judge of circuit), as one of them. It appears to have required all that gentleman's strictness to prevent his relation suffering from the bad choice he had made of one of his men of business.

"One of your attorneys," Sir Edward remarks[135], "is a man I never can, and never shall, accord with. I have several things to reveal to you when you come home. I believe, in order to take care of your interest, and (as I think) to protect your property, I must file a bill in Chancery. When you arrive, you shall have an account of it: I don't think any labour troublesome to serve you, but assure you (and Mr. King knows it) I have had a great deal.

"It is a great pleasure," adds this respectable Judge, "to know that, considering your father and his large family, God Almighty has put it into your mind, as well as your power, to make him and them happy. Assisting a parent must be the most agreeable sensation to good hearts. I happened, in a small way, to have that happy opportunity. I call it happy, and it affords me many agreeable reflections."

[135] Letter to Clive, 24th of December, 1759.

A few months after Clive sailed for India, his eldest sister[136] married Sir James Markham, Bart.; and when he returned, he found that three more had entered the matrimonial state, being much indebted (if we are to believe their sprightly cousin already noticed) for their happy settlement to the good fortune of having an Indian Colonel for their brother.

Clive never forgot those to whom he was in any degree indebted for his advancement. Several of his letters are addressed to Mr. Chauncey, a gentleman who, though then retired, had, at one period, taken a very active part in Indian affairs. In one of these letters[137], after communicating to him the peace with Suraj-u-Dowlah, Clive observes, "If I have been in any way instrumental in the late revolution, the merit is entirely owing to you, who countenanced, favoured, and protected me, and was the chief cause of my coming to India in a station which rendered me capable of serving the Company. Accept, Sir, of my gratitude, and sincerest wishes for your welfare. May you enjoy the blessings of peace and retirement, and may success and every other happiness in this life forsake me, when I forget how much I am obliged to you!"

However, a sense of gratitude had more value from being expressed in the moment of victory, and from being addressed to an individual who had no longer any power of promoting his views. I notice such facts, not only because they are the truest indications of character, but as they account for the zeal and attachment which Clive's numerous and respectable friends displayed on many trying occasions. Neither his wealth nor his fame could have inspired such feelings. Sincerity and warmth of heart alone can kindle corresponding sentiments in honourable minds.

Of Clive's friends in India I have already spoken. His ties with them had been formed in the course of public service, and remained unbroken, except in the rare cases, where he thought individuals parted from those principles of action upon which his esteem was founded. His deep and affectionate gratitude towards Colonel Lawrence has been mentioned. His friendship for Mr. Pigot remained unchanged: not so that for Mr. Orme. We find in one of his father's letters an observation upon his being reconciled to that gentleman on his return to India in 1755. Mr. Clive expresses his hope, in this letter, that Mr. Orme's History would be speedily published, as the objections[138] on account of Mr. Chauncey were at an end.

Clive, though his experience had rendered him singularly well acquainted with the character of all classes of the natives of India, was very little, if at all, versed in the languages of that country; but he appears not only to have been most solicitous to avail himself of the aid of those who had this advantage, but, when he found the acquirement accompanied by integrity and talent, to recommend them, and place them in the highest stations in the service. His notice and patronage of Mr. Watts, Mr. Vansittart, and Mr. Hastings, afford ample proof of this fact; and,

[136] Lady Markham is still alive, and, although upwards of ninety, in the enjoyment of all her faculties.

[137] 23d of February, 1757.

[138] What these objections were, or the cause of their termination, is not explained; but Mr. Clive's letter proves that the first part of the history was written before 1755.

on almost all occasions, public and private, when he brings forward the names of those individuals, he adds some observations on the great advantages they enjoy over others, from their knowledge of the languages, the manners, and the habits of the people of India.

During his expedition to Bengal, Clive had only one of his relations in his family, Mr. George Clive, for whom he cherished a very sincere affection. The two persons to whom he appears to have been most attached were Mr. Walsh and Mr. Luke Scrafton, both civil servants of the Company, whose names have been frequently mentioned in the course of the narrative. They continued through life in habits of the strictest intimacy with their friend and patron. Of Mr. Walsh, Clive never speaks without expressing great respect for his character; and of his regard for Mr. Scrafton, whose lively disposition suited his own, we have many proofs. Bad health obliging that gentleman to go to Madras, Clive wrote by him to Sir George Pocock, in a style which evinced his kind and anxious solicitude.

"The bearer of this[139]," he observes, "Mr. Luke Scrafton, is a young fellow of great worth and honour. Much I fear he is too far gone to be recovered by the coast air: he has been a constant attendant of mine in all our expeditions, and can solve any question you may have to ask on the subject of Bengal. For God's sake return him to me in good health and condition!"

Clive was also on the most intimate terms with Captain Latham, a distinguished officer of His Majesty's navy; and this intimacy was increased from that gentleman's marriage to a relation of Mrs. Clive, who had accompanied her to India. I have found numerous private letters from Captain Latham, which are all written in the open manly style of a British seaman, and bear a convincing testimony to the tone of Clive's mind on all points connected with his friends. From the tenor of one, in answer to a letter from Clive, written immediately after the enthronement of Meer Jaffier, it would seem that Mrs. Latham was one of those whom he considered (from the relation in which she stood to him) entitled to participate in his good fortune. His conduct on this occasion appears to have given sincere pleasure to Mrs. Clive; as the letter in which his kindness and liberality are noticed is superscribed with the word "Charming," in her own handwriting.

I have before mentioned the origin of Clive's regard for Colonel Forde; the grounds upon which he selected him for the command of Bengal, and the degree in which he deemed himself indebted to him for his great and brilliant achievements. We have also seen the poignant feelings with which he regarded the conduct of the Court of Directors towards this able and gallant officer, who, immediately after the capture of Masulipatam, had the mortification to find himself superseded by Colonel Coote, who, a year before, had been his junior in Adlercron's regiment; but, returning from India with fortune and reputation, had obtained a Colonel's commission, and had just landed at Madras in command of a regiment destined for Calcutta.

Though Colonel Coote had evinced, on the expedition to Bengal, those qualities as an officer which subsequently made him so renowned, neither his oppor-

[139] 14th of September, 1759.

tunities nor his achievements bore as yet any comparison with those of Colonel Forde; but the successes of the latter were not known in England at the period of Coote's appointment. Many, therefore, will deny the justice of Clive's complaint of the conduct of his superiors on this occasion; but even these must admire that warmth and decision, with which he pledged himself to support an officer with whom he had no private friendship, except such as had been formed in consequence of his eminent public services.

The news of Colonel Coote's arrival reached Clive about the same period as the account of Major Forde's capture of Masulipatam, and of the conclusion of the treaty with the Subahdar of the Deccan. Desiring, at such a moment, to afford every consolation to the mind of that meritorious officer, he not only stated his opinion as to his superior claims to those of the officer by whom he was superseded, but gave him the most unqualified assurances of his future support.

"I can easily conceive," he observes in a letter[140] to Colonel Forde upon this occasion, "that such rank and honour bestowed (I think I can say without flattery) on one so much your inferior in every respect, must give you much concern. I assure you it has affected me greatly, and is one of my principal motives for wanting to push home with the utmost expedition on the 'Royal George.' I flatter myself, the request I have to make will not be denied me, which is, that you will stay in Bengal all next year, provided Coote remains on the coast. If within that time I do not get you a colonel's or lieutenant-colonel's commission, and an appointment of Commander-in-chief of all the forces in India, I will from that instant decline all transactions with Directors and East India affairs."

Clive's resentment at the Court of Directors was increased by their subsequently annulling Colonel Forde's appointment to Bengal, while his attachment to that officer was greatly heightened by his admirable conduct in the destruction of the Dutch armament. But there were other feelings which may have influenced his mind. He certainly entertained at this period a strong prejudice against Colonel Coote, which may possibly have originated from the prominent manner in which that officer, when only a Captain, was brought forward at Calcutta to support the alleged rights of his Majesty's service against those of the Company. But we have, nevertheless, proofs that Clive appreciated his talents from his employing[141] him on all occasions, and particularly in detaching him, after the battle of Plassey, in pursuit of the French corps. But at the same time that he entertained this high opinion of his military talents, he considered, from his whole conduct in Bengal, that he was mercenary and prone to intrigue, and consequently an unfit person to be intrusted with great powers on such a scene. I do not find among Clive's papers any specific grounds to justify this opinion; and in the absence of all such documents, we must conclude, from the high reputation which Colonel Coote attained and supported, that it was erroneous; or, at all events, that, if this eminent commander evinced in his youth any such dispositions as those of which he was suspected, they were early corrected: for though he never displayed any remark-

[140] 24th of August, 1759.

[141] Captain Coote commanded the troops detached to take Hooghley, and he was, before the battle of Plassey, sent with the advance to attack Kutwa.

able talents as a statesman, he assuredly became as qualified for the chief military command in India as any person that ever held that station; and during his latter years, the love and esteem in which he was held by his countrymen was even exceeded by the affectionate regard and attachment of the native troops, whom he so often led to victory.

In giving this tribute to a soldier, whose memory I have venerated from my earliest years, I must do justice to Clive by declaring my sincere conviction (formed from the perusal of his numerous letters upon the subject) that he was most sincere and conscientious in the opinion he expressed, and upon which he acted. With such impressions upon his mind, he certainly thought he was doing his duty to the public by his endeavours to keep Colonel Coote at Madras; and he was so solicitous to effect this object that he consented to the request of the government of Fort St. George, that the regiment of that officer should remain for some time at that presidency.

He enters fully upon this subject in his correspondence, both with Mr. Pigot and Mr. Vansittart; but his letters contain merely a repetition of his opinions as to Colonel Coote's unfitness for the general command of the forces in Bengal, while he recognises the benefits to be derived from his services in the mere military operations on the coast of Coromandel. The success of Clive's efforts on this occasion proved fortunate for the reputation of Colonel Coote, who, during the subsequent year, established a high military character by the battle of Wandewash and the capture of Pondicherry.

I have been compelled to enter more at length upon this subject than I desired, from its being intimately connected with those disputes regarding the employment of officers in India in which Clive became involved on his return to England. Colonel Coote, when he revisited his native country after the campaign of 1757, was received with favour and distinction. He was possessed of a small fortune, his connections were respectable, and his manners and address manly and agreeable. He became more prominent from being the senior King's land officer employed on the expedition to Bengal; and, from the comparatively low estimation in which the Company's[142] officers were held at that period, his fame was advanced to detract from their pretensions. He was represented as a rising officer, of whom Clive was jealous; and it was believed by many (till contradicted several years afterwards by his own evidence), that it was through his advice and remonstrances that the army advanced to the field of Plassey. Besides the influence and popularity which those combined causes gave to this officer, he enjoyed the marked favour and friendship of Mr. Sulivan, the Chairman of the Court of Directors, whose subsequent rupture with Clive is in a great degree to be attributed to their difference in opinion with regard to the respective pretensions and merits of Colonels Coote and Forde.

Clive, at the period of his second visit to his native country, was thirty-five years of age. We collect from his private correspondence, that he retained much of that hilarity of disposition for which he had been remarkable in youth. He was fond of female society; and many of his letters show that he was by no means indif-

[142] Though Clive held the King's commission as Lieutenant-Colonel, he was always considered as a Company's officer.

ferent to those aids by which personal appearance is improved. It was the fashion of the period to dress in gayer apparel than we now do; and the European visiter at an Indian Durbar, or Court, always wore a rich dress. We find in a letter[143] to Clive, from his friend Captain Latham, a description of a Durbar suit he was preparing for him, in which he says he has preferred a fine scarlet coat with handsome gold lace, to the common wear of velvet. He has also made up, he writes, a fine brocade waistcoat; and he adds to this intelligence, that "it is his design to line the coat with parchment, that it may not wrinkle!"

In a commission which Clive sent to his friend Mr. Orme, there is an amusing instance of his attention to the most trifling parts of his dress.

"I must now trouble you," he observes[144], "with a few commissions concerning family affairs. Imprimis, what you can provide must be of the best and finest you can get for love or money; two hundred shirts, the wristbands worked, some of the ruffles worked with a border either in squares or points, and the rest plain; stocks, neckcloths, and handkerchiefs in proportion; three corge[145] of the finest stockings; several pieces of plain and spotted muslin, two yards wide, for aprons; book-muslins; cambrics; a few pieces of the finest dimity; and a complete set of table linen of Fort St. David's diaper made for the purpose."

In the list of packages which Mr. Richard Clive sent to his son in Bengal, one is a box of wigs! Whether Clive had resorted to this ornament from want of hair, or from deference to the fashion of the period, I know not; but there is[146] an authentic anecdote of his boyhood, which proves how essential a wig was considered to all who were full dressed. Clive had, when very young, been admitted by a relation, who was Captain of the Tower, to be one of the spectators when his Majesty George the Second happened to visit that fortress. Nothing was wanted in the boy's dress to prepare him for the honour of approaching majesty except a wig! To supply this want one of the old Captain's was put upon his head; and his appearance in this costume was so singular as to attract the notice and smiles of the King, who inquired who he was, and spoke to him in a very kind and gracious manner.[147]

In concluding this chapter on the private occurrences of Clive's life during a period so eventful to his fame and fortune, I shall estimate, as far as I have the means, the wealth he carried to England, as well as the amount which he had, before he left India, given to, or settled upon, his friends and relations. I have already shown, in the fullest manner, how his great riches were acquired; and it is a grateful task to record the generous manner in which a considerable portion of them was distributed.

Clive, from what has been stated, may be said, when he returned to India in 1755, to have been worth little or no money beyond what he had vested for

[143] 5th of August, 1757.

[144] 1st of August, 1757.

[145] A corge is twenty pair.

[146] This anecdote of his father was communicated by Lord Powis.

[147] It is added that he was sent to school in a wig; but, as may be supposed, was soon quizzed out of it by his play-fellows.

redeeming the small family estate, and giving his parents an annuity. When he took possession of the government of Fort Saint David, he embarked in trade, like others who filled similar stations; but, to judge from his correspondence, he had not much success in his commercial pursuits. We read of nothing but bad markets, or the want of means of those who owed him money. He appears, before he embarked on the expedition to Bengal, to have made a large speculation in benjamin, which turned out badly. It is entertaining, when associated with the scenes in which he became engaged, to pursue his remarks upon his unprofitable adventure in this and other articles of trade.

After desiring his friend and agent, Mr. Orme, not to demand payment of the money owing to him by Messrs. Pybus and Roberts, and that the interest of the debt should be only 4 per cent., he observes[148], "You have given me a most curious account of my adventure in the Grampus. If I had not made better strokes in war than in trade, my money concerns would by this time be drawing to a conclusion."

The whole of Clive's money, when he returned to India in 1755, appears to have been in that country; for we find, from his correspondence, that he had hardly sufficient uninvested cash in England to pay for his annual supplies. He became anxious, however, after he attained great wealth, to remit it home; but this, owing to various causes, was very difficult. The public treasury was so rich from the successes in Bengal, that, for a period, no bills were drawn upon the Directors; Clive, therefore, had recourse to the Dutch Company, through whom he sent the greater part of his fortune; he also transmitted a considerable sum in diamonds[149] (a common mode at that time), and the rest in private bills; and, latterly, two on the Company.[150]

I have carefully examined his letters to his agents, from the 21st of August, 1755, when he advised them of his first remittance, till January, 1759, when he made one of his last; and the amount of property sent to England during that period is, as nearly as the difference of exchange and the loss[151] on bills enable us to judge, 280,000*l.* Of this I calculate that he received 210,000*l.* on the enthronement of Meer Jaffier; and the remaining 70,000*l.* is made up by part of his former fortune, his prize-money at Gheriah and Chandernagore, the receipts from the high stations[152] he held, and the accumulation of interest upon a considerable part of his property during the last five years of his residence in India.

---

[148] 11th of March, 1758.

[149] Clive sent sixteen thousand gold mohurs to his agents at Madras, Messrs. Orme and Vansittart, with directions to purchase diamonds as a remittance.

[150] One of the bills on the Company was for 8000*l.*, and the other for 32,881*l.* 12*s.* 2*d.* He advises his agents of these bills on the 9th of November and 23d of December, 1758.

[151] Clive expected the bills on Holland to produce 183,000*l.*, but, after a vexatious delay, they were paid with great deduction. His father states the loss upon this transaction as amounting to 10,000*l.*

[152] I consider the statement of the Committee of the House of Commons, of Clive's receipts at Moorshedabad, to be exaggerated; but we shall have occasion to notice this statement hereafter, particularly the note annexed to it, in which it is asserted, in direct opposition to truth, that Clive's jaghire was obtained at the same period as the donation from Meer Jaffier. Mr. Mill copies the statement and note without remark. (Vol. iii. p. 326.)

From what has been stated we may assume that Clive's fortune, before the jaghire was settled upon him, did not amount to 300,000*l.* It appears from documents before me that, previous to this grant, he had given away, or vested for annuities, a sum not less than 50,000*l.*[153] (more than one sixth of his fortune), to render comfortable and independent those for whom he cherished affection and gratitude.

Clive was, subsequently to these acts of generosity, enriched by the grant of the jaghire, which he himself estimates at 27,000*l.* per annum. With this addition, we may conclude he had an income of upwards of 40,000*l.*; a large amount, but far below what this Indian Crœsus (for such he was deemed) was thought by his countrymen to possess.

[153] The following sums appear to have been given or settled upon his relations and friends:—

Present to his sisters		£10,000
Present to Captain Maskelyne and others		10,000
Money vested to produce an annuity for his father, of	£500	
Money vested to produce an annuity for his aunts, of	150	
Money vested to produce an annuity for Colonel Lawrence, of	500	
To keep a coach for his parents	300	
Yearly amount of annuities	£1450	
Sum vested to produce the above		30,000
Total		£50,000

CHAPTER XII.

Clive in England.—His Politics.—His Quarrel with Mr. Sulivan.—His Right to the Jaghire disputed.—Parties at the India House.—Disasters in India.—Clive called upon to resume the Government of Bengal—Consents—Sets out for India, 1764

Clive remained in his native country between three and four years; and it will be proper briefly to narrate the events of his private life during this period, to notice the part he took in the political transactions of the times, and the connections he formed with persons of power and influence, whether in the direction of Indian affairs, or of the more general interests of the British empire. The knowledge of such facts, connected as they became with his future career, is quite essential to our subject.

The constitution of Clive had never been robust. He had been, for the last two years in Bengal, freer than usual from the attacks of a spasmodic complaint, to which he appears to have been more or less subject from his earliest years. In 1759 he had a very violent attack of rheumatism, and feared, at one time, that it might settle into gout; but this apprehension vanished; and when he embarked at Calcutta he describes himself as in excellent health.

When Clive reached England, he was received with distinction by his Sovereign and the members of the administration; and, notwithstanding the deep offence taken at his last public despatch, the Court of Directors, and particularly their Chairman, Mr. Sulivan, welcomed him as one to whom the Company were deeply indebted. The enjoyment, however, of those flattering attentions was early interrupted by a violent and dangerous illness, which for many months threatened to terminate his existence.

Clive was not, for some time after his arrival, honoured by any public mark of royal favour. This seems to have arisen from two causes: one, his very long and serious illness; the other, his desire to obtain more than the ministers were willing to grant. He, probably, at first expected to enter the British House of Peers, and to have a red riband; but, after a considerable delay, he received only an Irish peerage.

In writing[154] to his friend Major Carnac upon this subject, he observes; "If health had not deserted me on my first arrival in England, in all probability I had been an English peer, instead of an Irish one, with the promise of a red riband. I know I could have bought the title (which is usual), but that I was above, and

[154] 27th of February, 1762.

the honours I have obtained are free and voluntary. My wishes may hereafter be accomplished."

Clive had assumed a scale of expenditure suited to his income. He engaged in elections to aid his friends in the administration, and to give him the influence he desired in the prosecution of his plans for his own advancement, and the furtherance of those which he thought essential to the prosperity and security of the Indian empire. The expenses into which he was early led, combined with his liberality to his family, amounted to a very large sum[155]; and we can easily conceive the alarm with which he received, while yet on a sick bed, an intimation from Mr. Sulivan, that the Directors showed an inclination to question his title to his jaghire.

He strongly and feelingly expresses his sentiments upon this subject in a letter to Mr. Amyatt; "My arrival in England," he observes[156], "was attended with every mark of respect that I could wish, and my interest in Leadenhall Street might have been of as much consequence as I could have desired, for the advantage of my friends; but a most severe fit of sickness overset all. For twelve months it was difficult to pronounce whether I was to live or die. In so dreadful a situation, I could not think much of India, or indeed of any thing else but death. It is very natural to think, the interest of a dying man could not be very great. Under these circumstances, I had hints given me that either some attempts would be made upon my jaghire, or some proposal made for giving it up to the Company after a certain time, on a supposition, perhaps, that I had not long to live. Accordingly I was given to understand by Sulivan, that the gentlemen of the Secret Committee would wait upon me on this subject. But health returning, this proposal was dropt, and I have heard nothing more of it since. Although I have such an interest at Court and in Parliament, that I should not be afraid of an attack from the whole Court of Directors united, yet all my friends advise me I should do nothing to exasperate them, if they are silent as to my jaghire. Indeed it is an object of such importance, that I should be inexcusable if I did not make every other consideration give way to it; and this is one of the reasons why I cannot join openly with the Bengal gentlemen in their resentments. It depends upon you, my friend, to make me a free man, by getting this grant confirmed from Delhi, and getting such acknowledgment from under the hands of the old Nabob, and the present Nabob, as may enable me to put all our enemies at defiance. In this, I am sure, you will be assisted by Vansittart."

The account of the deposition of Meer Jaffier, and the election of Cossim Ali Khan, which had been planned by Mr. Holwell immediately after Clive left Calcutta, will occupy the next chapter. I only so far notice this revolution at present,

[155] This fact he mentions in several letters. In one to Mr. Amyatt, after entreating that gentleman to remain a short time longer in Bengal, to succeed Mr. Vansittart in the government, he warns him against retiring till possessed of an ample fortune. He notices the disappointment experienced by many of their friends, by the discovery of their inadequate means, and adds, that he had already spent[*] (in a period of eighteen months) upwards of 60,000*l.*

[*] This letter is dated 27th of February, 1762. Clive could not have reached England before September or October, 1760, and had been a twelvemonth on a sick bed.

[156] 27th of February, 1762.

as to state its effect on Clive's private feelings; as it divided and rendered irreconcilable enemies the friends in India whom he most valued. Though he deplored the revolution, and anticipated its bad consequences to the reputation of the English Government, he believed Mr. Vansittart to have been both disinterested and conscientious in the part he took; and with this impression, while he admitted the manly sincerity and honourable principles which dictated the violent opposition of his friend Major Carnac, he decidedly blamed the warmth and want of respect with which he had addressed his superiors on this subject. Mr. Amyatt was much respected by Clive both for his talents and integrity. He wished him to succeed Mr. Vansittart in the Government, and was unwilling that his services should be lost by his continued opposition, grounded on a measure which, as Clive truly stated, however much to be regretted, was now past and could not be recalled.

With such sentiments, Clive endeavoured to reconcile his friends to each other. His efforts were not successful: but it is a remarkable testimony to his personal character, that, during this period of violent collision between the parties in Bengal, every individual engaged in the contest referred to him, as to one on whose honour and judgment they had implicit reliance; and his more particular friends, though opposed on all other points, appear to have united whenever his interests were concerned.

To understand the motives which induced Clive to take an active part in the affairs of the India House, it is necessary to explain the actual condition of the different parties who at this period took a share in the management of the Company's concerns.

The legislature had not as yet directly interfered in the administration of our Eastern possessions; but ministers and men of high rank and influence had, nevertheless, great power and weight, both in the Court of Directors and in the Court of Proprietors. This, however, appears to have been seldom if ever exerted but to serve individuals, and to have been more maintained to promote parliamentary influence, and as a means of rewarding and attaching friends, than with any view to the benefit of the public interests of either the Indian or the British empire.

Mr. Sulivan, as has been mentioned before, had attained an ascendency in the direction, of which he was in complete possession when Clive came to England. But though he had a majority of the Directors with him, he had many and virulent opponents among the Proprietors. The most prominent of these were gentlemen who had been in Bengal, who considered themselves injured by the frequent supersession of the servants of that presidency by those of Madras and Bombay, to which they considered Mr. Sulivan more attached, and particularly to the latter.

Though Mr. Sulivan, as has been shown, professed great admiration of Clive, and was much indebted to him for the station he had attained in the direction, he appears to have early regarded him as a dangerous rival. It is certainly to be concluded from what subsequently took place, that the intimation regarding his jaghire was meant to repress the ambition of Clive, as connected with Indian affairs; and for a period it had the desired effect. This we learn from several of his private letters. In one, to Mr. Pybus at Madras, he makes the following observations on this subject[157]:—

"The Court of Directors seem to be much in the same situation as when you left England. Sulivan is the reigning director, and he follows the same plan of keeping every one out of the direction who is endowed with more knowledge, or would be likely to have more weight and influence, than himself. This kind of political behaviour has exasperated most of the gentlemen who are lately come from India, particularly those from Bengal. They are surprised I do not join in their resentments; and I should think it very surprising if I did, considering I have such an immense stake in India. My future power, my future grandeur, all depend upon the receipt of the jaghire money. I should be a madman to set at defiance those who at present show no inclination to hurt me. I have so far fallen into their way of thinking, as to preside at a general meeting of a club of East Indians once a fortnight; and this has all the effect I could wish, of keeping Sulivan in awe, and of convincing him, that, though I do not mean to hurt him, I can do such a thing if he attempts to hurt me. Indeed I am so strongly supported by the Government and by Parliament, that I should not be afraid of an attack from the whole body united; but there is no necessity of wantonly exciting them to attempts against my interest."

Clive, soon after he recovered from his illness, appears to have established himself in great favour at Court; and the Queen stood godmother to one of his children. These marks of royal favour, and his connection with the administration, combined with his known opinion that the British legislature ought to take a share in the management of the national interests in India, tended much to increase Mr. Sulivan's jealousy, and to alarm his ambition. His feelings, indeed, for some time remained dormant; but from the first day of Clive's landing in England there existed no cordiality between them. That no rupture ensued during this period, is, in some degree, to be attributed to Mr. Sulivan being in 1762 out of the direction by rotation. Before next general election, circumstances occurred which decided Clive in the determination to combine his interests with those of the great majority of Indians[158], to oppose this autocrat of the India House.

We find, in one of Clive's letters[159] to Mr. Vansittart, what I believe to be an honest statement of his feelings at the period at which it was written; and it sufficiently indicates the part he afterwards took to prevent the re-election of Mr. Sulivan.

"There is," he observes, "a terrible storm brewing against the next general election. Sulivan, who is out of the direction this year, is strongly opposed by Rous and his party, and by part, if not all, of the East Indians (particularly the Bengalees), and matters are carried to such lengths, that either Sulivan or Rous must give way. * * * * * * I must acknowledge that in my heart I am a well-wisher for the cause of Rous, although, considering the great stake I have in India, it is probable

[157] 27th February, 1762.

[158] We have already noticed, that the most violent of Mr. Sulivan's opponents were the gentlemen from Bengal, who formed, on this occasion, a party, long afterwards known in the India House by the name of the "Bengal Squad."

[159] 22d November, 1762.

I shall remain neuter. Sulivan might have attached me to his interest if he had pleased, but he could never forgive the Bengal letter[160], and never has reposed that confidence in me which my services to the East India Company entitled me to. The consequence has been, that we have all along behaved to one another like shy cocks, at times outwardly expressing great regard and friendship for each other."

The appearance even of friendship could not long continue between individuals actuated by such different interests and feelings. Lord Clive was the first to avow openly his real sentiments; but, according to his own statement, he had the completest proof that Mr. Sulivan was the secret abetter of those who sought to ruin him both in fortune and fame; and he ascribed to the encouragement of that gentleman the numerous articles which appeared in the newspapers and other ephemeral publications, traducing his character. This belief was confirmed by a knowledge that the personal efforts of the ex-chairman were unremittingly applied to exalt the name of Coote to a rivalry with that of Clive. But what appears to have exasperated him in the highest degree was the production of a letter[161] which Mr. Sulivan had written to his friend Colonel Coote, in March, 1761, in which, when remarking upon some disputes that the Colonel had with the government at Madras, he observes; "The behaviour of the then Bengal gentlemen to you being similar to their treatment of their masters, it puts an end to all reasoning. Still your detention at Madras verifies that reflection of Pope upon human foresight, 'Whatever is, is best;' and how much are we indebted to Providence for this disobedience to our orders. Your country and your friend share the honour of your masterly and prosperous conduct."

In the same letter, when referring more immediately to Colonel Coote's quarrel[162] with the gentlemen of Fort St. George, Mr. Sulivan adds:—

"Our people at Madras, we find, are hot-headed, but they are able, generous, and open. I can smother their rebukes; but the ungrateful wretches, late of Bengal, have hurt my temper. I pray keep up a friendly correspondence with General Lawrence,—he is great and good. I adore him for his distinguished and noble spirit."

The allusions in the latter paragraph of this letter were too plainly directed against Clive to be mistaken; and considering that, at the period when it was written, Mr. Sulivan was on professed good terms with him, he deemed the expression of such sentiments unpardonable. But, on the other hand, it might have been urged by Mr. Sulivan's friends, that these sentiments, though brought to light by some breach of confidence, were meant only for a private friend, and that there could be no breach of friendship where none existed; that Lord Clive and Mr. Sulivan belonged to different parties in politics; that their personal connections and views,

[160] For this letter, vide *antè*, p. 51.

[161] In the heat of the canvass at the India House, in the beginning of 1763, a copy of this letter was obtained and circulated. One was sent to Clive, who transmitted it to Mr. Vansittart, with expressions of the most unqualified indignation.

[162] Colonel Coote, when he took Pondicherry, supported by the Admiral, desired to keep that fortress for the King of England, and appointed an officer to command it. Mr. Pigot, and the gentlemen in Council at Fort St. George, refused to advance pay to the army till the fortress was given up; and having thus compelled that concession, removed the commandant nominated by Colonel Coote.

particularly as connected with the Indian administration in England, were opposed to each other; and that, if Mr. Sulivan had been led by considerations of interest to preserve outward terms of cordiality with Lord Clive, his Lordship had been alone restrained from attacking him by similar prudential considerations.

Amid the causes which tended to hasten a rupture between these individuals, we must not omit the irritation produced by their difference of opinion as to the merits and claims of the Company's servants in India. Clive was the bold and persevering advocate of all those who had gained and merited his friendship by the aid they gave him in the performance of their public duties. Several of his recommendations to Mr. Sulivan met with attention; but others were treated with slight or delay. I have already mentioned Clive's feeling respecting Colonel Forde. However great the claims of that officer, the more recent successes of his rival, Colonel Coote, had fully justified those who furthered his promotion in England; but Major Carnac had distinguished himself in Bengal by the defeat of the Shah-Zada, the surrender of that prince, and the capture of M. Law and the French who were attached to him. These services, Clive thought, gave him a claim to a superior commission. He was also very anxious to obtain a majority for Captain Knox, who, independent of his services under him, had, on several late occasions[163], established a reputation for skill and gallantry, superior to any one of his standing in India.

At this period it was not uncommon to give superior commissions to those who greatly distinguished themselves. Clive was the advocate of a system, which, considering the actual state of the service, he thought indispensable to reward and encourage men of talent and enterprise. Mr. Sulivan, though he did not deny the merits of the persons brought to his notice by Clive, appears to have been very reluctant to promote them, at the hazard of creating discontent to others. He was, like other members of the Court of Directors at that period, prompt to attend to the frequent appeals made to them against the local government; and such appeals were usually from those who had no pretensions to preferment but that of seniority, and who were often persons quite unfitted, by their habits and character, for the delicate and arduous duties which, at this period, devolved upon officers intrusted with high military command. Clive, by his notes in answer to the Chairman on these points, appears to have been very impatient of the general reasoning with which his applications were answered. He conscientiously felt, in supporting those he brought forward, that he acted from no motive but that of the public good; he saw that by such maxims our Indian empire never would have been gained; and he was quite satisfied that the system which Mr. Sulivan desired to establish, of directing the attention of the civil and military servants in India to the government in England, was calculated to subvert all authority in the local administration, and, in its results, to distract, weaken, and distress our yet infant empire in the East. Sulivan's were the principles of the head of a commercial company; Clive's those of the founder and sustainer of an empire.

To understand all the motives which influenced Clive's conduct at this period,

[163] The rapid march of Captain Knox to the relief of Patna in 1760, and the severe action he afterwards fought with a handful of men against Cuddim Hussun Khan, who had a considerable army, were exploits worthy of Clive himself.

it is necessary to advert to the changes in the British administration, and especially, in so far as these affected the individuals with whom he was most intimately connected.

The personal influence exercised by Lord Bute over the mind of his young sovereign counteracted the wise and vigorous measures of Pitt; who, on being thwarted in his design of anticipating the hostile intentions of Spain, retired with his friends from the cabinet.[164] Aware of the great popularity of his predecessor, Lord Bute (who succeeded Mr. Pitt) tried every effort to increase the number of his adherents. Amongst others, Clive was courted to give his support to the new administration. His fame, his wealth, and the votes he commanded, gave importance to his aid; and the terms offered him were alike tempting to his ambition and interests: but his respect for the integrity and great talents of Mr. Pitt had been increased by personal acquaintance[165], and he cherished the sincerest attachment to Mr. George Grenville, who, on Pitt's retirement, had resigned his situation as Treasurer of the Navy. Besides these personal considerations, the measures of Mr. Pitt were congenial with every sentiment of his mind; and he augured no benefit to the nation from the less energetic character of his successor, whose avowed eagerness for peace (he anticipated) would prevent its being concluded on such favourable terms as the successes of the war gave grounds to expect.

Governed by these motives, Clive rejected the overtures of Lord Bute. He states the grounds of his conduct in a letter to Major Carnac, written a month after the change of ministers occurred.

"Now that we are to have peace abroad," he observes[166], "war is commencing at home amongst ourselves. There is to be a most violent contest, at the meeting of Parliament, whether Bute or Newcastle is to govern this kingdom; and the times are so critical that every member has an opportunity of fixing a price upon his services. I still continue to be one of those unfashionable kind of people who think very highly of independency, and to bless my stars, indulgent fortune has enabled me to act according to my conscience. Being very lately asked, by authority, if I had any honours to ask from my sovereign, my answer was, that I thought it dishonourable to take advantage of the times; but that when these parliamentary disputes were at an end, if his Majesty should then approve of my conduct by

[164] Mr. Pitt resigned on the 5th October, 1761.

[165] We find in Clive's correspondence many allusions to his intercourse with Mr. Pitt, whom he describes as impressed with the fullest conviction of the importance of India to England. In a draft of a private note to the Chairman of the Directors, (which is not dated) he observes; "A few days ago I was with the Duke of Newcastle and Mr. Pitt. The discourse of the former was truly in the courtiers' style—many professions of friendship and regard, many offers of service, without the least meaning in them; but the discourse of the latter, which lasted an hour and a half, was of a more serious nature, and much more to the purpose. The subject was the support and welfare of the East India Company. Mr. Pitt seems thoroughly convinced of the infinite consequence of the trade of the East India Company to the nation; he made no scruple to me of giving it the preference to our concerns in America. Indeed, a man of Mr. Pitt's influence and way of thinking is necessary to oppose to the influence of Lord Anson, who certainly is no friend to our Company."

[166] 23d November, 1762.

rewarding it, I should think myself highly honoured in receiving any marks of the royal favour."

When the treaty of peace between France and England was in the course of negotiation, the opinion of Bussy[167] was taken on all points connected with the interests of his nation in India. No similar reference appears to have been made to Clive, whose knowledge far exceeded that of every other individual, on this important subject. But he was too earnest in his desire to promote the future peace of India to allow any party motives to prevent his offering every information that could aid ministers in that part of the negotiation which related to our Eastern possessions; he transmitted, therefore, a memorial to Lord Bute.

In this memorial Clive stated, that it was not now more than fifteen years since the European nations, who had established factories in India, were as much regulated and controlled in their concerns by the native governments as the natives themselves. To the extortions to which this exposed them, to the expense of their establishments, and to the decrease in value in the Indian manufactures, he attributes the disappointment of the expectations originally formed of great profits from this trade. Dupleix (he observes), on the ground that commerce alone must, under such circumstances, be a losing concern, suggested to his government the policy of making conquests in India; territorial revenue being, in his opinion, the only source by which a European nation could derive wealth from that country.

"Acting upon the principles he recommended," to use the words of the memorial, "Dupleix engaged in the contentions of the princes of the country, and had, at one time, in a great measure, obtained his aim. There remained nothing to complete it but the expulsion of the English out of Hindustan. We were at that time wholly attached to mercantile ideas; but undoubted proof of M. Dupleix's projects obliged us to draw the sword, and our successes have been so great that we have accomplished for ourselves, and against the French, exactly every thing that the French intended to accomplish for themselves and against us."

After stating these facts, Clive proceeds to detail, in this memorial, the extent to which concessions may be made at a general peace. He expresses great anxiety that the French should, if possible, be limited as to the number of men they are to maintain upon the coast of Coromandel; but, under every circumstance, he is strenuous against their re-admission to Bengal, except as merchants.

Lord Bute expressed his obligations to Lord Clive for this communication.

"I have received[168]," he states, "your Lordship's letter, and the paper accompanying it, in which you have offered your sentiments on the interests of this country with respect to our possessions in the East Indies, in a very clear and masterly manner. The lights you have thrown on the subject could not fail of being acceptable to me. I return your Lordship thanks, therefore, for the communication; and you may be assured that I will make a proper use of them."

---

[167] Bussy carried home a very large fortune, and through its influence he attained great consideration. The favour he enjoyed at court was increased by his connection with the Duc de Choiseul, whose niece he married soon after his return to France.

[168] Letter from Lord Bute, 1st September, 1762.

Every attention possible was given to Clive's suggestions; and by the definitive treaty of peace, concluded in February, 1763, the French government agreed not to maintain any troops in Bengal, or in the northern circars. These were the chief objects to which he had directed the attention of Lord Bute; but that minister (consulting only his friend Mr. Sulivan, and the Directors) had inserted an article into the preliminary treaty, by which the recognition, by the French, of the title of Mahommed Ali Khan, as Nabob of the Carnatic, was obtained by the English recognising the title of the ally of the French, Salabut Jung, as Subahdar of the Deckan. Nothing could be more preposterous than this guarantee (for to such it amounted) of the title of two Indian princes standing in the relations the Subahdar of the Deckan and the Nabob of Arcot did to each other, and to their European allies. Besides, Salabut Jung had for some years ceased to be the ally of the French, and was the ally of the English Government.

Clive, it would appear from the documents in my possession, only heard by accident of this extraordinary article. He hastened to Mr. Wood, the Under Secretary of State, whom he soon convinced of the embarrassment and danger it might produce. Lord Bute being also satisfied by his reasoning, it was, in forming the definitive treaty, so altered and amended, that (as I have elsewhere remarked) it might have remained innoxious, "had it not been subsequently converted by his Majesty's ministers into a pretext for one of the most unjustifiable and mischievous acts[169] of interference with the powers of the Company that is to be found on the page of Indian history."

Clive was dissatisfied with the peace, and voted in the minority that condemned that measure. His having come forward, under such circumstances, to give his aid in improving the treaty, as far as the interests of the Company were concerned, greatly increased his popularity with the proprietors. He continued in opposition, though to the sacrifice of his personal interests; nor was his conduct, on this occasion, dictated by any hope of Mr. Pitt's restoration to power. He evidently thought that great statesman had, by his own acts, barred himself from all chance of future employment.

Writing to Mr. Vansittart, Clive observes[170]; "Mr. Pitt, notwithstanding his great abilities and the many eminent services he has rendered this nation, has become the most odious man living to the King, nobility, and both parliaments. The King can never forgive him that unfortunate visit to the city on the Lord Mayor's day, his popularity was such, that it seemed as if *King William* instead of *King George* had been invited to that grand entertainment. As to the Privy Council, he has honoured them in Parliament with the names of state cowards and political misers. In short, his whole interest in Parliament is lost, and it is very improbable, if not impossible, he should ever come into employment again."

Ministers, unable to gain Clive, desired to give him every annoyance, and by diminishing his wealth and reputation, to lessen his influence. Lord Bute was Mr.

[169] The act to which I here allude is the appointment of Sir John Lindsay, ambassador from the King of England to the Nabob of Arcot. For an account of this transaction, vide Political India, vol. ii. p. 36.

[170] 2d February, 1762.

Sulivan's friend and patron; and the latter was a willing leader in this attack. The measures taken by his opponents satisfied Clive that he had no means of supporting his own interests but by a successful opposition to Mr. Sulivan at the ensuing general election at the India House.

The share of stock, which at this period, entitled a proprietor to vote, was 500*l.*; and though it was supposed to be the *bonâ fide* property of the individual who voted, the law was not so strict but what it could be avoided; and there is abundant evidence in the papers before me, that, in these annual contests for the administration, all parties "split votes" (as it was termed) to a very great extent.

Lord Clive, in the election of 1763, mentions his having employed 100,000*l.* in this manner; and we find in the following season, when his friends (after he had left England) so far triumphed over Mr. Sulivan as to bring Mr. Rous into the chair, that a bill[171] was brought into the House of Commons, and ultimately carried, by which the proprietor was compelled to swear, not only that the stock was *bonâ fide* his property, but that it had been in his possession a twelvemonth. This measure put an end (as was intended) to a practice, which, from being general, had ceased to be a reproach to individuals; and which, when resorted to by one party, left the other no option but following a bad example[172], or submitting to defeat.

Clive engaged in the contest at the general election at the India House with all the ardour which belonged to his character. His first intention appears to have been limited to the support of Mr. Rous; but I am led to conclude, from a few papers still preserved upon this subject, that he came forward personally as a candidate.

In a letter to Mr. Vansittart[173], adverting to what passed at a numerous meeting of the proprietors, he observes:—

"That tremendous day[174] is over. I need not be particular about it; you will have it from many hands. I should imagine there were present not less than eight hundred proprietors. Numbers of neutral people went off; and no small number of our friends, thinking our majority so great, that there was no occasion for their presence. Indeed, upon the holding up of hands, I thought we were at least two to one. This is really a great victory, considering we had the united strength of the whole ministry against us.

---

[171] The history of this bill is very curious, and is fully given in the letters of Mr. Walsh and others to Clive. It was brought forward in 1764, and read twice; but owing to some informality in its wording, was thrown out that session. This was imputed by Mr. Sulivan to the measures of his opponents, many of whom would have been disqualified, from not having had the stock for the prescribed period: they, on the other hand, accused Mr. Sulivan of having so timed the bill, as to establish his own votes and destroy those of his opponents.

[172] Mr. Walsh, in a letter to Lord Clive, of the 14th of February, 1765, after telling him of Mr. Sulivan's having split a number of votes, and of Mr. Divon (a partner of Child's house) having split 30,000*l.* to support him, informs Clive that he means to do the same with some of his money. He adds, "I am splitting mine to the amount of 20,000*l.* It is a troublesome and dangerous business, but the act of parliament will put an end to it."

[173] 19th March, 1763.

[174] Clive here alludes to a quarterly meeting of the Court of Proprietors.

"Our cause gains ground daily, I should think we shall be stronger at the election than we were in the General Court. However, this time only can show, and I do not choose to be very sanguine, our opponents being very active."

In a subsequent part of the same letter, anticipating success as certain, he enters into particulars as to the share he proposed to take in the affairs of the Company, and the arrangements he hoped to be able to carry into effect. It is a relief, when accompanying him into such scenes, to have the proof which this letter affords, that the expectation of being better able to promote the interests and strengthen the empire of India, was the leading motive which induced him to seek a station, which he may deem it most fortunate for himself and the interest of his country that he failed in attaining.

"If we should succeed," he adds in the letter before quoted, "I have no thought of ever accepting the Chair; I have neither application, knowledge, nor time, to undertake so laborious an employ. I shall confine myself to the political and military operations; and I think I may promise, you shall have a very large military force in India, such a force as will leave little to apprehend from our enemies in those parts. I propose having all the troops regimented; that there shall be kept up at Bengal three battalions of infantry, consisting of seven hundred and eighty men each battalion, and three companies of artillery, and four battalions of sepoys; the same at Fort St. George. A much less number will serve for Bombay. But more of this by the latter ships, when we see the event of the thing."

From letters addressed to his friends in India, during the first two years of his residence in England, it may be inferred that Clive, on his return to his native country, had no intention whatever of involving himself so deeply with the parties at the India House, and for some time he had little intercourse with any of the Directors.

"The situation I am in at present," he observes in a letter to Mr. Lushington[175], "and the part of the town where I now reside, seldom gives me an opportunity of seeing any of the Directors, to whom I have been very sparing of applications, since I do not like refusals."

From this and other facts we may collect that the desire to repel attack, on one hand, and the zeal and confidence of friends, on the other, hurried him into the contest in which he became engaged. His cause was warmly espoused by many noblemen and gentlemen of the first respectability. Almost all those who had served in India were of his party, and brought with them their friends and connections. These classes of proprietors were all-powerful at the quarterly meetings of the General Court; but when Directors were balloted for, the election was chiefly decided by persons in different walks of life, many of whom seldom, if ever, attended those Courts; but, having bought stock, either as a good investment of capital, or as the means of establishing an influence with the Directors, or with Administration, they gave their votes at elections as suited their respective interests. Mr. Sulivan had in his favour a great majority of the Directors, and he was actively supported by ministers; his strength was consequently great with this class of vot-

[175] 28th February, 1762.

ers, and with persons employed in England by the Company, and the officers and dependents of Government. He numbered also, among his friends, many of the merchants and tradesmen in the city, and nearly the whole of the ship-owners and others connected with the trade to India.

No election ever excited more interest than that now pending. Each party summoned all its forces; but Clive was destined to sustain his first defeat in a contest, in which we cannot but regret he should ever have engaged. His victorious opponents lost no time in making him feel the full weight of their resentment.

It has been already stated that Clive received his jaghire in 1759: the grounds upon which it had been granted and accepted were, at that period, placed upon the records of Government. He had enjoyed it four years; receiving, annually, its amount from the Company. Immediately after his return to England an intimation was conveyed to him, by Mr. Sulivan, that the Secret Committee of the Directors desired to communicate with him regarding this grant. He expressed his willingness to meet them, and enter into any explanation; and, considering the jaghire only as a life-rent, he was disposed to meet any fair arrangement that could be suggested; but the subject had not been re-agitated. Three years had passed, and his revenue from this source was regularly paid by the Bengal Government to his agents in Calcutta. Under such circumstances, whatever he might have apprehended from the hostility of Mr. Sulivan, whom he had certainly provoked by an open and determined opposition, he could not but be astonished to hear that the first step the Directors took, after the election of 1763, was to transmit orders to the Bengal Government to stop all further payments on account of Lord Clive's jaghire, and to furnish them with an account of all sums which had been paid to that nobleman and his attornies since the date of the grant.

I find, among the MSS. in my possession, a short narrative of the progress of this transaction, which presents, in a very compressed form, a series of facts, a knowledge of which is quite essential to the clear understanding of this question; I shall therefore give them in the words of the writer.[176]

"By the ninth article of the treaty between the Company and Meer Jaffier, at the time of the revolution in 1757, certain lands to the south of Calcutta were ceded to the Company as perpetual renters, the Nabob reserving to himself the lordship and quit-rents, which amounted to near 30,000*l.* yearly; and the Company could never be legally dispossessed so long as they continued to pay that quit-rent. The Company farmed out these ceded lands for above 100,000*l.* a year, and paid the quit-rent regularly to the Nabob till the year 1759, when the Nabob, in consideration of the great services rendered him by Lord Clive, assigned over to his Lordship, for life, that quit-rent. The assignment passed through all the forms usual in the country; and Lord Clive became grantee of the rent, under the same authority, precisely, as the East India Company had become grantee of the lands. From this period the rent was duly paid to Lord Clive, instead of to the Nabob; nor was there any intermission of the payment until differences arose between the noble Lord and Mr. Sulivan. It was intimated to his Lordship that some scruples were enter-

[176] The extract here quoted is part of a larger paper in defence of Lord Clive's conduct, and believed to be written by the late Sir Henry Strachey.

tained concerning any further payment; and Mr. Sulivan himself, at last informed him, that the Court of Directors were of opinion it ought to be retained for the Company's use. Lord Clive replied, that he was entitled to it as well by the laws of England as by the laws of India; that his right to the reserved rent was established upon the same authority as the Company's right to the ceded lands; that he was, notwithstanding, ready to concur in its devolving to the Company after he should have enjoyed the possession of it a reasonable number of years; and that he was desirous of a conference with the Court of Directors upon the subject, any day they might be pleased to appoint.

"It might have been imagined that the Court of Directors, if they had no other objects upon this occasion than the honour and interest of the Company and justice to an individual, would have paid some attention to an acquiescence of this nature. But their resolution, under the influence of their leader, was to resent the offence given them by the noble Lord in the attempt he was meditating against their power; and this was to be done, not by entering into the discussion of any terms of accommodation, in which each party, contending for the right above mentioned, might have met, but by putting an immediate stop to the payment of the jaghire, and leaving upon his Lordship the difficulties and vexation of recovering his property by a suit at law.

"There was, however, another secret motive to this violent and unjust measure. It happened that Lord Clive and his parliamentary friends had, for some time, acted in opposition to the court-party; and in this country, where ministers maintain their power by the inflicting of punishments, as well as by the distribution of rewards, it is no wonder that they should endeavour to weary out by oppression those whom they cannot allure by corruption. The Chairman of the East India Company was known to be at enmity with Lord Clive. Him, therefore, they considered as the aptest instrument with which the noble Lord might be tortured into a change of political conduct; and the plan of mutual resentment was no sooner resolved upon than executed.

"By one of the first ships which sailed for Bengal after the contested election, the Court of Directors sent orders to the Governor and Council, that they should no longer pay to the attornies of Lord Clive the rent granted him by Meer Jaffier, but that they should in future detain it in their hands, and carry it to the credit of the Company; and that they should transmit to the Court of Directors an exact account of all the sums already received by Lord Clive or his attornies on that head, as his Lordship's pretensions to the jaghire would be settled in England. The public letter conveying these orders assigned no reason for their being issued; but a private letter[177] from Mr. Sulivan to Mr. Vansittart, then Governor of Bengal, which was soon after produced on oath in the Court of Chancery, declared that the payment of the jaghire was stopped, because all cordiality between the Court of

[177] The contents of this private letter to the President of the Council at Bengal were as follows:—"That all cordiality being at an end with Lord Clive, the Court of Directors had stopped payment of his jaghire; a measure which would have taken place years ago, had it not been for him (Mr. Sulivan); and that, on this head, the said President was to obey every order which he might receive from the Court of Directors; and that more was not, nor must be expected of him."

Directors and Lord Clive was at an end. This vindictive plea, confidentially communicated by the Chairman to his friend the Governor, could not, however, be set up in a court of equity in justification of a flagrant violation of right. The Company had, for some years, paid the jaghire without objection; and even at this time of litigation they neither claimed any title to it themselves nor pretended that there was any other claimant than the present possessor. It is not necessary to enumerate the absurd arguments and mean subterfuges to which the Court of Directors were reduced, in answer to the bill filed against them by Lord Clive in the Court of Chancery. It is sufficient to observe, that the principal reasons which they assigned for discontinuing the payment were, that the Company might one day or other be called to account by the Emperor[178] of Hindustan for the money paid under the head of this jaghire; that, therefore, Lord Clive was accountable to them even for the sums he had already received; that, if the Nabob, Meer Jaffier, had a right to grant the jaghire out of his own revenues, (which, however, the Court of Directors did not admit,) yet as that Nabob had been deposed by the Company's agents, the grant became of no effect.

"Such were the grounds upon which the right to the jaghire was contested; and we may judge how very futile they were, by the sentiments entertained of them by all the eminent lawyers of the time; for the Court of Directors consulted gentlemen of the first reputation in the profession. Among these were Mr. Yorke, the Attorney-general, and Sir Fletcher Norton, the Solicitor-general, the substance of whose opinions was, that it did not appear to be material to enter into such objections as might be made either by the Emperor of Hindustan or the successors of Meer Jaffier, to the form or substance of the grant of the lands to the Company, or of the reserved rent to Lord Clive; that they both claimed under the same granter, and that the East India Company could not raise an objection against the grant to Lord Clive, founded on the want of right and power in the Nabob, which would not impeach their own; that the question was to be considered, not upon the strict absolute words (according to the laws and constitution of the Moghul empire), but relatively as between the East India Company, the grantee of the lands from Meer Jaffier, and Lord Clive, the grantee of the same Nabob, of a rent issuing and reserved out of those lands when granted to the Company; that the question ought to be determined between his Lordship and the Company upon the same

[178] Lord Clive, in his address to the proprietors in 1764, answers all these objections in a very full and conclusive manner. In treating of the supposed claims of the Emperor and the want of power in the Nabob to grant a jaghire, he remarks, that the arguments used against him by the Directors are exactly those which the Dutch government had recently brought against them, in the affair of the destruction of their armament in 1760; and he refers the Court, in answer to their present plea, to the memorial they lately submitted to his Majesty; in which, after justly describing the Emperor of Delhi as possessing, beyond very narrow limits, only a nominal power, they observe; "The Nabob makes war or peace, without the privity of the Moghul; that there appears still some remains of the old constitution in the succession to the state of Nabob; yet, in fact, that the succession is never regulated by the Moghul's appointment: the Nabob in possession is desirous of fortifying his title by the Moghul's confirmation, which the court of Delhi, conscious of its inability to interpose, readily grants. The Nabob of Bengal is, therefore, *de facto*, whatever he may be *de jure*, a sovereign prince."

principles as the like question would be determined, arising between the owner of lands in England subject to a rent, and the grantee or assignee of that rent, in a case where both parties derived from the same original granter; that it was incumbent upon the Court of Directors, in this instance, to turn chancellors against themselves; and that it was for the honour of that great Company to act upon such principles, not only with foreign merchants, trading companies, and foreign states and sovereigns, but with their own servants.

"Such was the opinion of the greatest lawyers. But the Court of Directors, actuated, it should seem, rather by a spirit of resentment than by principles of equity, although they could not hope for a decision in their favour, determined still to withhold the jaghire, and to protract the judgment of Chancery by such stratagems or delays as the forms of judicial proceedings might chance to furnish them with."

Lord Clive complained (and apparently with great justice) of the mode in which this measure relating to his jaghire was to be carried into execution. The letter regarding it was sent to India without any intimation to him; and when, on hearing that the government of Bengal had been directed to stop all future payments to his agents, he applied to the Court of Directors for a copy of their proceedings in a case so deeply affecting his fortune and his reputation, they peremptorily refused compliance with his request.

Under such circumstances, he had nothing left but to institute (as he did) a suit in Chancery, and to give to his agents abroad the best general instructions his want of minute information enabled him. Mr. Vansittart, the Governor, was his principal agent; but conceiving that his duty to him and that to his superiors might clash, he desired him on such occurrence to devolve the charge of his interests on Major Carnac, and in case of this gentleman not thinking proper to act, he nominated Mr. Amyatt, Mr. Lushington, and Mr. Amphlett[179], his attornies.

The situation and feelings under which he acted on this remarkable occasion are fully explained in the following letter to Mr. Vansittart:

> "My dear Friend,
>
> "Last night I received advice that the Directors had sent orders to their President and Council of Bengal to pay into their cash the amount of my jaghire, and not to grant me any bills of exchange on that account. Without enlarging upon this subject, so arbitrary and ungrateful a proceeding will give you a just idea of the principles of those who have the management of the Company's affairs at present.
>
> "I am really at a loss what to desire of you about so delicate a matter. Upon the whole, act like an honest man, and a man of honour: do justice to your friend without injuring the Company; for I am satisfied, the more this affair is inquired into, the more it will be to my honour. At the same time, I am obliged to take every

[179] Mr. Amphlett (a connection of Lord Clive) was a civil servant of Bengal; but his abilities as an engineer had led to his being employed in improving the works at Fort William.

step both against the Directors and the Governor and Council that the law will admit of.

"Enclosed you will receive a letter to that purport, and if you should judge it not improper to act as my attorney on this occasion, I request you will act accordingly. I have sent Carnac a duplicate of the power of attorney sent you by this conveyance, and you will observe I have appointed the Major, Lushington, and Amphlett, to act as may be thought most proper by you and Carnac, with whom I request you will consult on this occasion.

"If you should find my information not exactly true, and that the Directors allow you some latitude of judging of my right to the jaghire, before you take such a step, these precautions of mine may be laid aside for the present; but I have too good authority for what I write; notwithstanding the Directors have refused giving me a copy of the paragraph sent by this conveyance, which I demanded in form.

"I am, dear Sir,
"Your affectionate friend and servant,
(Signed) CLIVE.

"Berkeley Square,
"April 28th, 1763.
"To Henry Vansittart, Esq."

In a letter to Major Carnac of the same date, after giving him similar information regarding the conduct of the Directors, he observes:—

"Your friendship and regard for justice will, I am persuaded, induce you to take every step in support of both my fortune and reputation; and the more this affair of the jaghire is inquired into, the more honour it will do me, and make the ingratitude of the Directors appear in blacker light.

"What I wrote you last year is become now absolutely necessary,—that the old Nabob, as well as the present one, should acknowledge my right to the jaghire in the strongest terms. Meer Jaffier will be surprised at this step, and may, if he pleases, address a letter to the Company upon the occasion; a translation of which must be enclosed.

"The opinion of the lawyers is, that the Directors' orders are illegal; that the President and Council cannot, consistent with their own safety, put them in execution; for which purpose I have addressed a letter to the President and Council, forbidding them to comply with the orders sent them, at their peril.

"Enclosed you will receive a power of attorney to act for me, if you shall think necessary, provided Vansittart should decline it from his being Governor. I have desired Van. to consult with

> you on this matter; and you will observe that I have nominated Lushington and Amphlett to act as my attorneys, if you should not think it proper, or for my interest, to act for me.
>
> "In case the Governor and Council should retain my money, or refuse giving bills of exchange, you (or whoever acts as my attorney) are immediately to commence a suit at law against the Company, and to transmit a very exact account of all your proceedings, that it may be taken up in England. I am not in the least doubt of making the aggressors pay dear for the attempt; but their purpose will, in some respect, be answered by their lawsuit, as it prevents me becoming a Director next year. However, this will not prevent me from bringing in my friends, which will be the same thing."

Lord Clive wrote to his friend, Mr. Amyatt, in much the same terms: he observes, in the conclusion of this letter[180],—

> "You, who know the honourable manner in which I acquired my jaghire, will not be wanting to do me justice; at the same time, do your duty to the Company as far as is consistent with equity and your own safety; for I tell you very plainly, that if the Governor and Council obey the orders received from the Company, they must do it at their peril, and that I shall immediately commence an action against them by my attorneys in Bengal.
>
> "The letter I send to the Governor and Council, I am persuaded, you will look upon as an act of necessity, in order to save my undoubted property from the worst of enemies,—a combination of ungrateful Directors."

From the sentiments entertained and expressed by Mr. Vansittart and Lord Clive's other friends in Bengal, and the result of communications with the Nabob and Emperor[181], there is no doubt that every step would have been taken, and every document obtained, that could have confirmed his right to the jaghire; but an arrangement which took place in the ensuing year at the India House rendered all further proceedings unnecessary.

The violent animosities of parties in Bengal, which spread to England, were brought to a crisis, in that country, by intelligence of the dreadful massacre at Patna, and the murder of Mr. Amyatt, and those by whom he was accompanied, at Moorshedabad. These events will be fully noticed in the next chapter. Suffice it here to say, that they produced the greatest alarm in the mind of every one connected with India.

The proprietors now turned all their attention to the state of Bengal; where, besides what had occurred with the native government, the recriminations of the opposed parties among their own servants had brought to light a scene of cor-

[180] 28th April, 1763.

[181] The Shah-Zada (Shah Alum) had, before Clive's letters arrived, succeeded to the throne of Delhi.

ruption, division, and distraction in their internal rule, which, if not early remedied, threatened to bring complete ruin upon their affairs, and to disappoint all the golden dreams of profit from their possessions in that quarter of India.

Under such circumstances it is not surprising that the eyes of almost all should have been turned on Clive, as the only person fitted to remedy the mismanagement and misrule of their Indian empire. At a very full General Court he was unanimously solicited to return to India.

At the same time, the proprietors proposed to the Directors the instant restitution of his jaghire; nor can there be a doubt (according to the narrative[182] now before me) that this vote would have been carried by a great majority; but Lord Clive, who was in Court, not thinking it strictly honourable to take advantage of this sudden spirit of generosity, and to carry, merely by his popularity, a case which was depending at law, rose, and requested they would desist from their liberal intentions; adding, that from being sensible of the impropriety of going abroad whilst so valuable a part of his property remained in dispute, he would make some proposals to the Court of Directors, which would, he trusted, end in an amicable adjustment of this affair.

Lord Clive had now thrown off all disguise with Mr. Sulivan; they were open and irreconcilable opponents. His Lordship, on this occasion, pursued a course quite suited to the boldness and decision of his character. After stating what he had done about the jaghire, he concluded by observing, "There was another and more weighty obstacle to his undertaking the management of the affairs in Bengal, without the removal of which he thought it incumbent upon him to apprise them of his positive determination to decline entering again into their service: that he differed so much from Mr. Sulivan in opinion of the measures necessary to be taken for the good of the Company, that he could not consider that gentleman as a proper Chairman of the Court of Directors; that it would be in vain for him to exert himself as he ought, in the office of Governor and Commander in Chief of their forces, if his measures were to be thwarted and condemned at home, as they probably would be, by a Court of Directors under the influence of a Chairman, whose conduct, upon many occasions, had evinced his ignorance of East India affairs, and who was also known to be his personal and inveterate enemy; that it was a matter totally indifferent to him, who filled the chair, if Mr. Sulivan did not; but that he could not, consistently with the regard he had for his own reputation, and the advantages he should be emulous of establishing for the Company, proceed in the appointments with which they had honoured him, if that gentleman continued to have the lead at home."[183]

Mr. Sulivan, fearing he might fall a sacrifice to the resolution which he saw the Court entertain of possessing on any terms the services of Lord Clive, and knowing too well the frame of his Lordship's mind to expect any change in sentiments he had so decidedly avowed, rose, and expressed his concurrence in the opinion of the General Court as to the talents of Lord Clive, with whom he could conceive

[182] MSS. of Sir Henry Strachey.

[183] I have extracted this summary of what Lord Clive said upon this subject from the MSS. before quoted.

no reason why he should be at variance, it having been his desire to live in friendship with him. After these professions, and some general observations of the same tendency, Mr. Sulivan proceeded to represent the impropriety of superseding (by the civil and military powers proposed to be granted to Lord Clive) Mr. Vansittart, Governor of Bengal, and Major-General Lawrence, who had lately been induced to return to Madras. He also stated the disappointment which the nomination of Lord Clive would create to Mr. Spencer, a Bombay servant lately nominated to the head of affairs at Bengal. But the General Court were in no temper to listen to such reasoning, and with one voice insisted upon the Directors making the appointment. The Directors, as a last resource, desired to try the question by ballot; but the bye-laws of the Company establish that no ballot shall take place except by a requisition of nine proprietors. Though upwards of three hundred were present, this number could not be found to sign their names to such a requisition; and the Court, in consequence, adjourned.

The Court of Directors, thus compelled to attend to the wish of the Court of Proprietors, nominated Lord Clive Governor and Commander in Chief of Bengal. There was some hesitation about the military commission interfering with that of Major-General Lawrence, who, though advanced in years, and infirm, had accompanied his near relation Mr. Palk, when that gentleman was appointed Governor of Madras. But Clive intimated, that it was far from his wish to supersede his old commander: all he required was, that neither Major-General Lawrence nor any other officer should have the power of interfering with his command in Bengal.

Lord Clive received his appointment[184] within a month of the general election; and the Directors hurried their preparations for his departure, from a desire that he should leave England before that took place; conceiving, no doubt, that his doing so would evince a confidence in their support, and prevent that opposition which several of them expected, on the ground of their known hostility to the popular Governor. A letter was, in consequence, written to Lord Clive by the Secretary, informing him that a ship was ready to receive him. He replied, that, for reasons he had assigned at the General Court, he could not think of embarking, till he knew the result of the election of Directors, which was to take place in the ensuing month. The Directors, when they received this answer, declared that they considered it as a resignation of the government. They therefore summoned a General Court, at which one of the proprietors in their interest moved, that, as Lord Clive declined the government of Bengal, they should proceed to a new nomination; but his Lordship's declaration at the late Court had made too deep an impression to be easily erased. The proprietors saw nothing in his conduct but manly consistency with the sentiments he had before so decidedly avowed; and, on the other hand, viewing the conduct of the Directors as an unworthy artifice to evade compliance with their wishes, they threw out the proposition with violence and clamour.

On the 25th of April, 1764, a very warm contest took place. Mr. Sulivan brought forward one list of twenty-three Directors; and Mr. Rous (who was supported by Clive) produced another. Notwithstanding his friend, Lord Bute, was no longer minister, Mr. Sulivan succeeded in bringing in half his numbers; but we cannot

[184] March, 1764.

have a stronger proof of the degree in which the attack of Lord Clive had shaken the power of this lately popular Director, than the fact that his own election was only carried by one vote. In the subsequent contest for the chair, Mr. Rous succeeded; and Mr. Bolton, who was also of Clive's party, was nominated his Deputy.

Soon after the election of the Directors, the Court took the subject of the settlement of Lord Clive's jaghire into consideration; and a proposition, made by himself, was agreed to[185], confirming his right for ten years, if he lived so long, and provided the Company continued, during that period, in possession of the lands from which the revenue was paid.

Lord Clive, previous to his departure, communicated his sentiments to the Directors, very fully, upon all points connected with affairs in Bengal. The subject of his letters will be noticed hereafter. Suffice it to say, that the same emergency which caused his nomination led to his being vested with extraordinary powers; and he was, aided by a committee of persons of his own naming, made independent of his Council. His recommendations of different military officers were also attended to. The King's troops being at this period recalled, all officers in his Majesty's service were ordered to England. Major Caillaud, promoted to the rank of Brigadier General, had been appointed to Madras; Major Carnac's services were rewarded with a similar commission, and the command of the troops in Bengal; Sir Robert Barker was appointed to command the artillery; Majors Richard Smyth and Preston were nominated Lieutenant-Colonels of the European corps; and Major Knox advanced to the rank of Lieutenant-Colonel, to command the sepoys.

The victory which Lord Clive obtained at the India House was followed up by his friends, who, on the next general election (1765), strengthened their party among the Directors very considerably; and Mr. Sulivan, notwithstanding the active exertions of his adherents, was again defeated. This success gave Clive the support he required during his short but important administration of the affairs of Bengal. It laid, however, the foundation of the future troubles of his life; for those over whom he now triumphed cherished their resentments[186]; and their ranks

[185] This agreement between the Company and Lord Clive is as follows:—

> "By indenture bearing date the 16th May, 1764, between the United Company of Merchants of England trading to the East Indies on the one part, and Robert Lord Clive on the other part, it is agreed, that the said Company shall, for the term of ten years, cause to be paid to Lord Clive, his administrators, &c. out of their treasury in Bengal, (to be computed from the 5th May, 1764,) the full amount of the said jaghire rents; provided nevertheless, that in case the said Lord Clive should die before the expiration of the said ten years, the Company shall make good the payment of the jaghire only to the time of the death of him the said Lord Clive; provided also, that in case the Company shall not be in actual possession of the lands out of which the said jaghire issues, and the revenues thereof, to and for their own use, and during the said term of ten years, then and in such case, the said Company shall not be compellable or subject to pay any further part of the jaghire than shall accrue due during the said Company's actual possession of the said lands out of which it issues."

[186] Mr. Sulivan was not defeated without an active struggle. Mr. Walsh, in a letter

were early recruited by numerous malcontents from India, whom Clive's reforms had either deprived of the means of accumulating wealth, or exposed to obloquy. The efforts of his confederated enemies will be noticed hereafter: the subject is mentioned here merely as a consequence of his engaging personally in the politics of Leadenhall Street. How far that step was one of wisdom, or of necessity, it is very difficult to determine.

The twenty-four Directors were at this period elected annually; and they had no sooner taken their seats than they were obliged to commence an active canvass to maintain them. Their patronage was the great means by which this was effected; and as that extended to almost every office in India, the value of which rose in proportion to the undue exercise of local authority, the Directors, generally speaking, might be said to derive strength from the continuance of those abuses which, as managers of the Company's concerns, it was their duty to correct. At the period of which I am writing, a great change had taken place in this body. Within the last ten years a number of the servants of the Company had returned to England with large fortunes; all of those bought India stock, to give them weight as proprietors; and many sought the direction, either to support their own interest, or that of their friends. Their efforts to influence elections brought them sometimes into violent collision with each other, but oftener with those classes of individuals who, before this change, had almost wholly monopolised the management of the affairs of the East India Company.

To judge from the papers and pamphlets written by the different parties concerned in the general elections, and the means taken to create and influence the votes by ballot, we should pronounce that the India House, at this period, presented, annually, a scene in which there was little more of temper, and decorum of language, than at any popular election in the kingdom. No person better knew the nature of these contests than Lord Clive; and no one could be more anxious to avoid them. The resolution he took and declared, of preserving himself personally clear of them, was communicated to all his friends; and there can be no doubt that he was sincere in desiring to abstain from mixing in a scene where he might lose, but could not gain, reputation. But England is a country where men who require support must give it. Lord Clive had grounds, from his first landing in his native country, to dread an attack upon his fortune. He ascribes (and no doubt justly) the forbearance of his opponents to their dread of his influence, particularly with ministers and at court; but that was now at an end, when his attachment to Mr. Pitt and Mr. Grenville, and his disapprobation of the peace, led him, as we have stated, to reject the overtures of Lord Bute, when that nobleman added to his power, as the court favourite, that attached to the station of Prime Minister of his country.

Lord Clive, under such circumstances, had no choice between bartering his independence to obtain security to his fortune, and strengthening himself, through other means, in order to resist the attack with which he was threatened. He had

to Lord Clive of the 5th April, 1765, speaking of the contest, observes:—"Lord Bute joined him (Mr. Sulivan) very strenuously, and got the Duke of Northumberland to do the same. This change may appear extraordinary; but abject submissions on the one part, and tender solicitations on the other, are said to have brought it about!"

many and warm friends among men of the first rank and respectability in England; and a numerous body of Indians were attached to him, either through gratitude, or from admiration of his character. But all these persons had their own objects to serve; and a continuance of their attachment could not have been expected by one who, thinking only of himself, chose to be neutral in affairs which nearly concerned their honour or their interest. To prevent, therefore, his being left defenceless and at the mercy of those in whom he had no confidence, Clive, we must suppose, was compelled to come forward; and, once in the field, defensive measures (however prudent) were altogether unsuited to his character. He immediately became the assailant; and his short but active campaign at the India House, though chequered with defeat and victory, was ultimately successful, from the same causes which had made him so often triumph in very different scenes. His bold, open, and uncompromising mind gave courage to his friends, and filled with dismay the ranks of his enemies. But never was that good fortune which attended this extraordinary man through life more conspicuous than when it preserved him from sinking into the leader of a party at the India House, and restored him to his proper sphere, to improve and consolidate his former labours, and fix beyond dispute his claim to the title of the Founder of the British Empire in India.

Lord Clive, notwithstanding the opinion he expressed of the imprudence of Mr. Pitt, continued to entertain the greatest veneration for that statesman. In a letter to Major Carnac, he expresses his delight at the feelings of indignation with which Mr. Pitt heard of the conduct of the Directors in stopping the payment of his jaghire. But the person to whom Clive appears to have most completely attached himself was Mr. George Grenville; and the connection between them rested upon principles alike honourable to both. It was by the advice of Mr. Grenville that Clive came to a compromise with the Directors; and he interfered, personally, to bring the dispute between his Lordship and that body to an amicable conclusion.

When Clive left England, he took care to free himself of all political connections, except with his friend Mr. Grenville; and he requested the members whom he brought into parliament, and those friends who from gratitude chose to give him their personal aid, to make the support of that statesman the rule of their conduct. We learn these facts from the letters of Mr. Walsh to Clive, after the departure of the latter from England.

In one letter, written when Mr. Grenville was in office, Mr. Walsh observes, "There is no alteration in the administration; the coldness and jealousy between them and Lord Bute seem to continue, and rather to increase. Your friend Mr. Grenville maintains his ground very well; indeed he appears to me to confirm his power daily, by his vast application to business, and by the moderation and circumspection with which he conducts himself. He is very sparing of promises, and therefore, as I take it, means to keep those he makes, which is the sure foundation for a durable administration. I am much inclined to think that while he has any influence, there will be no unpopular steps taken by the ministry. The day of the general warrants held till five in the morning, when an amendment that destroyed the motion was carried by a majority of thirty-nine. Before the debate, I spoke to Mr. Grenville, and reminding him of what had passed when you introduced me to him, I remarked that it was upon such occasions as the present that he had the most want of assistance from his friends; and that I was apprehensive my being no longer neutral, as I was last year, would, instead of being of use to him as I meant it, be of detriment; and that, therefore, I left it to his option, whether I should come down that day or not; upon, which, he very handsomely desired me to come down by all means, and be determined by the merits of the cause, and not only that day, but during the whole session. I accordingly was there, and staid till one in the morning, when the debate, having got amongst the lawyers, grew excessively dull and tedious, and not being very well at the time, I retired without voting at all."

In a subsequent letter[187], Mr. Walsh informs Lord Clive of the unexpected change that had taken place in the administration. After describing the different political parties that had arisen, and were likely to arise, he adds, "As to me I do not propose being absolutely of either party; your interest does not appear to me by any means to require it, nor do my inclinations at all lead me to it. Mr. Grenville, it is true, I consider as entitled personally to all your assistance; but his connections are no ways to be justified. The man, therefore, not his party, should have your support, and, agreeably to what you yourself told him in my presence, that your ministerial attachments would cease for ever with his quitting the administration, your plan henceforward should be independency."

Lord Clive had a most tedious voyage to India. The ship put into Rio Janeiro, from whence we find letters to all his friends in England. Constantly alive to every object which affected, in the most remote degree, the interest of his country, he communicated to Mr. Grenville the observations which occurred to him upon the state of the colony, which he had very unexpectedly visited.

"As a well-wisher to my country," he observes[188], "I cannot avoid representing to you the deplorable condition of this capital settlement of the Portuguese. I should think myself deserving of everlasting infamy if I did not, with a battalion of infantry, make myself master of Rio Janeiro in twenty-four hours. They have nothing here that deserves the name of fortification: an unflanked garden wall with a rampart, with some old unserviceable and honey-combed cannon, constitute the chief strength of this place; and if the capital be in this defenceless condition, what are we to think of the subordinate settlements on the coast of Brazil. Bad as the Spaniards are, they could not fail, upon a future war, of making a speedy and easy conquest of all the Portuguese possessions in this part of the world, which would be of much more consequence to Spain than the conquest of Portugal. If a hint of their weakness could be conveyed to the court of Portugal, and the reformation already begun there could be extended to the coast of the Brazils, it might be the means of preserving their valuable possessions from falling into the hands of the Spaniards sooner or later."

Mr. Grenville, after he left office, acknowledged the receipt of this letter and some small presents from the Cape. He refers, in this communication, to the change of administration which had so recently occurred; and I quote his observations less from their connection with the life of Clive than from the value which

[187] 13th December, 1765.

[188] 14th October, 1764.

attaches to every sentiment of one of the most honourable and eminent statesmen who belonged to this period of English history.

"I take this opportunity," Mr. Grenville observes[189], "of repeating to your Lordship my thanks, for the honour of your letter from the Brazils, and for the sensible and useful observations contained in it; which I immediately endeavoured to make the best use of in my power. I have since then received an account of your very obliging present of some wine, a sea-dog, and some birds from the Cape. The sea-dog was unluckily lost in the voyage home, by jumping overboard, and the birds I have not yet been able to get; but when I return to town, I shall apply to Mr. Walsh for his assistance. The wine is safely lodged in my cellars, and by the account of it, I make no doubt will prove excellent.

"Your Lordship will have heard long before this letter can reach your hands, of the change which the King has been advised to make in his administration, in consequence of which I have no longer the honour to be in his Majesty's service. You will certainly have received many comments upon this very sudden (and, from the situation of public affairs when it happened, very unexpected) alteration; but as I am too nearly concerned in this event to make them, I will only say, that I sincerely wish it may be productive of benefit to the King and to the kingdom, instead of being attended with that confusion and disorder which is generally expected, if the present system should continue, though that is thought not likely. For my own part, I can only say, that I am in the same opinions, and shall endeavour to promote the same plan for the public business out of office, which I did whilst I had the honour to hold one. In these sentiments, those who are now in his Majesty's service will probably not agree with me; but on the other hand, I have reason to hope for the approbation of those who have done me the honour to approve my conduct. I shall earnestly wish in every situation, to preserve the good opinion and kindness which my friends have so strongly expressed towards me upon the present occasion, and to cultivate the good will and friendship which your Lordship has shown to me. Our accounts here of the state in which you will find affairs in the East Indies are too uncertain for me to be able to make any pertinent observations upon them; I will, therefore, content myself with expressing to you my warmest and most hearty wishes, that you may be attended with the same success and honour to yourself, and the same benefit to the public, in your present command, as your former conduct in those countries so deservedly acquired."

Lord Clive had been flattered during his stay in England, by having a vote passed that his statue should be placed in the India House along with those of General Lawrence and Sir George Pocock. A medal[190] had also been struck at the

[189] 14th October, 1765.

[190] The following is the account of this medal given by Mr. Stuart (commonly called Athenian Stuart) by whom it was designed. "The medal commemorates the battle of Plassey, and is in honour of Lord Clive. On one side is his Lordship, holding the British standard in one hand, and with the other he bestows the ensign of Subahship on Meer Jaffier. In the space between, are grouped together a globe, a cornucopia, and an antique rudder, to which the legend refers. The cornucopia symbolises the riches with which Meer Jaffier atoned for the injuries done to our countrymen by his predecessor; the rudder is for the augmentation of our navigation and commercial privileges; and the globe, for our territori-

desire of the Society for Promoting Arts and Commerce, in commemoration of the victory of Plassey, and its great and important results. These honourable marks of regard and respect could not but be gratifying; and, combined as they were with the enjoyment of domestic[191] happiness, and the society of friends to whom he was attached, they naturally rendered him very reluctant again to leave his native country. The bad health he had for the first twelvemonth after his return made him dread the effects of an English winter; but latterly he appears to have overcome that feeling, though we meet, in his letters, with occasional expressions of despondency, which indicate that depression of spirits consequent on the nervous attacks to which he continued to be subject.

Lord Clive purchased, as his town residence, the lease of the excellent and spacious house, which still belongs to his family, in Berkeley Square. He made several improvements on Styche; but the house and lands being on a limited scale for his fortune, he bought the estate of Walcot, and employed a celebrated architect[192] to render the mansion suitable to the residence of his family. His kind attentions to his parents appear to have been greater than ever; and when on the eve of returning to India, though his agents' letters show that the purchases he had made and the stoppage of his jaghire had so embarrassed him, that he had no money at command, he generously gave a bond to each of his five sisters for 2,000*l.*, in addition to the present to the same amount which he had before given them.

Lord Clive carried to India Mr. Strachey, and Captain Maskelyne, a brother to Lady Clive. He exerted his utmost efforts to forward the interests of her other brother, Mr. Nevil Maskelyne of Cambridge; and these efforts, supported as they were by the great science and high character of that gentleman, obtained for him the Regius professorship at Woolwich.[193]

Mr. George Clive, who (as has been before stated) brought home a moderate fortune, improved it by marriage; and was too comfortably settled to return to India. Mr. Scrafton had become a Director; but his grave duties do not appear to have deprived him of his usual high spirits. In one letter, he warns Lord Clive, that he is now in a different relation to him, being "one of his honourable masters." In another, he gives a humorous account of some of their mutual acquaintances and

---

al acquisitions; all of which were consequences of this victory. In the exergue is written, '*A Soubah given to Bengal.*'

"On the other face of the medal is a victory seated on an elephant, bearing a trophy in one hand, and a palm-branch in the other. The inscription is '*Victory at Plassey,*' '*Clive Commander.*' In the exergue is the date of the victory, and the mark of the Society for Promoting Arts and Commerce."

[191] In the collection of letters in my possession are many which prove the happiness Lord Clive enjoyed, at this period, in his family; but he was not exempt from severe afflictions. I have before mentioned the loss of an infant boy, when he sailed on his second visit to India. When he left Calcutta in 1760, his youngest boy was so ill, that he could not embark; the child was left in charge of Mr. Fullarton, and died. A daughter, as has been mentioned, was born to Lord Clive after his arrival in England; and Lady Clive, when he sailed, was on the point of being confined again.

[192] Mr. (afterwards Sir Robert) Chambers.

[193] Dr. Nevil Maskelyne is better known as Astronomer-Royal at Greenwich.

friends.

"I add this letter," he observes, "to give you an account of that arch Tory Harry[194], who, having shook off a load of gout at Mortlake, is come to town so pert, so envenomed with toryism, that he is quite unsufferable. He goes about boasting of your Lordship's conversion, abuses Mr. Pitt, impeaching his patriotism and honour, because a private gentleman has left him an estate which he swears he has no right to, and that the will should be set aside, for that the man who made it must have been *non com.*; trumps up the Duchess of Marlborough's legacy, the Hanover millstone, &c. &c.; swears Lord Bute is the only man of merit, and Tories the only true patriots. * * * * Young Walcot has married a parson's daughter *sans un sol*; and Walsh has married a country-house, that will run away with more money, and give him more plague, than half the wives in England. Poor Daddy King is half eat up with the gout; has just one hand left to play at cards, and the free use of his tongue, so that he has as much enjoyment of his faculties as if his whole body were at ease."

Lord Clive's friend Mr. Pigot returned to England before his Lordship left it: his fortune[195] was reported to be very large; and through the influence it enabled him to establish, he attained first a baronetcy, and afterwards a peerage.

Mr. Orme had settled in England; and from his correspondence appears (at this time) to have been engaged in finishing the second part of his history. In a letter[196] now before me, he complains of the obstructions which forms create to his examination of the records of the India House; while he expresses his hope of meeting more facility from the kind attentions of Lord Clive. Writing to that nobleman, he observes, "I have had permission to poke into the records of the India House, and have discovered excellent materials for the exordium of my second volume; but the difficulty of getting them away is immense, for every scrap of an extract that I desire is submitted to the consideration of the Court of Directors; so that in three months, and after making twenty-five journeys to the House, I have not got half what I want. All because they wo'n't lend me old books, of which not a soul in England suspected the existence until my rummages discovered them. I am afraid, my Lord, that these gentlemen suspect that I shall make a fortune by my book; and therefore think all the trouble and impediments I meet with to be what I have no reason to complain of, as it is in the way of trade.

"You, my Lord, have treated me differently; and pray continue to do so. Make me a vast map of Bengal, in which not only the outlines of the province, but also the different subdivisions of Burdwan, Beerboom, &c. may be justly marked. Get me a clear idea of the different offices and duties of Duan, Bukhshee, Cadgee, Cut-

[194] Mr. Harry Clive.

[195] Mr. Watts estimated Lord Pigot's fortune at 400,000*l*. It had chiefly been made (according to the same authority) by lending money at high interest to the Nabob, the chiefs, and managers of provinces. This practice was then too common to be considered as in any way discreditable; though it was soon afterwards discovered to be one of the most baneful and injurious to the public interests that the Company could tolerate in any of their servants, but above all, in those high in station.

[196] 21st November, 1764.

wall, and all other great posts in the government. Take astronomical observations of longitude, if you have any body capable of doing it. I send you a skeleton of the Bengal map I intend for my second volume, and I will hereafter send you the first sheets of the book itself; which will contain matter entirely new, even to us East Indians; but that cruel India House, and my paper constitution, keep me back most terribly."

Among those he had left in India, Lord Clive regarded none with more sincere friendship than Major Carnac[197]; and when he feared that that officer would resign the service from disgust at the treatment he had received, he wrote him in the most urgent manner, to take no such precipitate step. He informs him, in one letter[198], that he had exerted himself to the utmost, and would continue to do so while he lived, to promote his views; and "if any accident happens to me," he adds, "I have left you an annuity of 300*l.* per annum."

Mr. Amyatt had established himself very high in the opinion of Lord Clive, with whom he maintained, for several years, a very intimate correspondence, to which frequent reference has been made. Lord Clive thought equally well of this gentleman's talent and integrity; and was deeply grieved at hearing of his death. He had, it is true, recommended Mr. Vansittart to be his successor, in preference to Mr. Amyatt; but the latter was quite satisfied that this was done from a conscientious conviction of Mr. Vansittart's superior competency to the station; and he knew that Lord Clive had endeavoured, though unsuccessfully, to obtain for him the succession of the government of Bengal, which had been given to Mr. Spencer, a member of Council at Bombay, a gentleman whom Clive had recommended to be at the head of his own presidency, but against whose present nomination he remonstrated in the strongest manner, on the ground of his abilities and character (though respectable) not being such as to warrant the supersession of so many civil servants at Bengal, and particularly of Mr. Amyatt.

We have often had occasion to notice the intimate footing on which Clive had lived for many years with Mr. Vansittart, and the high opinion he entertained of his virtue and abilities. Though condemning the dethronement of Meer Jaffier, he ascribed the chief blame of that measure to Mr. Holwell, and believed that his friend Van. (as he termed him) had acted from necessity: but when Cossim Ali was left uncontrolled to pursue his own course, and the Governor, acting on the system of non-interference with the Nabob's authority, abandoned to his mercy the rich Hindus and others, who had long looked to the English for protection, Clive was unqualified in his condemnation of a policy which he deemed calculated to injure the reputation, and with it the strength, of the British Government. The opinions he gave on this subject were in direct opposition to those contained in the minutes and memorials published by Mr. Vansittart in defence of his conduct; and their wide difference on a subject of such importance led to their being of opposite parties in the India House.

Mr. Sulivan became the advocate of Mr. Vansittart, whose modesty, moder-

[197] Major Carnac, in 1760, came to St. Helena with Lord Clive, and from thence returned to Bengal.

[198] June, 1764.

ation, and great virtue he contrasted with the bold, grasping ambition of Lord Clive; and this circumstance, more than any other, tended to loosen those bonds by which the two friends had been so long united.

When persons are in the situation of Lord Clive and Mr. Vansittart, every trifle obtains importance, and serves to widen the breach. Lord Clive appears to have been, during the whole of his residence in England, very desirous to establish himself well at court. Among other attentions, he studied to gratify the curiosity of the King, by obtaining for him some of the most remarkable animals of the East. He wrote[199] several times to Mr. Vansittart to aid him in this object. Some time after his application, Lord Clive received a letter from that gentleman, intimating that he had sent home two elephants[200], a rhinoceros, and a Persian mare, which he requested his Lordship would, along with his brother, Mr. Arthur Vansittart, present to his Majesty.

When these animals reached England, Mr. A. Vansittart requested Lord Clive would accompany him to court, to present them. The following answer to this letter shows the first impression which this transaction made upon his Lordship's mind.

"Upon the receipt of your letter," Lord Clive observes, "enclosing a copy of a paragraph from your brother, I can plainly perceive, that Mr. Vansittart, declining to comply with the request I made him, of purchasing and sending home, on my account, an elephant, to be presented to his Majesty by me, has taken that hint to send one home on his own. This unkind treatment I neither deserved nor expected from Mr. Vansittart. I am persuaded his Majesty will not think I am wanting in that respect which is due to him, if I decline presenting, in another person's name, an elephant which I intended to present in my own. At the same time, I shall take care his Majesty be informed of the cause of my desiring to be excused attending you to his Majesty, with Mr. Vansittart's presents."

An explanation took place upon this subject; and it appears by a letter[201] from Lord Clive to Mr. Vansittart in the following year, that some blame attached to the captain of the ship, who acted, according to Lord Clive's opinion, at the instigation of Mr. Sulivan. But it is a justice we owe to the memory of the latter gentleman to state, that Lord Clive was in such a frame of mind at the time he listened to this accusation, as readily to believe that every thing (whether public or private) which tended to annoy or injure him originated with or was aggravated by, his rival for

[199] One of Lord Clive's letters to Mr. Vansittart is dated 17th December, 1762. The passage alluded to is as follows:—"I must again repeat my desire of having a large elephant embarked for his Majesty, if the thing be practicable, of which you must be a better judge than I, who are upon the spot; and if you can send me any curiosities, such as antelopes, hog-deer, nilgows or lynxes, I shall be much obliged to you."

[200] One of the elephants was so large that it could not be embarked.

[201] In this letter, which is dated January, 1764, Lord Clive observes; "I am sorry there should be any mistake about the elephant; and although I was somewhat affected at first at the commission you gave me to present the elephant to his Majesty in your name, instead of my own, yet the thing in itself appears to me to be of too trifling a nature for either of us to think any more about it. Your brother will inform you in what manner Sampson has acted, owing, I believe, to the instigation of Sulivan."

supremacy at the India House.

Though several causes combined to interrupt that cordiality which had once subsisted between Lord Clive and Mr. Vansittart, no open rupture took place. The latter had left Calcutta before his successor arrived, and returned to his native country with a moderate fortune[202], and a character for integrity that was never impeached, even by those who censured most severely the weakness and impolicy of many measures of his government.

Lord Clive, in the hurry of leaving England, forgot to include Mr. Call, the chief engineer at Madras (with Mr. Campbell[203] and Mr. Preston), in his recommendation for a brevet commission as Colonel. He wrote[204] from Rio Janeiro to the Chairman, Mr. Rous, entreating he would rectify his mistake, and prevent so excellent an officer being hurt by neglect. In the same letter he called his attention, in a very forcible manner, to the merits of Colonel Forde.

"If Caillaud," he observes, "should not go to the coast of Coromandel, pray do not forget Colonel Forde, who is a brave, meritorious, and honest officer. He was offered a jaghire by the Subah of the Deckan, but declined taking it upon terms contrary to the interest of the Company. Lord Clive, General Lawrence, and Colonel Coote, have received marks of the Directors' approbation and esteem; Colonel Forde has received none. The two captains who fought and took the Dutch ships in the Ganges received each a piece of plate; but Colonel Forde, the conqueror of Masulipatam, who rendered the Company a much greater service by the total defeat of all the Dutch land forces in Bengal, has not been distinguished by any mark of the Company's favour."

I here close the account of Clive's second visit to his native country, in which he resided more than three years. I have been minute in relating the events of this period. They had, both as they related to the friendships he formed and improved, and the hostility which his open and warm temper provoked, a serious influence upon his future career; and a knowledge of them is quite essential, both to the developement of his character, and to the understanding of the subsequent part of these volumes.

---

[202] Mr. Walsh writes to Lord Clive, that Mr. Vansittart told him his fortune did not exceed 2,500*l.* per annum.

[203] Afterwards Sir Archibald Campbell, Governor of Fort St. George.

[204] 14th October, 1764.

CHAPTER XIII.

State of India during Lord Clive's absence, 1760-5.—Mr. Vansittart's Government.—Deposition of Meer Jaffier.—Elevation of Meer Cossim.—Massacre of Patna.—Restoration of Meer Jaffier.—Disorders in Bengal

Before resuming the narrative of Clive's life, and accompanying him on his last visit to India, it will be necessary to take a general and concise view of the events which had occurred in that country during the short period of his absence. It would, indeed, be impossible, without such a review, to understand the nature of the scenes in which he became engaged, or the motives and grounds of the measures he adopted.

He was succeeded in the administration of the affairs of Bengal by Mr. Vansittart; who, as he owed his elevation to Clive, was disposed, we may conclude, to pursue the course of policy which Clive had marked out. But however easy it may be for a man of moderate talent to follow genius in a smooth and beaten track, it becomes impossible, where the road is rugged and indistinct, and where the slightest deviation leads inevitably to the widest separation from him who preceded.

This was the case with Mr. Vansittart. He had a clear perception between right and wrong, in the abstract; but his letters and minutes, soon after he was appointed governor, show that he was quite incompetent to take a comprehensive view of the great and conflicting interests committed to his charge, and still less to quell the violent passions that were in action. He found evils of much magnitude, and he conscientiously desired to remedy them; but he appears to have looked no further, and, consequently, to have often exchanged bad for worse. Volumes have been written for and against the measures he adopted: they will be here noticed only in a very cursory manner.

I have stated, in the tenth chapter, that at the period of time when Clive sailed for England, accounts had been received of the advance of the Shah-Zada towards Patna; and that Colonel Caillaud had been detached with a force to aid Ram Narrain in repelling the invasion. Alumgeer the Second had been murdered by his minister, Umad-ul-Moolk[205]; and the Shah-Zada[206], on becoming emperor, had assumed the title of Shah Alum[207]; nominating, at the same time, Sujah-u-Dowlah

[205] More commonly called Ghazee-u-Deen.

[206] Prince Royal.

[207] Shah Alum signifies "King of the World."

(the ruler of Oude) his vizier.

The young emperor was successful in his first action with Ram Narrain; but the latter being reinforced by Colonel Caillaud and Meeran, the invaders were, in their turn, defeated[208], and compelled to retire from before Patna. The Emperor, however, instead of retiring towards Benares, took the route of Moorshedabad, whither he was pursued, and obliged to retrace his steps; and, after another ineffectual attempt to take Patna, he retreated to Hindustan. The triumph of the Nabob's arms was completed by the defeat of the rebel Raja of Purneah, by Captain Knox; but, in the midst of these successes, an event occurred, which became the proximate cause of another revolution in Bengal. The Prince Meeran, who has occupied so conspicuous a part in this narrative, was killed[209] by lightning. This violent young man had been at once the support and dread of the less energetic Meer Jaffier. Though Meeran was sensible of the necessity of the aid of the English, he was impatient of the state of dependence and control in which the alliance with that nation had placed him; and the continual conflict of his interests and passions rendered him turbulent and dangerous. To Clive, alone, he was obedient; and a sentiment of attachment and respect for that commander appears, on many occasions, to have checked him in schemes that must have terminated fatally for himself, or his father. This prince, with all his vices and errors, was generous to his dependents and army; who, after his death, afraid of losing their arrears, surrounded the palace, and threatened the life of their sovereign, against whom many of his dependents took up arms; and, as if the misfortunes of the country were to be complete, it was visited by a predatory incursion of the Mahrattas.

Amid these scenes of war, mutiny, rebellion, and plunder, Mr. Vansittart assumed the government of Bengal.[210] Mr. Holwell, who had been in temporary charge, cherished the greatest prejudice against the reigning Nabob. Meer Jaffier was, according to him, the author of all these evils; and so entirely did he succeed in impressing the new governor with the same sentiments that, within two months[211] from Mr. Vansittart's arrival at Calcutta, a treaty was concluded with Meer Cossim Ali, son-in-law to the Nabob, the general of the army, engaging that the Nabob should invest him with full power as ruler of Bengal, Bahar, and Orissa; in return for which, he made over to the Company the fruitful provinces of Burdwan, Midnapore, and Chittagong.

The ostensible causes of this revolution are honestly, indeed, but not very satisfactorily, stated by the Governor himself in his narrative[212], and seem to have been chiefly the financial difficulties of the Company's affairs. The Nabob was to a certain extent in arrear, and other pressures were felt. "The season had now begun," says Mr. Vansittart, "when our forces were to take the field against a powerful enemy, whilst we had scarce a rupee in our treasury to enable us to put them in motion. The easy channel in which the Company's affairs ran, whilst the sums stipulated by the treaty (with Meer Jaffier) lasted, had diverted their atten-

[208] 22d February, 1760.

[209] 2d July, 1760.

[210] August, 1760.

[211] This treaty was concluded on the 27th September.

[212] Vol. I. p. 98.

tion from the distresses which must unavoidably fall on them, whenever that fund should be exhausted; and continuing to act on the same extensive plan in which they set out, they now found themselves surrounded by numerous difficulties, which were heightened by the particular circumstances of the country at this period, and weighed down with the very advantages which they had acquired; that is, an establishment which had lost the foundation on which it was built; a military force proportioned to their connections and influence in the country without the means of subsistence; a fortification begun upon the same extensive plan, at a vast expense; and an alliance with a power unable to support itself, and threatening to involve them in the same ruin."

Mr. Vansittart adds, that had indolence and weakness been the Nabob's only faults, destructive as they were to the welfare of the country and of the Company, he would have felt more severely the necessity of measures the tendency of which was to dissolve the engagements between him and the Company; but that in addition to this, he found a general disaffection to his government and detestation of his person and principles in all ranks of people. Even from this representation of the person principally concerned in the revolution, it is plain that the measure "of not only breaking a solemn treaty without previous warning and negotiation with the prince with whom it was contracted, but even of dethroning that prince, without attempting to remedy by some convention the temporary evils complained of, was a rash and unjustifiable measure, particularly where the change and all the articles of the new treaty were so obviously for the advantage of one of the parties only."

The Governor went to Moorshedabad in the hope of persuading Meer Jaffier to resign a power which he endeavoured to convince him he was alike unfit and unworthy to use, and to place it in the hands of Cossim Ali, who was his nearest connection, and the commander of his army. We cannot be surprised that the Nabob should indignantly repulse these attempts to render him the willing instrument of his own degradation. He refused to be associated, in any way, with the proposed arrangements for the better government of his dominions; and stipulated for nothing but permission to retire to Calcutta, that his life might be safe from that danger to which it must be exposed, if he remained at his own capital. His request was granted; and Cossim Ali was proclaimed Nabob.[213]

[213] A curious and minute account of the progressive steps taken in effecting this revolution is given in a letter to Clive (dated the 3d December, 1760,) from Mr. Lushington, who held the situation of linguist to the army, and who was an eye-witness of the incidents he describes. After detailing Mr. Vansittart's visit to Moorshedabad accompanied by a hundred and eighty Europeans, six hundred sepoys, and four pieces of cannon, that force might be used in case Meer Jaffier should refuse to comply with his demands, and mentioning that he had delivered to the Nabob three letters explanatory of his intentions, to which he waited a final answer, Mr. Lushington proceeds:—"We waited all the next day; but no answer coming, the Governor thought it proper not to lose any time, and therefore ordered Colonel Caillaud to go by water with his detachment, so early that he might surround the palace at daybreak; sending at the same time a letter, acquainting the Nabob that he had sent the Colonel to settle those affairs which he had conferred with him about, and to which he had promised to give an answer, but none was brought. The Nabob sent word to the Colonel he would give no answer until the troops returned to Moraudbaug, as he never expected such

The character of this chief stood high before his elevation. Of the crime of guilty ambition, it is vain to think of clearing him; but if he afterwards committed the greatest atrocities, and if his memory has become, from his cruel deeds, an object of just abhorrence with the English, it must not be forgotten that he was stung to madness, by the conduct of individuals of that nation; that he was rashly raised to power, by men who could not support him in its exercise, and driven to extremities by others, who, in the pursuit of their own interests and political views, appear to have thought all means justifiable, that could accelerate his downfall.

There is no page in our Indian history so revolting as the four years of the weak and inefficient rule of Mr. Vansittart. He was, as an individual, virtuous and respectable, and his intentions were pure; but these personal qualities were altogether insufficient to carry him through such a scene as that in which he became involved. His apologists have imputed his failure to the want of support from his associates in power, to that spirit of cupidity and rapacity, which had been kindled by the successes of Clive, and to the hopes and intrigues of the natives, which were cherished and excited to action by those that were hostile to the Governor and his plans.

These assertions are all true, but they only serve to prove the want of that superiority of mind, that spirit of command in Mr. Vansittart, which would have enabled him to sway the minds of his own countrymen, as well as the want of that foresight which should have led him to abstain from the adoption of measures extremely questionable in themselves, and which he did not very clearly see that

---

treatment from the English. Some few conferences were afterwards held by Mr. Hastings and myself with several of the Nabob's ministers; but as nothing could be agreed on I was sent back to Moraudbaug, to give an account of our proceedings to the Governor, and to have his final order whether we should storm the palace in case the Nabob refused to comply. He answered he wished not to spill the blood of a man whom he raised to such dignities, but that the affair must be finished before sunset. With this I returned; and found, to my great surprise, Cossim Ali Khan's standards, and the nobits[*] beating in his name. Colonel Caillaud now told me that the Nabob had sent out the seals to his son-in-law, and offered to resign the government if the English would be security for his life. This was immediately agreed to, and a meeting was held between the Colonel and the Nabob, who made the following speech, as well as I can remember:—'The English placed me on the musnud; you may depose me if you please. You have thought proper to break your engagements. I would not mine. Had I such designs I could have raised twenty thousand men, and fought you if I pleased. My son, the Chuta Nabob (Meeran), forewarned me of all this. I desire you will either send me to Sabut Jung (Lord Clive), for he will do me justice, or let me go to Mecca; if not, let me go to Calcutta; for I will not stay in this place. You will, I suppose, let me have my women and children; therefore, let me have budgerows and be carried immediately to Moraudbaug.' The Governor saw him soon after this, and he made much the same speech to him, adding, he could be nowhere safe but under the English protection."

That Mr. Lushington did not concur very cordially in the measures described, may be inferred from his concluding observations. "The Company," he observes, "are to receive the countries of Burdwan, Midnapore, and Chittagong, for this service. I, therefore, should be glad to know how this Nabob will be any more able to pay his people than the old man, after having given away a third part of his revenues."

[*] Large drums.

he could carry through. The only ground of apology for *him, and that not a very sufficient one,* is, that he allowed himself to be surprised in adopting the measure at all; and that even in the instrument which he employed for executing the work, he was deceived in the character of Meer Cossim, whose financial skill and ferocious energy were both equally unforeseen. The truth, however, is, that many of the acts of Mr. Vansittart's administration were less his own than those of a selfish and domineering council.

The first year of the new Nabob's reign was marked by success against his foreign enemies. Major Carnac, who now commanded the English troops in Bengal, defeated the Emperor at Gyah; and a rebellion of the chief of Beerboom and Burdwan was repressed by the aid of a detachment under Major Yorke. Major Carnac, who had obtained just reputation from his military operations, had acquired more with the natives of India by his generous treatment of M. Law, who was compelled to surrender to him, and by his humane and politic behaviour to the unfortunate emperor, whom he had defeated, but whom he afterwards waited upon and attended as one of his subjects.

The courteous behaviour of Major Carnac to the French commander excited, according to the author of the Seer Mutakhareen, equal astonishment and admiration. We cannot refrain from giving an account of the surrender and treatment of M. Law in the words of the native historian.[214]

"When the Emperor left the field of battle, the handful of troops that followed M. Law, discouraged by this flight, and tired of the wandering life which they had hitherto led in his service, turned about likewise and followed the Emperor. M. Law, finding himself abandoned and alone, resolved not to turn his back; he bestrode one of his guns, and remained firm in that posture, waiting for the moment of his death. This being reported to Major Carnac, he detached himself from his main, with Captain Knox and some other officers, and he advanced to the man on the gun, without taking with him either a guard or any Telingas (sepoys) at all. Being arrived near, this troop alighted from their horses, and pulling their caps from their heads, they swept the air with them, as if to make him a *salam;* and this salute being returned by M. Law in the same manner, some parley in their language ensued. The Major, after paying high encomiums to M. Law for his perseverance, conduct, and bravery, added these words:—'You have done every thing which could be expected from a brave man; and your name shall be undoubtedly transmitted to posterity by the pen of history; now loosen your sword from your loins, come amongst us, and abandon all thoughts of contending with the English.' The other answered, 'that if they would accept of his surrendering himself just as he was, he had no objection; but that as to surrendering himself with the disgrace of being without his sword, it was a shame he would never submit to; and that they might take his life if they were not satisfied with that condition.' The English commanders, admiring his firmness, consented to his surrendering himself in the manner he wished; after which the Major, with his officers, shook hands with him, in their European manner, and every sentiment of enmity was instantly dismissed on both sides. At the same time the Major sent for his own palankeen, made him

[214] Seer Mutakhareen, vol. ii. p. 164.

sit in it, and he was sent to camp. M. Law, unwilling to see, or to be seen, shut up the curtains of the palankeen for fear of being recognised by any of his friends at camp; but yet some of his acquaintances, hearing of his being arrived, went to him. The Major, who had excused him from appearing in public, informed them that they could not see him for some days, as he was too much vexed to receive any company. Ahmed Khan Koreishee, who was an impertinent talker, having come to look at him, thought to pay his court to the English by joking on the man's defeat; a behaviour that has nothing strange, if we consider the times in which we live, and the company he was accustomed to frequent; and it was in that notion of his, doubtless, that with much pertness of voice and air, he asked him this question; 'And Beeby (Lady) Law, where is she?' The Major and the officers present, shocked at the impropriety of the question, reprimanded him with a severe look and very severe expressions: 'This man,' they said, 'has fought bravely, and deserves the attention of all brave men; the impertinences which you have been offering him may be customary amongst your friends and nation, but cannot be suffered in ours, which has it for a standing rule, never to offer an injury to a vanquished foe.' Ahmed Khan, checked by this reprimand, held his tongue, and did not answer a word. He tarried about one hour more in his visit, and then went away much abashed; and, although he was a commander of importance, and one to whom much honour had been always paid, no one did speak to him any more, or made a show of standing up at his departure. This reprimand did much honour to the English; and it must be acknowledged, to the honour of those strangers, that as their conduct in war and in battle is worthy of admiration, so, on the other hand, nothing is more modest and more becoming than their behaviour to an enemy, whether in the heat of action, or in the pride of success and victory. These people seem to act entirely according to the rules observed by our ancient commanders, and our men of genius."

The Emperor of Delhi this year[215] invested Cossim Ali as Subadar of Bengal, Bahar, and Orissa; the latter agreeing to pay an annual tribute of twenty-four lacs. The aid of the English was desired to fix the Emperor upon the throne of Delhi; and in return, an offer was made of the Dewanee of Bengal, Bahar, and Orissa; but, though the project was entertained at Calcutta, the want of funds for the expedition, and alarm at the embarrassments in which it might involve the Company, prevented its acceptance.

The consequence of the success of his arms, was a desire, on the part of the Nabob, to avail himself of it to confirm his power, and to enable not only to raise funds to discharge the heavy burdens imposed upon him as the price of his elevation, but to enrich himself. No means appeared more likely to effect these ends than the plunder of Ram Narrain, the celebrated governor of Patna. Mr. Vansittart had anticipated this desire, and had furnished Major Carnac with orders to protect a man, who had so often merited, and so often received pledges of protection from the British government. Happy would it have been for the English name and interests, had the Governor persevered in this resolution!—but deceived by the artful representations of Cossim Ali, and irritated by the opposition and remonstrances

[215] 1761.

of Major Carnac, who had (as his friend Clive thought[216], most unnecessarily,) joined his opponents, Mr. Vansittart appointed Colonel Coote to the command of the troops at Patna, as preparatory to abandoning its ruler. But Coote, like Carnac, refused to be passive, much less to be the instrument of a measure which they both deemed a violation of pledged faith to an individual; and as such, derogatory to the honour, and injurious to the interests of the British nation. The consequence of this opposition, which, however laudable the motives, was quite indefensible in military officers, was the removal of Colonel Coote; after which Ram Narrain was seized, but no wealth was found in his possession. His imprisonment, and subsequent execution, by order of Meer Cossim Ali brought just reproach upon the English government: for nothing but direct rebellion, or the most flagrant violation of his duty, could have warranted the abandonment of one whom we had so repeatedly, and so specifically, guaranteed against the apprehended avarice and resentment of his superior's passions, which were aggravated by the protection that policy had compelled us to give to this Hindoo ruler. That the conduct of Cossim Ali was not to be anticipated, is a weak and inadmissible excuse. The faith of the British nation should not have been committed to such hands: for if there exists one ground of strength more than another to our empire in India, it is the strict maintenance of such guarantees as that which had been given to Ram Narrain. They can never be made without creating hostility in the parties whose power they limit, or to whose interests they are, or seem to be, opposed. Every artifice, and every effort, therefore, will be used to induce us to break them; and when we do so, we may be satisfied, that we lose more of real strength, by every such act, than can be gained by the most brilliant victory.

One of the chief causes of the discord which prevailed in Bengal was the exemption from duties on their private trade, claimed by the Company's civil servants, who at that period were remunerated by their trade rather than their salaries. The system of collecting customs on the transit of goods in the interior of the country prevailed all over India; and in Bengal much inconvenience was felt, and many quarrels arose, from the number of tolls and inspections to which the Company's goods were liable, in common with all others, in their transit to and from the marts of purchase and sale. To obviate these, it was arranged with the Nabobs, in explanation of the Emperor's firman, that the Company's flag and *dustuck*[217], in their boats and other conveyances, should secure their goods from search; and as their trade consisted solely of goods from foreign parts for sale in the country,

[216] In a letter to Major Carnac, dated the 7th of May, 1762, Clive observes, "Although I am convinced of the goodness of your heart and intentions, yet there is a warmth and fire in your disposition which often carries you beyond the rules of prudence; and, whatever your friends in India may say of the letter you sent the Board, I wish you never had wrote it, for it gives room to such designing men as Sulivan to do you more prejudice than you can imagine."

The same sentiments had been previously expressed by Clive, in a letter to Mr. Vansittart, 3d of February, 1762. "I am most heartily concerned," he says, "that Carnac has been induced to take part with your enemies in the Council. He has an excellent heart, and a very good understanding; but the warmth of his temper in this instance has got the better of both."

[217] Dustuck, a permit, exempting goods from the payment of duties.

or of country goods for foreign exportation, the privilege only partially interfered with the trade of the interior. While the Nabobs and their officers were in full power, any abuse of this privilege was easily checked. But when, after the accession of Meer Jaffier, the English had become all-powerful, and it was dangerous to interfere with their acts, or to question their proceedings, the Company's servants, who had still the privilege of trading on their own account, not only covered their private adventures, by passports under the Company's name, but all their servants and dependents claimed an exemption from internal duties on the same plea, and besides entered deeply into the internal trade of the country. During the vigorous administration of Clive such attempts had been rare; but when all fear of correction was lost in the increasing weakness of his successors in the government, men set no limits to their efforts to enrich themselves. The Nabob's revenue was injured, and his authority insulted, in every quarter of his dominions, by the exemptions claimed for the trade of European agents, and the respect demanded for the persons of the lowest of their servants. Against their pretensions and excesses he made the most forcible remonstrance, but in vain. Many of the persons of whom he complained were members of Council; and it was not surprising, therefore, that difficulties should occur in any attempt made by the Governor to check and reform such abuses. Cossim Ali became impatient of delay; and finding his representations produce no effect, and that the orders of the government were either evaded or disobeyed, he himself took, and authorized measures of violence, that increased the discontent and hostility of the party opposed to Mr. Vansittart; many of whom were the persons chiefly benefited by the abuses complained of, who represented him as leaving British subjects and public servants of the Company at the will and mercy of a capricious tyrant whom he had unjustly raised to the throne.

To remedy these evils, Mr. Vansittart negotiated a treaty, by which, while some advantages were left to the servants of the Company, many of the privileges they had claimed were done away. This treaty, though exceptionable in some of its clauses, might have operated well, had Mr. Vansittart's Council been disposed to listen to reason, and had Cossim Ali been more temperate. Trusting to his judicious and active administration of the customs as one of the sources out of which he was to discharge the heavy pecuniary obligations under which he had come to the English, he adopted the strictest measures for enforcing their collection. The adjudication and enforcement of all fiscal demands by the articles of the treaty had (unfortunately as affairs stood) been left to the Nabob's officers. Numerous collisions instantly ensued in all parts of the country. "In truth," says Mr. Verelst[218], a dispassionate observer, "it soon became a personal quarrel. Meer Cossim, in the orders issued to his officers, distinguished between the trade of his friends, and of those who opposed him, treating individuals with indecent reproach." The opponents of Mr. Vansittart, who thought their interest injured, and who now formed the majority of Council, combined in measures which soon led to an open rupture.

So excessive were the claims made by the English and their native servants, for carrying their goods free from the duties paid by the Nabob's own subjects,

[218] Verelst's View, p. 47.

that the whole commerce of the country was thrown into confusion, and ruin was threatened to the Nabob's finances. As a measure of justice to his own subjects, and to prevent the daily breaches of the peace which occurred, he saw no remedy left, but to abolish all customs in his dominions. An order was accordingly issued abolishing all tolls and customs for the space of two years.

This act of the Nabob, though extorted by necessity, and so injurious to his own revenue, was loudly exclaimed against as an infringement of his engagements with the Company; and two agents[219] were sent to demand its annulment. But before they could adjust differences, events were brought to a crisis, principally through the impressions made upon the Nabob's mind by the conduct of the majority of the Council.[220]

[219] Mr. Hall and Mr. Amyatt.

[220] "The question is," Mr. Vansittart observes, in a letter to Clive, dated the 25th of February, 1763, "whether the salt, beetle-nut, and tobacco trade shall be carried on with the Company's dustuck, or pay duties to the country government, and go with their dustuck. I am of the latter opinion, and assured the Nabob I would not grant dustucks for these articles, but that myself and any other English gentlemen who had a mind to trade in them, should pay the government's duties and take out their dustuck. This, and some rules I proposed for restraining the overgrown power of the English gomastahs employed in carrying on this trade, and giving the officers of the government their due authority, were disapproved by the rest of the Council; and it was resolved to call down the members from the subordinates to make the necessary regulations upon these points at a full board. * * * * Where the abuses will end I know not; for where the Nabob's officers have the power and the courage to oppose and prevent the unlawful attempts of our gomastahs, they are not contented with that, but, in their turn, oppress and injure in a most extravagant and insufferable manner, so that it is a difficult matter to keep a proper balance; and I shall be obliged to you if you will take an opportunity of giving Mr. Sulivan your sentiments on the subject."

A very different view of this subject is taken by Major Carnac. In a letter to Clive, dated the 26th of February, 1763, he observes: "Mr. Vansittart's interview with the Nabob, instead of removing our grievances, has occasioned their being exceedingly multiplied and carried beyond sufferance. He, in conjunction with Mr. Hastings, without consulting the rest of the Board, established a set of regulations, whereby a duty of 9 per cent. is laid upon all articles of inland trade without exception; and the disputes of our gomastahs and others in our employ are subjected to the decisions of the Nabob's officers. These concessions are so evidently shameful and disadvantageous to us, that it is not to be conceived they could ever have been submitted to, except by persons who were bought into them; and, indeed, it is confidently asserted, and generally believed, that Mr. Vansittart got seven lacs by his visit to Mongyr. The members of the Council, then at Calcutta, passed a severe minute of censure upon the President's procedure, and summoned the absent members, in order to devise a speedy and effectual remedy for the complaints received from every quarter. They have been some time assembled, and have absolutely forbid the regulations being complied with, and have issued out orders to repel by force any insults that shall in future be offered, or obstructions to our trade. It is, indeed, high time," he adds, "to overset the ruinous system which Mr. Vansittart has so industriously endeavoured to establish: by a strange contradiction, he deposes one Nabob under pretence of mal-administration, and then asserts the successor to be independent, and master of his own actions, and uses all possible means to render him so, and to increase his power. We have so sensibly felt the ill use made thereof by Cossim Ali Khan, that the man must be wilfully blind who does not see the necessity of immediately checking his career, and the consequences that must result from his being

Mr. Vansittart informs Lord Clive of his measures for regulating trade; but states his apprehensions of the result. These were but too fully verified. The Nabob, alarmed by the assembly of all the Council from the out-stations, and outraged by their seizure of some aumils (or revenue officers) for the performance of his orders, became most violent, and was rendered more so from the daily reports of the conduct of Mr. Ellis, chief of Patna, who, from the first, had been the determined opponent of his elevation. A knowledge of the disposition, and a belief of the hostile intentions of this public agent, led him to stop two boats proceeding to Patna with arms; and he added to this act of aggression a demand for the removal of Mr. Ellis, and the English detachment from Patna. This conduct was regarded as very little short of an open declaration of war; and as such, it was treated by the majority of the Council, who issued orders to Mr. Ellis, giving him the power (if he thought it right to exercise it) to anticipate the Nabob's hostile designs by seizing upon the citadel of Patna. The reins of government had fallen from the hands of Mr. Vansittart, and were guided by a selfish and sordid majority.

It was in vain that Mr. Vansittart and Mr. Warren Hastings protested against giving such discretionary power to a man known to be so violent. They too truly anticipated the result. At the very moment Cossim Ali (alarmed at having proceeded too far) released the boats, he heard of the Fort of Patna being surprised and taken by the English troops, acting under the orders of Mr. Ellis. Though it was immediately re-taken by his troops, Cossim Ali's rage, at what he deemed a treacherous commencement of hostilities, knew no bounds; and throwing away the scabbard, he became furious in his resentment against the whole English nation, and all who had adhered to them. Mr. Amyatt[221], one of the deputies sent to Monghyr, was murdered on his way back to Calcutta. To Ram Narrain's death was added the execution of the two Hindu Seits (or bankers), who had always been supposed attached to the English interests; and notwithstanding the entreaties and threats

suffered to run on." From these observations, it may safely be concluded, that the gallant Major was a better soldier than statesman.

[221] The following letter, dated the 15th of June, 1763, which we find entered in the copy book of Mr. Amyatt, was meant to report to Mr. Vansittart the failure of his mission. The original never reached its destination. "I am favoured with yours of the 8th and 9th instant. We waited on the Nabob, and delivered him your letter: he was highly incensed, and expressed great contempt for us and our forces, and told us he expected nothing else than a war; that we might go and remain at our tents till we received the Council's orders, and then signify the same to him by writing—which he supposed would be much the same as your letters to him; if so, he should dismiss us, but expected Mr. Hay to remain a hostage till those prisoners we had of his were released. The stopping our arms is not equal to the seizing his aumils, he says; and our troops being in his pay, they shall not remain at Patna; and peace or war depended on their removal, which he found would not be the case. All my endeavours to establish a friendship and confidence have been in vain; nor can I convince him we did not intend breaking with him, or to disgrace him by being obliged to seize his aumils, but necessitated so to do. He seemed inclined to quarrel, or rather resolved we shall have no influence, or free intercourse, or trade through his country, but what he pleases. I have had a very disagreeable time with him, and shall be heartily glad when free from this embassy, which I have, to the utmost of my power, endeavoured to conclude, in bringing about a lasting peace and friendship, and reconcile the Nabob to every body; but to no purpose, nor can it be effected."

of the Governor, and the more direct menaces of Major Adams, commanding the British forces, he glutted his vengeance with the deliberate murder of Mr. Ellis and all the English (except one) who had been taken prisoners at Patna. Their numbers amounted to one hundred and fifty, of whom fifty were military or civil officers.

Subsequently to this act of atrocity[222], Cossim Ali and the German[223], Sumroo, (who had been the instrument of the massacre,) fled before the British troops, and found refuge in the territories of Oude. Sujah-u-Dowlah, the prince of that country, not only refused to deliver them up on the demand of the British commander, but, acting as an ally of Cossim Ali, advanced to attack the English army, then under Major Munro, from whom he received a signal defeat at Buxar. He was afterwards pursued into his own country, and again discomfited, though he had been joined by the Mahratta chief, Mulhar Row Holkar. So situated, this ruler adopted a very politic and decided course. He would not, he said, bring a stain upon his honour, by surrendering men who had sought his protection; but he commanded Cossim Ali and Sumroo to quit his dominions, and repaired to the British camp, throwing himself entirely upon the clemency of his enemy. To this he was chiefly induced by the accounts which had been received of the return of Clive, whom he could not hope to oppose, and whose resentment he hoped to disarm by unqualified submission. His conduct and character were represented in the most favourable light by Major Carnac, who earnestly recommended that he should be treated with generosity, and confirmed in his dominions. Such a measure, this sensible and liberal officer remarked, would be more beneficial to our interests and reputation, than any change we could make in this quarter of India.

The events that have been described led to the re-elevation of Meer Jaffier to the Musnud; and we must, therefore, shortly revert to the history of that prince.

Before Clive left India, Meer Jaffier had committed many acts that might have been construed into infractions of the treaty with the English, and more, that, strictly viewed, would have proved him ill suited for the high station to which he had been raised: but Clive considered that his conduct was less to be attributed to his character, which was weak and vacillating, than to the galling nature of his dependent condition; and as the relations between the Nabob of Moorshedabad and the English could not be changed, without danger to the very existence of the latter, he judged wisely, that, while Meer Jaffier abstained from hostility, however glaring his defects, any change in the head of the native government would be impolitic, and attended with consequences alike injurious to the reputation and interests of the British government.

The departure of Clive was the most serious of all misfortunes to Meer Jaffier. He required the most liberal toleration that enlarged policy could give to his measures. He had, besides, a respect for the character and a dread of the displeasure of Clive, which operated as a check upon his excesses. Mr. Holwell (the temporary successor to Clive) could not succeed to his influence over the mind of the Nabob,

[222] 1763.

[223] A well-informed friend of the author remarks, that he was not a German, but a Frenchman or Swiss, of the name of *Sombre*, which, perhaps, had been his *nom-de-guerre* when in the French service.

whose want of personal deference must have aggravated the bad impressions the new governor appears to have previously entertained of his character. But, though Mr. Holwell has laboured to prove that Meer Jaffier, subsequent to his combination with the Dutch, carried on a correspondence with the Shah-Zada hostile to the English, the fact is not clearly established; and if it were, the sound principles that regulated the conduct of Clive would have led to its being passed over. The unhappy death of Meeran, however, was the event which tended most to accelerate the revolution. It threw, as has been shown, the army and country into equal confusion; and the step taken by the Nabob of elevating his nearest connection[224] and most efficient military leader, Cossim Ali, to the condition before held by his son, proved the proximate cause of his ruin.

Cossim Ali's ambition was of too active a nature to render him content to await the death of his father-in-law and benefactor; and he found, in the distracted state of the Nabob's government, and in the prejudices of those intrusted with the administration of the Company's affairs in Bengal, ample grounds to proceed upon. He had also recourse to what he no doubt deemed more certain means of effecting his object. He promised (and the promise was afterwards made good[225]), large sums to those of the select committee who had favoured his elevation. He anxiously desired to extend his gifts to the members of the committee who were opposed to the measures of the Governor; but they rejected his offers, and made such rejection a strong ground of the sincerity of that protest[226] which they had entered against the proceedings of the Governor and his party on this memorable occasion.

The letter written by the secret committee of Bengal to the Court of Directors, at the period of Clive's departure for England, has been already noticed. It was, of course, deemed most contumacious; and as a mark of their displeasure, the Court

[224] Cossim Ali was his son-in-law.

[225] Mr. Vansittart, in his communications with the Nabob, rejected this present previous to the treaty, as it might appear the price of its stipulations: but he intimated, at the same time, that there would be no objection to such present after the obligations of the treaty were fulfilled. The following is a list of the presents acknowledged to have been received on this occasion:—

Mr. Vansittart	rupees 500,000	£58,333
Mr. Sumner	240,000	28,000
Mr. Holwell	270,000	30,937
Mr. M'Guire	180,000	20,625
Mr. Smyth	134,000	15,354
Major Yorke	134,000	15,354
General Caillaud	200,000	22,916
Mr. M'Guire	75,000	8,750
		£200,269

Vide Parl. Reports, vol. iii. p. 311.

[226] This protest, which is in the form of a letter, is dated the 11th of March, 1762.—Vide Parl. Rep., vol. iii. p. 252.

dismissed from their service the four civil councillors.[227] Three of those dismissed were zealous supporters of Mr. Vansittart; and their removal threw the power into the hands of a majority, whose violence, in their opposition to him and Cossim Ali, led to measures which precipitated the rupture with the latter, and all the horrid acts by which it was attended.

On the breaking out of the war, the restoration of Meer Jaffier was urged by the majority of the Council; and when the excesses of Cossim Ali put an end to all hopes of a settlement with him, Mr. Vansittart and Mr. Hastings, who were at first opposed to the measure, concurred in it. The re-elevation was attended with few changes. He confirmed the concessions[228] made by Cossim Ali, and restored the advantages of trade to the English which that prince had taken from them. Meer Jaffier survived his restoration to power but a short period; and that was disturbed by mutinies in his army, and by the intrigues and corruption of his court. He imputed all his misfortunes to the absence of Clive; and he anxiously desired to protract his existence till the arrival of one, whom, notwithstanding all their disputes and differences, he appears throughout to have considered as his only true friend. The gratification of his wish was denied him. He died a few months before Clive's arrival[229]; but the warm and often-expressed sentiments of Meer Jaffier, on this point, show that he was neither destitute of good feeling nor discernment. The sincerity of his attachment was proved by the last act of his life, which was to leave a legacy to his friend. The amount and destination of this bequest shall be hereafter mentioned.

On the death of Meer Jaffier, doubts arose as to his successor. The first claimant was Nujum-ud-Dowla, a youth of twenty, and son of the deceased; and the second, his grandson (the son of Meeran), who was only six years of age. After some deliberation, the decision was in favour of the former.

By the treaty[230] concluded with this prince, the military defence of the country entirely devolved upon the English; the Nabob agreeing to keep no more troops than were necessary for purposes of parade. The most remarkable feature of this arrangement was, the agreement of the young Nabob to appoint, with the advice and concurrence of the English government, a Naib Subah (or vicegerent), to conduct the civil administration of his country. At the time when Meer Jaffier was restored, the choice of his minister was, of course, considered as being of the greatest importance. While at Calcutta, he proposed to appoint to that office Nundcomar[231], a Hindu of the worst character. To this Mr. Vansittart strongly objected, recommending Mahommed Reza Khan, a Mahommedan noble of talent and of reputed integrity, but who was opposed (probably for those very qualifications) by the intriguing and corrupt faction which had long governed the court of

[227] Messrs. Holwell, Pleydell, Sumner, and M'Guire.

[228] The provinces of Burdwan, Midnapore, and Chittagong.

[229] February 6, 1765.

[230] February, 1765.

[231] This man has been before mentioned. He was justly objectionable to the British government on account of the various intrigues and treasons in which he had been detected; and was imprisoned at Calcutta for his correspondence with its enemies during the reign of Cossim Ali.

Moorshedabad. The Nabob soon after left Calcutta, when Nundcomar followed; and, in spite of Mr. Vansittart's remonstrances, being supported by the majority in Council opposed to the Governor, he was intrusted with the direction of the Nabob's affairs. Mr. Vansittart had left Bengal before the death of Meer Jaffier; on which event, by the treaty that followed, Mahommed Reza Khan (then at Dacca) was elevated to the rank of Naib Subah to his successor, Nujum-ud-Dowla.[232]

Mr. Vansittart, or rather his council, has been reproached[233] (as Clive was) for making Nabobs, without any reference or respect for the legitimate authority of the Emperor of Delhi, or his Vizier, Sujah-u-Dowla. But however politic it might have been to have gained the sanction of such authorities after the measure was adopted, a previous application would have been the height of folly and of weakness. Whatever latitude of interference, or right of approbation, had been given to the Emperor or his minister, would assuredly have been exercised for venal and ambitious purposes; and the embarrassments, that must ever attend such proceedings, would have been multiplied tenfold. Sujah-u-Dowla, it is true, upbraided the English with their conduct in this particular. He accused them of casting down and putting up Nabobs at their pleasure; but this was to gain opinion, and afford a pretext for the hostilities he meditated against their power. The very chief who made this accusation was the proclaimed minister and servant of the Emperor; but he yielded him neither obedience, nor a participation in the revenues of the wide and rich territories of Oude. Names and forms, as connected with the different relations of authority in the empire of India, continued to be observed, and were so far of importance; but, as connected with the substance of power, they had been, for a long period, wholly neglected; and though we may agree with the historical antiquary, who judges from the principles of times long past, and looks only to the theory of Indian government, that the English were wrong, yet, if we take a dispassionate and comprehensive view of the actual condition of India, we must, I conceive, not only deem them defensible upon this point, but pronounce that, under the circumstances in which they were placed, it was quite impracticable for the local authorities at Calcutta to pursue any other line, without sacrificing the interests committed to their care, and greatly increasing the anarchy and bloodshed in the country, regarding the administration of which the disputes existed.[234]

The changes that took place at Madras during Clive's absence from India have little relation to these Memoirs, as that presidency continued, during his second administration, almost unconnected with Bengal. Suffice it, therefore, to say, that the power of the English Nabob (as he was termed), Mahommed Ali Khan, was

---

[232] Vide Mill's British India, vol. iii. p. 318.

[233] There is some confusion in Mr. Mill's account of this transaction (vol. iii. p. 330.), from that accurate historian having overlooked the fact, that the appointment of Nujum-ud-Dowla was managed by Mr. Spencer and his council, Mr. Vansittart having previously set out for Europe.—See 3d Report of Committee of 1773, p. 21.; and Scott's Hist. of Bengal, vol. ii. pp. 439-447.

[234] An exception must be made of the deposition of Meer Jaffier: Suraj-u-Dowla, and Cossim Ali respectively forfeited their authority in consequence of their unsuccessful attempts to destroy the power of the English.

fully established[235]; the strong fortress of Vellore was besieged, and taken from Mortiz Ali Khan, and part of the Carnatic was assigned, as a jaghire, to the Company.

Another event occurred during this period[236], which created a great sensation. The gallant Mahommed Esoof, who had so greatly distinguished himself in the early campaigns of Lawrence and Clive, had been continued in the management of Madura and Tinnevelly, which he had been the chief instrument of reducing to order. He was, in this situation, subject to the Nabob, to whom, and those around him, he was not long in becoming an object of jealousy and hatred. The defalcation of revenue from exhausted countries, and the haughty replies made by a proud soldier to reproaches, added to the preparations he made to guard against the designs of those he justly deemed his enemies, furnished ample pretexts for accusing him of malversation and rebellion. The Company's troops were combined with those of the Nabob for his reduction; which was not, however, effected, without great waste of blood and treasure, and at last accomplished by an act of treachery. A Frenchman in his service, of the name of Marchand, betrayed him; and he was put to death by the Nabob, Mahommed Ali. This gallant soldier, no doubt, became a rebel to the prince he served; but he may be deemed, in some respects, the victim of those disputes for power which ran so high, at this period, between the English and the Nabob. Mr. Pigot, according to Mahommed Ali, forced Mahommed Esoof upon him as the manager of the countries of Madura and Tinnevelly; and by his support and countenance encouraged him in acts of contumacy and disobedience. Educated as the Vellore Subadar had been, and knowing that the real power was vested in the English, he appears to have looked exclusively to them, and to have paid little attention to one he considered as having no more than a nominal authority. But the departure for England of his friend Mr. Pigot, and the succession of Mr. Palk, whose policy conceded to the Nabob the real dominion of his country, left Mahommed Esoof without hope; and, in the desperate struggle he made for his life, the former faithful soldier of the English not only corresponded with their enemies, the French, against whom he had so often and so gallantly fought, but declared himself the subject, and displayed in his fort and country the banners, of that nation. This last act of his life has not deprived his memory of the honours that belong to it, as the bravest and ablest of all the native soldiers that ever served the English in India.

Mr. Palk, formerly clergyman at Fort Saint David, who had risen, by his moderation, good sense, and experience, to different offices of government, was, when Clive returned to India, Governor of Madras. His appointment to this station induced his friend and near connection, General Lawrence, to quit his retreat, and revisit, as commander of the troops, the scene of his former fame.

At Calcutta, Mr. Spencer from Bombay had succeeded to Mr. Vansittart. He was governor at the time of the elevation of Nujum-ud-Dowla, and participated in the money[237] that was distributed on that occasion. These presents have been just-

[235] 1763.

[236] 1764.

[237] Vide Parliamentary Reports, vol. iii. p. 312.

ly arraigned, as furnishing powerful motives to the Company's servants for making revolutions by which they were enriched; and it is one of the heaviest charges against Clive, that his example was the origin of this baneful practice. The fact is not disputed; but it happened in this case, as in most others, where small men attempt to imitate great, that they reach only the defects, and fail in every other part.

The princely presents which Clive merited and received were the rewards of great services rendered to the parties by whom they were given, and in which his first efforts were prompted by considerations that were decidedly uninfluenced by sordid motives. Add to this, that whatever he undertook prospered, and that all the individuals whom he elevated he preserved, not only from their native enemies, but from the still more galling encroachments and rapacity of the Company's servants. By such acts he won the good opinion of all ranks in India. From the King to the peasant the name of Clive inspired sentiments of respect and confidence.

What a contrast was presented by his successors in power! Money for themselves was, in every engagement, one of the stipulations, and *appeared,* though in some cases it might not have *been,* the leading motive of their measures. All their measures failed: every one connected with them was ruined. The character for good faith, which at Clive's departure stood so high, was lost. No one trusted the word of an Englishman. Many of those who engaged in these scenes were able and virtuous; but there was no leading genius among them. The jealousy and party spirit that pervaded the government at home multiplied checks and cherished insubordination in those abroad; till nothing was heard but accusations and recriminations.

The army, both European and native, had fallen into a very insubordinate and mutinous state. The officers evinced this spirit on almost every occasion where they deemed their personal interests affected; and many of the privates deserted to the native powers. A most serious mutiny occurred at the period when Major Munro took the command of the army[238] at Patna. A battalion of sepoys left camp to join the enemy: they were intercepted by a body of troops, and twenty-four of the ringleaders were brought before a native court-martial, and sentenced to death. They were all executed; and we are informed by an officer who was present, that an incident occurred on this occasion, which not only created a great sensation at the moment, but left a lasting impression on the native soldiers of Bengal, being truly characteristic of their proud and dauntless spirit.

When the orders were given to tie four of these men to the guns, from which they were to be blown, four grenadiers stept out and demanded the priority of suffering, as "a right," they said, "which belonged to men who had always been first in the post of danger." The calm manner in which this request was made, and the anxiety that it should be granted, excited great sympathy in all who beheld it. The officer[239] on whose authority this fact is stated, and who was an eye-witness of the scene, observes; "I belonged on this occasion to a detachment of marines. They were hardened fellows, and some of them had been of the execution party that shot Admiral Byng; yet they could not refrain from tears at the fate and con-

[238] 1764.

[239] Captain Williams' Memoir of the Bengal Native Army.

duct of these gallant grenadier sepoys."

When a strong sense of imminent danger, and a fear of total ruin to the affairs of the Company and of the English nation in Bengal, excited universal attention and alarm, all eyes were naturally turned on Clive, as the only human being who could restore the reputation and interests of this nation in India. He was in consequence, as has been stated, called upon to proceed once more to that country, and he had courage to obey the call, though convinced that the scene presented difficulties which were almost insurmountable, and that he would have to perform duties that were personally invidious, and calculated not only to interrupt but to destroy all his prospects of future enjoyment.

There can be no doubt that Clive, in consenting, under such circumstances, to return to India, was chiefly, if not solely, actuated by an honourable ambition, and by an ardent desire to promote the interests and glory of his country. His first stipulation, however, was, that his stay should be limited to a very short period; and he pledged himself (and the pledge, as will be shown hereafter, was nobly redeemed) not to enrich himself one farthing by any pay or emoluments he might receive from the high station to which he was nominated.

Though Clive had been restrained by many considerations, as well as by the rapidity of events, from taking personally any decided part in the disputes in Bengal, he had not been an unconcerned observer of those scenes. Each party had addressed him with an equal solicitude that he should approve and support them; but we do not meet in his private correspondence with any full expression of his sentiments. He regretted, it appears from his letters, the removal of Meer Jaffier from the throne; but uninformed of the minute circumstances that had produced that measure, he did not withdraw his confidence in the wisdom of the administration of one, whom he so highly valued as Mr. Vansittart, till he saw him depart step by step from all those maxims of policy he had laid down as the rules of his own conduct, both in regard to native princes and other men of rank and consequence in India.

The opposition of his views to those of his successor, as well as his own difficulties, are clearly expressed in a letter he wrote to the Court of Directors immediately before his embarkation.

"In obedience to your commands," Lord Clive observes[240], "I now transmit the purport of what I had the honour to represent to you by word of mouth at the last Court of Directors, with some other particulars which slipped my memory at that time.

"Having taken into consideration your letter sent me by the Secretary, as also the request of the General Court of Proprietors, I think myself bound in honour to accept the charge of your affairs in Bengal, provided you will co-operate with, and assist me in such a manner that I may be able to answer the expectations and intentions of the General Court.

"As an individual, I can have no temptation to undertake this arduous task, and nothing but the desire I have to be useful to my country, and to manifest my

[240] This letter is dated 27th April, 1764.

gratitude to this Company, could make me embark in this service, attended as it is with so many inconveniences to myself and my family. I cannot avoid acknowledging that I quit my native country with some degree of regret and diffidence, on leaving behind me (as I certainly do) a very divided and distracted Direction, at a time, too, when unanimity is more than ever requisite for the carrying into execution such plans as are absolutely necessary to the well-being of the Company.

"I shall now enter into a short discussion of your political, commercial, and military affairs in Bengal. Without searching into the causes of the unhappy revolution in favour of Cossim Ali Khan, I shall only remark, that if the same plan of politics had been pursued, after he was placed upon the throne, as that which I had observed towards his predecessor, he might with great ease have remained there to this day, without having it in his power to injure either himself or the Company in the manner he has lately done. Indeed, Mr. Vansittart's ideas in politics have differed so widely from mine, that either the one or the other must have been totally in the wrong. Soon after Cossim Ali Khan was raised to his new dignity, he was suffered to retire to a very great distance from his capital, that our influence might be felt and dreaded as little as possible by him:—he was suffered to dismiss all those old officers who had any connection with, or dependence upon us; and, what was the worst of all, our faithful friend and ally, Ram Narrain, the Nabob of Patna, was given up; the doctrine of the Subadar's independency was adopted, and every method was put in practice to confirm him in it. We need seek for no other causes of the war, for it is now some time that things have been carried to such lengths abroad, that either the princes of the country must, in a great measure, be dependent on us, or we totally so on them.[241] That the public and continued disapprobation of Cossim Ali Khan's advancement to the government, expressed by the gentlemen of Calcutta, increased the Nabob's jealousy, is most true; and that it was the duty of every one, after the revolution was once effected, to concur heartily in every measure to support it, cannot be denied. It is likewise true, that the encroachments made upon the Nabob's prescriptive rights by the Governor and Council, and the rest of the servants trading in the articles of salt, beetle, and tobacco, together with the power given by Mr. Vansittart to subject our gomastahs (or agents) to the jurisdiction and inspection of the country government, all concurred to hasten and bring on the late troubles; but still the groundwork of the whole was the Nabob's independency. It is impossible to rely on the moderation and justice of Mussulmen. Strict and impartial justice should ever be observed; but let that justice come from ourselves. The trade, therefore, of salt, betle, and tobacco having been one cause of the present disputes, I hope these articles will be restored to the Nabob, and your servants absolutely forbid to trade in them. This will be striking at the root of the evil. The prohibition of dustucks to your junior servants will, I hope, tend to restore that economy which is so necessary in your service. Indeed, if some method be not thought of, and your Council do not heartily co-operate with your Governor to prevent the sudden acquisition of fortunes, which has taken place of late, the Company's affairs must greatly suffer. What power it may be proper to vest me with, to remedy those great and growing evils, will merit your

[241] Clive's clear and practical mind here puts the question on its real basis. There is no other alternative.

serious consideration. As a means to alleviate in some measure the dissatisfaction that such restrictions upon the commercial advantages of your servants may occasion in them, it is my full intention not to engage in any kind of trade myself; so that they will divide amongst them what used to be the Governor's portion of commercial advantages, which was always very considerable."

Clive then proceeds to offer some observations upon the state of the Company's military affairs in Bengal; and suggests the necessity of keeping up an European force of four, or, at least, three thousand men.[242] While he pays a just tribute to the high character of the Indian army, and to the honour they had gained by their gallant exploits, he laments the want of due obedience and subordination, so essential to the interests of the service. To remedy this (which was rendered more necessary by the removal of the King's troops at this time), he recommends an immediate increase of field officers; and points out to the Court the different individuals, who, from their character and services, had the strongest claims upon their notice.

"I would recommend," he observes, "the appointing three field officers to every battalion, a colonel, lieutenant-colonel, and major; and the officers I would choose to command the battalions should be Majors Carnac, Richard Smith, and Preston. You have already done justice to Major Carnac's character by reinstating him in the command of your forces in Bengal, and by acknowledging his services in the most public manner. This gentleman will, I flatter myself, stand as high in your esteem as Brigadier General Caillaud; and will, I hope, have the same rank and appointments. The military merits of the other two gentlemen you are likewise well acquainted with, having both received from the Court marks of approbation for their distinguished services. To command your artillery I would recommend Sir Robert Barker, whose abilities in that department have been exceeded by no officer that ever was in your service. Your sepoys are already commanded by Major Knox, whose merits I could wish to have rewarded with a lieutenant-colonel's commission. Your horse, when raised, should be commanded by a lieutenant-colonel, or major.

"I have very strong reasons to wish this idea of regimenting your troops may take place; for without such a subordination I shall not be able to enforce your orders for the reduction of your military expenses, which have been a constant dead-weight, and have swallowed up your revenues. I could wish, that whatever emoluments are unavoidable may fall to those few who, having been long, are high in your service, whether civil or military. Thus will the expense be scarce felt by the Company, in comparison to what it is at present, when, for want of due subordination, every one thinks himself entitled to every advantage; and the juniors in your service be excited to exert themselves, from a certain knowledge that application and abilities only can restore them to their native country with fortunes honourably acquired."

[242] "For the good of the Company," Clive observes in the letter already quoted, "I would propose that you should always have, in Bengal, four, or at least three, thousand Europeans; to consist of three battalions of seven hundred each; four companies of artillery of one hundred each; and five hundred light horse."

In concluding the subject of military affairs, Clive submits to the consideration of the Court his ideas and opinions on the proper mode of levying troops in England. The method pursued at this period he considered to be, in many respects, objectionable. In order that due attention might be paid to the selection of recruits, and to insure, at all times, a proper supply of efficient men, to meet any unexpected demands that might arise in cases of sudden emergency, he suggests, that the Company should apply to his Majesty for permission to maintain two battalions, of five hundred men each, in England, with a proper proportion of officers; and, as a reward to the important services of Colonel Coote and Colonel Forde, he recommends that these two officers should be nominated to command them.

Clive appears to have referred much of the spirit of opposition that arose in Bengal to the jealousy among the public servants of that presidency of appointments, which they deemed supersessions, of civilians from Madras and Bombay, to be governors of Bengal.

"The heart-burnings and disputes," he observes, "which seem to have spread and overrun your settlement of Calcutta, arose, I must fear, originally, from your appointment of Mr. Vansittart to the government of Bengal from another settlement; although his promotion was the effect of my recommendation. The appointment, therefore, of Mr. Spencer, from Bombay, can only tend to inflame these dissensions, and to destroy all those advantages which the Company only can expect from harmony and unanimity amongst their servants abroad. The resignation of Messrs. Verelst, Cartier, and many others of the senior servants, which must be the consequence of Mr. Spencer's appointment, will deprive me of those very gentlemen on whose assistance I depend for re-establishing your affairs in Bengal."

The following letter from Clive relates to the same subjects, and contains too many sound observations and wise reflections upon the actual state of the affairs of India at this period to be omitted. Though the Court of Directors did not comply with the wish of Clive, that he should have the power (since vested in Indian governors) of acting, when occasion demanded, upon his own responsibility, they did what was almost tantamount,—they vested the power required in a select committee[243], composed of persons from whom he had no opposition to apprehend, and who were competent to all acts of administration, independent of the other members of Council.

"I shall not enter," Clive observes, "into the motives which caused the deposition of Meer Jaffier, nor into the fundamental cause of the present war with Cossim Ali Khan. It is sufficient to say, that these two events have lost us all the confidence of the natives. To restore this, ought to be our principal object; and the best means will, in my opinion, be by establishing a moderation in the advantages which may be reserved for the Company, or allotted to individuals in their service.

"If ideas of conquest were to be the rule of our conduct, I foresee that we should, by necessity, be led from acquisition to acquisition, until we had the whole empire up in arms against us; and whilst we lay under the great disadvantage of fighting without a single ally, (for who could wish us well?) the natives, left

[243] This select committee was composed of Lord Clive, General Carnac, Mr. Verelst, Mr. Sumner, and Mr. Sykes. The two latter accompanied Lord Clive from England.

without European allies, would find, in their own resources, means of carrying on war against us in a much more soldierly manner than they ever thought of when their reliance on European allies encouraged their natural indolence. The last battle fought against Cossim Ali Khan is a proof of this assertion, for never did the troops of India fight so well.

"Nothing, therefore, but extreme necessity, ought to induce us to extend our ideas of territorial acquisitions beyond the amount of those ceded by Cossim Ali Khan, in his treaty with Vansittart. This necessity can only arise from finding that nobody will trust us; and that the people of the country are determined to try their strength with us to the utmost.

"But by this system of moderation it is not intended that the Nabob should be left entirely independent of us. The moment he fancies himself in this situation he will look upon us as enemies who have taken too much from him, and whom it will be necessary, either to reduce to our ancient state of mere merchants, or to extirpate. This, therefore, was the error of Mr. Vansittart's conduct: he advised the Nabob to regulate his treasury, save money, to form and discipline an excellent army, and to pay them well and regularly, contrary to the practice of all the princes of India. By following this advice punctually, Cossim Ali, in two years, thought himself in a condition to bid us defiance, and was near being so.

"It ought, therefore, to be our plan to convince the Nabob that our troops are his best, his only support against foreign enemies; and that our friendship will be his best support against the plots and revolutions of his own officers. Necessitated, by the extent of his dominions, to repose large governments and great trusts in particular men, jealousies will be perpetually subsisting. On the nice and disinterested management of these will depend our importance. The principal officers must be convinced that we will protect them from any capricious violences of their sovereign; and, on the other hand, the Nabob must be convinced, that we will give them up to his just resentment the moment their ambition alone leads them to strike at him.

"To carry this balance with an even hand, the strictest integrity will be necessary in every one who shall have a vote in your councils abroad. I found myself every day assaulted by large offers of presents, from the principal men of the province, not to support the Nabob in resolutions contrary to their interests; and from the Nabob, to sacrifice them to his capricious resentments.

"But even this conduct alone will not be sufficient to keep us from giving umbrage. During Mr. Vansittart's government, all your servants thought themselves entitled to take large shares in the monopolies of salt, beetle, and tobacco, the three articles, next to grain, of greatest consumption in the empire. The odium of seeing such monopolies in the hands of foreigners need not be insisted on; but this is not the only inconvenience: it is productive of another, equally, if not more prejudicial to the Company's interests; it enables many of your servants to obtain, very suddenly, fortunes greater than those which in former times were thought a sufficient reward for a long continuance in your service. Hence these gentlemen, thus suddenly enriched, think of nothing but of returning to enjoy their fortunes in England, and leave your affairs in the hands of young men, whose sanguine expectations are inflamed by the examples of those who have just left them.

"This, therefore, will be the greatest difficulty which I shall have to encounter; to persuade, or, if necessary, to oblige your servants to be content with advantages much inferior to those which, by the prescription of some years, they may think themselves entitled to. Yet if this is not done, your affairs can never be settled on a judicious and permanent plan. My fortunes, my family, and the other advantages I may be possessed of, will naturally make me wish to accomplish my intentions for the Company's service abroad as soon as possible, that I may return to my native country, which, it cannot be imagined, that I quit without some regrets; but if I should meet in your councils abroad men whom private interest may render averse to my maxims, I shall, perhaps, instead of settling your affairs as may be expected from me, find myself harassed and over-ruled in every measure by a majority against me in council.

"It therefore rests with the Court of Directors to consider, seriously, whether they should not intrust me with a dispensing power in the civil and political affairs; so that whensoever I may think proper to take any resolution entirely upon myself that resolution is to take place. The French Company gave Mr. Godeheu sole and absolute control over all their settlements to the east of the Cape of Good Hope, at a time when their affairs were not in a worse condition than ours are at present. In India we ourselves have had examples of supervisors. I myself was intrusted with great powers by the gentlemen of Madras, when I went down to Bengal against Suraj-u-Dowlah: the use which I made of these powers will, I hope, justify my opinion, that I may, without danger, be intrusted with an authority so highly necessary at present. The occasions of exerting it will rarely happen, but will certainly happen at times, when all may be lost for want of it. Moderation, I will venture to say, was always a part of my character in political concerns; and as a means to induce the gentlemen abroad to contract their views of private advantage within the bounds essentially necessary to the interests of the Company, the first step I shall take will be, to give up to them every commercial advantage, as I did during my last residence in Bengal. I need not mention that these advantages are, to a Governor, great, and adequate to his station.

"To prevent dissensions, I am willing to receive a military commission inferior to General Lawrence's; but that gentleman has received from the Court of Directors so very extensive a power over all their forces in India, that the presidency, at which he resides, is, in fact, little less than the residence of a Governor-general over all your settlements in India. If ever the appointment of such an officer as Governor-general should become necessary, it is evident that he ought to be established in Bengal, as the greatest weight of your civil, commercial, political, and military affairs will always be in that province. It cannot, therefore, be expected that I should be subject to have any part of the military forces allotted for that province recalled or withheld from me at the will of an officer in another part of India; or that even the presence of that officer in Bengal should, in any way, interfere with my military authority in that province. It will likewise be necessary (at least until affairs in Bengal are restored to perfect tranquillity) that whatever troops, treasures, or other consignments may be destined from England to that presidency, shall not, as usual, be stopped and employed by any of the other presidencies at which they may chance to arrive in their passage towards the Ganges."

Such was the prospect, and such were the anticipations, with which Clive proceeded to India. The task was arduous, but his mind was resolved on its full performance; and the next chapter will show that his efforts were more than sufficient to surmount the obstacles that were opposed to his success, although they proved even greater than he had apprehended.

CHAPTER XIV.

Clive assumes the Government of Bengal, 1765.—State of the Country and of the various Services.—Military Arrangements.—Negotiations with the Nabob of Bengal.—Treaty with the Nabob-Visier.—Settlement with the King.—The Duannee acquired for the Company.—Discontents in the Civil Service, and Reforms effected

We have already adverted to the state of confusion in which affairs were at Bengal when Lord Clive landed.

Never had an individual a more arduous task of reform; but he came to it with great local knowledge, with a full acquaintance with the characters of those by whom he was likely to be aided or thwarted, and with a mind determined at all hazards to execute the great work to which he had been called, almost by acclamation.

The public letters, papers, and minutes which were laid before Parliament, regarding the transactions in Bengal, during the years 1765 and 1766, illustrated as they are by the debates of 1772, gave a full and accurate history of those two years; but it is in his volumes of private letters, more than even in any public documents, that we must look for the motives of Clive's conduct, during this most eventful period of his life. These are so numerous, that it is difficult to select from them such as will best give, in his own language, a just idea of the difficulties which he had to combat, and of that unyielding firmness and determined resolution by which they were overcome.

He writes to his friend General Carnac, under date the 3d May, 1765:—

> "I arrived here this morning to take possession of a government, which I find in a more distracted state, if possible, than I had reason to expect.
>
> "The measures taken, with regard to the country government, have been at best precipitate; and the gentlemen here, knowing that the arrangement of all affairs was absolutely vested in the committee, might, I think, have avoided going the lengths they have, till my arrival. But I am determined not to be embarrassed by the errors of others, if in my power to remedy them. At least, I will struggle hard that the disinterested purpose of my voyage prove not ineffectual. Your resolution, my dear friend, and principles, almost unparalleled in these climes, will, I am sure, co-op-

erate with me in every regulation for the public good. Verelst appears, as far as I can hitherto judge, to be a man of honour and integrity. Sykes may be thoroughly relied on, and Sumner must, for his own sake, be a friend to the Company. It is impossible, therefore, to doubt that we shall be able to settle every matter to the satisfaction of our employers. The young Nabob should be treated with respect, with dignity, and with that honour which ought to be characteristic of Englishmen in Asia as well as in Europe; but since we have experienced such a series of troubles from the mismanagement of Subahships, it is our duty to guard against future evils, by doing for ourselves what no Nabob will ever do for us; and never trust to the ambition of any Mussulman whatever, after what has happened. Peace upon a firm and lasting foundation must be established if possible. And to obtain this object, I conclude it will be necessary for me to march up to you at camp, not to continue long there, but to enter into some treaty with the King. Your long and extensive expedition I could wish had been avoidable; but of that and all other affairs I will speak more at large, when I have the pleasure of hearing from or seeing you. For the present, I can only say, that our views ought to be confined to Bengal and its departments, and so far I am sure may be gone with justice; nor do I doubt, that a committee of gentlemen, whose emulation is not excited by the distribution of loaves and fishes, may acquire at this juncture immortal honour to themselves, and lasting advantages to the Company. To-morrow morning I begin to read over the papers, and minutes of Council, that I may, by seeing what has been done, be able to form a clearer opinion of the plan we ought now to adopt. This business will, I suppose, employ my attention for two or three days, and then you shall hear from me."

In a letter to the same officer, under date the 6th May, Clive observes:—

"I shall now inform you of this day's proceedings. Having met in Council, after some debates, the field officers were established as follows:—General Carnac, Colonel Smith, and Sir R. Barker are Colonels of the first, second, and third regiments of Infantry; Sir R. Fletcher, Major Peach, and Major Chapman, Lieutenant-Colonels; Majors Champion and Stibbart, Majors. It was also proposed to fill up the other vacancy, which I objected to, until General Carnac's sentiments were known; a compliment I thought due to the commanding officer. You will therefore point out to me whom you would have the third Major, and he shall be appointed. I am informed you do not think Major Champion has had justice done him, when these appointments were made. Major Champion's merits were not known, or he would most certainly have stood next in rank to Colonel. However, Major Champion is satisfied with an assurance from me, that whatever the Directors shall order on that head shall be complied with.

"After this matter was settled, I desired the Board would order those paragraphs relative to the power of the committee to be transmitted to the chiefs and council of the subordinate settlements, to the Commander-in-chief of the army, and to the two presidencies of Madras and Bombay, that they might know what powers the committee were invested with. I then acquainted the Board, that the committee was determined to make use of the power invested in them, to its utmost extent; that the condition of the country, and the very being of the Company made such a step absolutely necessary. Mr. Leycester then seemed inclined to enter into a debate about the meaning and extent of those powers, but I cut him short, by informing the Board, that I would not suffer any one to enter into the least discussion about the meaning of those powers; but that the committee alone were absolutely determined to be the sole and only judges; but that they were at liberty to enter upon the face of the consultations any minutes they thought proper, but nothing more. Mr. Johnstone desired that some other paragraphs of the letter might be sent to the different subordinates, &c., as tending, I believe, in his opinion, to invalidate those orders. Upon which I asked him, whether he would dare to dispute our authority? Mr. Johnstone replied, that he never had the least intention of doing such a thing; upon which there was an appearance of very long and pale countenances, and not one of the council uttered another syllable. After despatching the current business, the Board broke up, and to-morrow we sit in committee, when, I make no doubt, of discovering such a scene as will be shocking to human nature. They have all received immense sums for this new appointment, and are so shameless, as to own it publicly. Hence we can account for the motive of paying so little respect to me and the committee; and, in short, every thing of benefit to themselves they have in this hasty manner concluded, leaving to the committee the getting the covenants signed, which they say, is of such consequence, that they cannot think of settling any thing final about them until Lord Clive's arrival.

"Alas! how is the English name sunk! I could not avoid paying the tribute of a few tears to the departed and lost fame of the British nation (irrecoverably so, I fear). However, I do declare, by that Great Being who is the searcher of all hearts, and to whom we must be accountable, if there must be an hereafter, that I am come out with a mind superior to all corruption, and that I am determined to destroy those great and growing evils, or perish in the attempt.

"I hope, when matters are a little settled, to set out for the army; bringing with me full power for you and me to settle every thing for the best."

His own situation and that of the country, at the period of his arrival, is forcibly depicted in a letter to Mr. Palk, Governor of Madras.[244]

"I wrote you a few lines last Saturday; since which matters do not go on so well as I could wish. Nasib Cawn, either through treachery or want of ammunition, has surrendered himself and army to the enemy; and Sir R. Fletcher, who was going to his assistance with one hundred Europeans, four battalions of sepoys, and four field-pieces, will find some difficulty to get back, as I understand the Rohillas, Mahrattas, and Sujah Dowla, intend to use their utmost efforts to prevent it. He has gained the banks of the Ganges, but I fear has no boats: however, as the General is marching to join him, I hope the enemy will not be able to make any impression before their junction, when I think there is not much to apprehend. Whether Sujah Dowla intends to try his fortune in another battle, or to harass and cut off our supplies, and detach into the Bahar province, we know not. However, we are providing against all accidents, by forming a second army from the reinforcements lately arrived, who are already upon their march for Patna, to cover that country or proceed further, as the situation of affairs may require. Thus circumstanced, you will see the necessity of reinforcing us upon all occasions when you can do it consistent with the safety of your own settlement.

"Mr. * * * * and all the council have been guilty of such barefaced corruption, that the committee have thought it absolutely necessary to make use of the power given them, in its utmost extent. You are addressed by this conveyance, and copy of the powers with which we are invested has been sent to you.

"At the first meeting, the gentlemen began to oppose and treat me in the manner they did Vansittart, by disputing our power, and the meaning of the paragraph in the Company's general letter. However, I cut that matter short, by telling them they should not be the judges of that power, nor would we allow them to enter into the least discussion about it; but that they might enter their dissents in writing, upon the face of the consultations. This brought matters to a conclusion, and spared us the necessity of making use of force, to put the Company's intentions into execution. We arrived on Tuesday, and effected this on Thursday. On Friday we held a committee; and on Monday was read before the council the following resolution from the committee book:—'Resolved, that it is the opinion of this committee, that the covenants be executed immediately by the rest of the council, and all the Company's servants.' After many idle and evasive arguments,

[244] 11th May, 1765.

and being given to understand they must either sign or be suspended the service, they executed the covenants upon the spot. From this you will see what I had the honour to inform you of, that I am determined upon an absolute reformation; but here we must act with caution, until a peace is established, which I do not despair of accomplishing during the rains.

"It gives me infinite concern to inform you that Mr. Spencer (of whom I had the highest opinion) is by no means the man of integrity or abilities that I took him to be; being deeper in the mire than the rest, and who appears to me to have been seduced and led astray by Johnstone and Leycester, having never had any will or opinion of his own, since he came to the chair. Indeed, the dignity of governor is sunk even beyond contempt itself; and the name of council only heard of in these parts. Would you believe that in his letters to the Nabob and others he has submitted to write, 'I and the council?'

"We are waiting the arrival of the Nabob and his ministry, to determine whether we shall suspend them the service, or represent matters in a general light leaving to the Directors to determine their state; though I am persuaded they will never wait such a decision, having all of them received large fortunes which they bare-facedly confess, for absolutely and precipitately concluding the late treaty with the young Nabob; not waiting for our approbation, or leaving it in our power to rectify the least tittle, without being guilty of a breach of faith.

"The large sums of money already received, and obligations given for the rest, on account of this treaty, are so very notorious through the whole town, and they themselves have taken such little pains to conceal them, that we cannot without forfeiting our honour and reputation possibly avoid a retrospection, as far back as the receipt of the covenants and Meer Jaffier's death. If we should call upon you hereafter for the assistance of Messrs. Broke, Russell, Kelsall, Floyer, and two or three more, we are persuaded your zeal for the service will not let you hesitate a moment about sending them by the first conveyance. However, you will keep the contents of this paragraph to yourself, till you hear from the committee or me upon the subject.

"I have employed Mr. Vansittart[245] as Persian interpreter, but cannot admit him to that share of confidence I wish to do, until those matters are ended entirely, out of a point of delicacy towards him."

Clive addressed a letter to Mr. Spencer at this period[246], which is singularly illustrative of that bold and open manner which led him to speak and write his

[245] Mr. George Vansittart, the brother of Henry, the late governor.

[246] 13th May, 1765.

sentiments with little if any of that reserve and discretion which are necessary to less vigorous minds to insure their unobstructed progress through life. Mr. Spencer was at this time still in Calcutta.

> "I have read over all the consultations from the death of the late Nabob, Jaffier Ali Cawn, to the 4th April, 1765, in which it does not appear to me that you and the gentlemen have given any solid reasons for thus precipitately concluding a solemn treaty with the present young Nabob. There could have been no danger in declining an absolute conclusion of the treaty, until our arrival, which you know was expected every day. I am most sensibly affected at the treatment I have received from you and the gentlemen touching my jaghire. The instructing your deputies to apply to the Nabob for a sunnud to confirm the agreement made by the Company and me was officious, and contrary to the instructions of the Court of Directors, who more than once, in their last letter of the 1st of June, say, this matter is to be conducted by Lord Clive in conjunction with the council. Such a proceeding carries with it a reflection upon my integrity, as if it was doubted whether I should make use of the power I was invested with to perform what I had so solemnly engaged to perform. However, before I leave India, I will endeavour to convince this part of the world upon what principles I act."

Clive was at this period most anxious to make peace with the native states; and among other reasons that led him to seek this object, one of the principal was, to establish subordination[247] in the army, and to correct abuses in the civil administration, neither of which it was easy to effect while war existed. One of his first steps had been to establish the supremacy of the committee, which consisted only of five members, over the council which had sixteen, including the chiefs of all the principal factories. The members of council could not be expected to suffer patiently the execution of measures, which not only reduced their influence and power, but threatened investigation into their past conduct, and destroyed their golden prospects for the future. A party was soon formed against Clive, the head of which was Mr. Leycester.[248] But one of the most able and energetic of Clive's opponents was Mr. John Johnstone, who had distinguished himself for his zeal and activity when employed with Colonel Forde at the capture of Masulipatam, and in various other services. Mr. Johnstone was, as has been stated, one of the members of the committee who had been the instruments of placing the young Nabob on the throne, and who had received presents which they were not disposed to return. On the contrary, they pleaded the example which others, and especially Clive himself, had given, and refused to admit that there was any just ground for considering conduct as criminal in them which had been approved in their predecessors, placed under circumstances which, according to their statement, were not essentially dissimilar.

[247] Vide letter to Mr. Sykes, 7th July.

[248] Vide letter to Mr. Palk, 14th July.

Clive[249], disregarding opposition, recorded his opinion that the treaty with the Nabob was formed with precipitation; and while he expressed in the most open and bold manner his opinion as to the motives which had influenced those by whom it had been concluded, he declared his determination to exercise his full powers to correct mal-administration, to enforce the signature, by the civil servants, of the covenant, as ordered by the Directors, which had hitherto been evaded[250]; and above all, to put a stop to the shameful abuses and wrongs which had arisen from Europeans in the civil service, and free merchants engaging in the inland trade.

He was quite aware of all the odium and hostility which the sudden and great reform he contemplated would bring upon him, both in India and England; but, from the whole tenor of his private letters of this date it is obvious, that the knowledge of this, so far from dispiriting, only encouraged him to the great efforts he made. The following is an extract of a letter to Mr. Sykes of the 29th June on the subject:—

> "I fear the military as well as civil are so far gone in luxury and debauchery, that it will require the utmost exertion of an united committee to save the Company from destruction. However, let us always appeal to the rectitude of our intentions, and we shall be enabled to complete the arduous undertaking with great satisfaction and honour to ourselves. Remember me to Verelst in the kindest manner; tell him the Company and myself have no other dependence, but upon the justness of his and your principles."

Lord Clive's anxiety to conclude a peace, made him determine, immediately after his arrival, to proceed to Patna. He had also several arrangements to effect at

[249] Vide letter to Mr. Spencer of the 13th May.

[250] The Court of Directors, by the Lapwing packet, which left England in June, 1764, sent positive orders, which reached Calcutta on the 24th January, 1765, that all persons in the Company's service should execute covenants, restraining them from accepting, directly or indirectly, from the Indian princes, any grant of lands, rents, or territorial dominion, or any present whatever, exceeding the value of four thousand rupees, without the consent of the Court of Directors. The letter further contained orders relating to private trade, and to batta to the troops. The council assembled next day, 25th January. It is remarkable that the subjects, both of the batta and of the private trade, are noticed in the consultation, but no allusion whatever is made to the matter of the covenants. At this crisis the old Nabob died; and Mr. Johnstone and Mr. Leycester were immediately empowered to negotiate with his son, the young Nabob, and accordingly did conclude a treaty, 6th February, as has been already mentioned. About twenty lacs of rupees were, on this occasion, promised, and the greater part of it received, as a present to the Governor and several members of council. (Verelst's Narrative, p. 51.; Third Report of Select Committee of House of Commons, p. 21.) As upwards of three months had elapsed at the time of Clive's arrival, and the Company's orders regarding the covenants had not yet been put in force, the Select Committee, immediately on meeting, issued an order for carrying them into instant effect. Clive, in his letters, expresses great indignation at the circumstances attending the treaty with the young prince; and it is impossible not to agree with him in thinking, that the delay in the signing of the covenants, and the subsequent presents from the young Nabob, reflect light on each other.

Moorshedabad[251], where affairs had fallen into great confusion. His intention was to proceed, after settling affairs in Bengal, to Bahar; and his colleagues in the committee delegated to him their power to conclude a settlement with Sujah Dowla and the Emperor of Delhi, with or without the aid of Brigadier General Carnac.[252] Lord Clive had, however, left Calcutta but a short time, before he was embarrassed by the wavering conduct of Mr. Sumner, the senior member of the committee. His Lordship had proposed, for strong and obvious reasons, that the members of council should be reduced from sixteen to twelve, and that the chiefs of subordinate factories should not be included. Their being in council, he argued, gave them an increased local influence and power, that was often abused; and the council were slow and reluctant to censure or punish the acts, however much they disapproved of them, of members of their own body. Another evil arose out of this system. Rise to council was in fact by seniority; for when nothing appeared on record against an individual, his claim to that station was almost invariably admitted. Mr. Sumner was adverse to any change of this system. Clive, though annoyed at his conduct, which he thought too compromising, endeavoured by every argument he could use, to reclaim him to that decided course which he conceived it the duty of the committee to pursue, and from which it was important they should not be diverted, either by the opinions or remonstrances of the council: Mr. Sykes continued firmly to support the Governor, but he was called away to his duties at the court of the Nabob at Moorshedabad; and Mr. Verelst had been before nominated to the station of supervisor of Burdwan and Midnapore.

Placed under these circumstances, Lord Clive made every effort to convince Mr. Sumner of the necessity of giving him a decided support against the opposition raised by the council.

"I hope," he observes on one occasion, "my last letter will have convinced you of the insignificancy of the struggles of the gentlemen of council, as well as of their power, when compared with that of the committee. If you will but convince yourself that they have laid themselves under such a censure that nothing can excuse them at home, and that the committee's upright and spirited conduct must gain the universal applause, you will treat them with that contempt which they deserve, by never suffering them to give a vote on any subject whatever, when once it has fallen under consideration of the committee.

"But to convince you what opinion even Mr. Sulivan and our enemies must have of our conduct, I refer you to the two enclosed letters of Mr. Palk, who is Mr. Sulivan's oracle. Besides, I have seen a letter of his to Mr. George Vansittart, wherein he speaks in the highest terms of what we are about, and the absolute necessity of a reformation.

"The behaviour of the council is so shameless, abandoned, and ungrateful, that I know not whether I shall not produce fresh accusations against them, in that the subordinate chiefs, down to the writers, have laid all the zemindars under contribution, of which I shall soon be in possession of the most authentic proofs."

In almost all Clive's letters written at this period he dwells upon the same sub-

[251] Vide letter to Mr. Sumner of the 26th June.

[252] Vide letter, Secret Committee, 21st June, 1765.

jects, expresses his opinion that the covenants should be executed, and depicts the extent and enormity of the prevailing abuses and corruption in the interior of the country, particularly by the natives, whom men with local influence and power have employed as agents. These have (as he states), by their exactions and tyranny, rendered the English name odious.

The sentiments he entertained of his council are fully given in a letter to Mr. Sykes, under date the 10th August.

> "The behaviour of the council has convinced me they are children and fools, as well as knaves, and I am not at all concerned, on the Company's account, that they have demeaned themselves in the manner you represent; for we may now, with great propriety, let the sentiments of humanity give way to justice. For my own part, I am determined, as one, to show them no more mercy; indeed it now becomes necessary, as well for our own vindication as for the advantage of the Company, to make an example of them, and represent them in their proper colours to the Court of Directors.
>
> "I wish you would get ready the Dinagepoor Rajah's evidence, as well as the evidence of others, concerning Mr. Gray's conduct at Malda, against we assemble at Calcutta; and also what other evidences of other gentlemen whose conduct deserves our censure. I can't help thinking Leycester has been guilty of other misdemeanours at Dacca, &c. Burdett I am sure has."

In a letter[253] from Lord Clive to the Directors, he has the following observations upon this subject:—"Upon my arrival, I am sorry to say, I found your affairs in a condition so nearly desperate, as would have alarmed any set of men whose sense of honour and duty to their employers had not been estranged by the too eager pursuit of their own immediate advantages. The sudden, and, among many, the unwarrantable acquisition of riches, had introduced luxury in every shape, and in its most pernicious excess. These two enormous evils went hand in hand together through the whole presidency, infecting almost every member of each department. Every inferior seemed to have grasped at wealth, that he might be enabled to assume that spirit of profusion which was now the only distinction between him and his superior. Thus all distinction ceased; and every rank became, in a manner, upon an equality. Nor was this the end of the mischief; for a contest of such a nature among our servants necessarily destroyed all proportion between their wants and the honest means of satisfying them. In a country where money is plenty, where fear is the principle of government, and where your arms are ever victorious, it is no wonder that the lust of riches should readily embrace the proffered means of its gratification, or that the instruments of your power should avail themselves of their authority, and proceed even to extortion, in those cases where simple corruption could not keep pace with their rapacity. Examples of this sort, set by superiors, could not fail of being followed, in a proportionable degree, by

[253] This letter is dated the 30th September, 1765. It is published in the Third Report of the Select Committee of the House of Commons, A. D. 1772.

inferiors. The evil was contagious, and spread among the civil and military, down to the writer, the ensign, and the free merchant."

In the answer from the Court of Directors to this letter[254] from Clive, they observe; "We have the strongest sense of the deplorable state to which our affairs were on the point of being reduced, from the corruption and rapacity of our servants, and the universal depravity of manners throughout the settlements. The general relaxation of all discipline and obedience, both military and civil, was hastily tending to a dissolution of all government. Our letter to the Select Committee expresses our sentiments of what has been obtained by way of donation; and to that we must add, that we think the vast fortunes acquired in the inland trade have been obtained by a scene of the most tyrannic and oppressive conduct that ever was known in any age or country."

In the letter of the same date as that of Lord Clive[255], from the Select Committee of Calcutta above referred to, they express themselves bound to lay open to the view of the Directors a series of transactions too notoriously known to be suppressed, and too deeply affecting their interest, the national character, and the existence of the Company in Bengal, to escape unnoticed and uncensured. "Transactions," they add, "which seem to demonstrate that every spring of this government was smeared with corruption, that principles of rapacity and oppression universally prevailed, and that every spark of sentiment and public spirit was lost and extinguished in the unbounded lust of unmerited wealth."

Lord Clive, in a letter to Mr. Sykes of the 20th August, informs him of the happy conclusion of his mission to Benares, and of his having obtained from the King the grant of the dewannee, or deed, for the administration of Bengal, Bahar, and Orissa; an arrangement to which he very justly attaches the greatest value, and which may be viewed as having crowned his efforts as a hero and a statesman, in fixing firm the foundation of the British empire in India.[256] It is difficult, at the present day, to appreciate that wisdom which appeared to attach a value to the form, almost beyond the substance, of power. It is impossible to satisfy those who judge such questions by philosophic rules, or others who apply a European standard to Indian policy, of the weight of the reasons which led Clive to give the consequence he did to an act, that may appear to them as being more likely to augment, than to lessen, the numerous obstacles which already opposed the good government of our Eastern territories. It is not easy to convince such persons of the degree in which he was enabled, by this grant, to reconcile to the rule of strangers the various communities which formed the vast population of India; nor can we compute the amount of strength which it took away from princes, who had long been enemies to those Europeans whom they deemed invaders and usurpers, but who were, from the moment the grant was made, in the eyes of a great proportion of their subjects, if not in their own, sanctioned in the exercise of the power they

[254] 17th May, 1766.

[255] 30th September, 1765.

[256] It may be mentioned, as a curious fact, that when the durbar for conferring the dewannee on the Company was held, the Emperor having none of the appurtenances of high condition or state along with him, an English dining table, covered over, made the throne on which he sat during the ceremony.

had attained, by the authority of one who, however fallen, was still considered the legitimate source of all rank and authority over that empire of which he was hardly more than the nominal head.

Philosophers may smile at such impressions, may despise those who act on such grounds; but as the bulk of human beings, in every country, are swayed by impressions and prejudices more than by reason, wise and great statesmen will continue to establish authority, and preserve peace, by adapting their measures to the habits and feeling of the community, instead of acting on theories which, taken in the abstract, have an appearance of wisdom, but reduced to practice, by running counter to the character and condition of the great mass of men, for whose benefit they are intended, produce bitter fruits from fair but deceitful blossoms.

Previous to the conclusion of the negotiations at Patna, Mr. Verelst[257], acting under the instructions of Lord Clive, had succeeded in obtaining the acquiescence of the Nabob of Moorshedabad and his ministers, to an engagement, by which it is stipulated, that 50 lacs of rupees should be assigned for his support[258], and that of his family, while the remaining revenue was allotted to the payment of restitutions, expenses of the army, and allowance to the King.

Lord Clive, in a letter which announced to the Court of Directors his having made peace, and obtained rights and privileges that gave them resources which, well managed, were more than competent to maintain the East India Company in that political power which a rapid succession of events had forced upon them, entered fully upon the subject of the future administration of their affairs, and, above all, the necessity of a complete reform in their civil and military establishments, which, in Bengal, he describes to be in the worst possible state, owing to many causes, but to none more than the rise of youth to wealth and high station, before they had either prudence or judgment; a rise inevitably succeeded by their falling into a state of indolence and luxury, that led to the increase of the evils it was his anxious object, and that of the Select Committee, to remedy.

The measures he adopted to enforce obedience to the orders of the Directors, regarding certain classes of their servants discontinuing trade, were accompanied by a distribution among the seniors, of a proportion of the profits of the salt monopoly, in shares accordant with their rank. These shares, though large, were considered as nothing by men who were enjoying the enormous profits that resulted from the privileges which their influence and authority gave them as merchants. This arrangement, consequently, caused great discontent among those whose interests it affected; which was increased by his removal of civil servants from many minor stations in the provinces, and ordering all free merchants, except those that were specifically licensed, to return to the presidency. An effectual check was also put, at this period, to that system of violence with which the native gomastahs, or agents of civil servants and free merchants, continued to enforce the passing their goods, not only without paying duties, but without dustucks or passes[259], which

[257] Vide letter from Mr. Verelst, 27th July, 1765.

[258] An addition of 386,131 was subsequently granted.

[259] Mr. Johnstone, who had resigned council, but who remained some time settling the commercial concerns with Mr. Bolts, complains of his salt being stopped; Lord Clive, in

were granted when it was deemed expedient or proper, on application. There is, in Clive's letter books, much correspondence upon this subject; the whole tenor of which proves, that the effort made by the committee to stop the inland trade, was one of the principal causes of that combination of civil servants, which rapidly increased in number and violence, when it was known, that Clive had requested that four of the senior and best qualified civil servants of Madras should be immediately sent to Bengal, in order to strengthen his administration of the latter presidency.

The conduct of Mr. Leycester, one of the council, who placed himself at the head of the discontented, forced the Select Committee to suspend him. Mr. Gray and Mr. Burdett, two other leaders, went home; and severe measures were taken with several juniors, who joined with their superiors in order to arrest reforms, which threatened to destroy those prospects of early and great wealth in which they so fondly indulged.

Clive heard, soon after his arrival, of Mr. Dudley being deputy-chairman; and we find a long private letter[260], written in 1765, to that gentleman. In this, after commenting with his usual freedom on the characters of persons connected with the conduct of Indian affairs, both at home and abroad, he particularly alludes to Mr. Sumner, his destined successor, who, however respectable, he was led to believe, from what he has seen and heard, would not be found to possess that energy and decision which were indispensable to carry into full effect the system which he had introduced.

He concludes this letter with some strong opinions, as to the measures that were necessary to insure the future welfare of Bengal:—

> "If the Directors will empower me alone, or me in conjunction with the present committee, to regulate matters, I can be responsible for the consequences after my departure; if not, I much fear, things will fall into the old channel, and to the advantages arising from salt will be added every other that can be obtained.
>
> "Remember the oath and penalty bond mentioned in my public letter.
>
> "If you could, by increasing the Governor's salary, or ordering his proportion of salt to be greater, insert in the oath, that the Governor should not be allowed the liberty of private trade, but attend only to the affairs of the Company, leaving trade to the second, &c., I think the plan of government would be much more perfect, as it would be less liable to abuses from the head.
>
> "With regard to the magnitude of our possessions, be not staggered. Assure yourself that the Company must either be what they are, or be annihilated. Hitherto, at least, one can see no alternative; for, in a moderate state, though the power might still be preserved, corruption and frequent revolutions, must in the end overset us. Never was there a time when affairs wore so strong an

reply, says he should have applied for a dustuck.

[260] Letter to Mr. Dudley, 29th September, 1765.

appearance of prosperity and stability as the present.

"Irruptions of the Mahrattas may now and then interrupt our trade, and impede the collection of our revenues; but I am persuaded that nothing can prove fatal but a renewal of licentiousness among your servants here, or intestine divisions among yourselves at home.

"I am sorry I cannot send the Directors, by this conveyance, a list of the revenues; but I am as much convinced as that I now exist, that when the revenues are all perfectly regulated, the Company will receive, clear of civil and military expenses, and without oppressing or overloading the inhabitants, a net income of 2,000,000*l.* sterling per annum.

"One arduous undertaking still remains behind; I mean, a thorough examination into all the civil and military offices. The difficulty is in the choice of men for a committee. We cannot easily find servants here endued with such strict principles of honour as to make them think it a duty they owe the Company to enter heartily into the scrutiny, and recommend such wholesome regulations as may in future prevent abuses.

"It is impossible for the Select Committee to go through the whole themselves, nor can they expect to see a thorough reformation take place, unless they are assisted with the zeal and assiduity of others. If the gentlemen of Madras whom I have recommended were here, I could be certain of having my plan soon completed. The Directors will, I am sure, be surprised when they see what a total inattention (to call it by no worse a name) there has been in the gentlemen of council, with regard to their employment, and what gross frauds have been committed by the natives acting under them.

"Still more will they be surprised, when they see the late military expenses, compared with the present; for there is now a system of economy, consistent with the true interest of the Company, and yet the allowances are not reduced below what they ought to be.

"Neither the general nor committee's letter is very full upon the subject of remittances. This year we shall probably draw upon you to the amount of treasure sent to China. There still remains 24 lacs of restitution money to be paid, 3 lacs of donation, 30 lacs of bonds and 10 or 12 lacs to be sent to Bombay; and if to this you add 20 lacs to be sent to China, the whole will amount to 87 or 89 lacs. Our treasury at present is low, as we have not yet received the benefit of our new grant; and large sums have been advanced for the investment, which will exceed 40 lacs this year.

"The trade of salt, betle, and tobacco is now become an object

> of the utmost importance, both to the Company and to individuals. If the profits should greatly exceed what they are stated at, as some are sanguine enough to imagine, you may be assured the Company shall receive the benefit; for, if the clear gain should exceed a certain sum, the indulgence will become too great. As matters are settled at present, the Company will receive one half of the advantages by allowing them a duty of 35 per cent. upon salt, which is the principal article. The proprietors pay 10 per cent. for the loan of money, and 5 per cent. may be allowed for the loss of boats and wastage."

The Court of Directors appear, from their general letters sent by Lord Clive, and those of subsequent date, to have been very anxious to put an end to the internal trade carried on by their servants and their native agents, which they considered as being alike oppressive to the inhabitants of the country, and injurious to the native governments. It constituted a great source of profit to individuals, but was, they stated, directly opposed to the interests of the Company, and from the mode in which it was carried on brought disgrace upon the English name. In the general letter of April 26th, 1765, the Court observes, with reference to the conduct of the civil servants who had charge of the government before the arrival of Lord Clive, and who pretended that their right to engage in the internal trade, and to have their goods passed free of duty, was founded on the Emperor's firman to the Company;—

> "Treaties of commerce are understood to be for the mutual benefit of the contracting parties. Is it then possible to suppose that the court of Delhi, by conferring the privilege of trading free of customs, could mean an inland trade in the commodities of their own country, at that period unpractised and unthought of by the English, to the detriment of their revenues and the ruin of their own merchants? We do not find such a construction was ever heard of, until our own servants first invented it, and afterwards supported it by violence. Neither could it be claimed by the subsequent treaties with Meer Jaffier, or Cossim Ali, which were never understood to give one additional privilege of trade beyond what the firman expressed. In short, the specious arguments used by those who pretended to set up a right to it convince us they did not want judgment, but virtue to withstand the temptation of suddenly amassing a great fortune, although acquired by means incompatible with the peace of the country, and their duty to the Company.
>
> "Equally blamable were they who, acknowledging they had no right to it, and sensible of the ill consequences resulting from assuming it, have, nevertheless, carried on this trade, and used the authority of the Company to obtain, by a treaty exacted by violence, a sanction for a trade to enrich themselves, without the least regard or advantage to the Company, whose forces they em-

ployed to protect them in it.

"Had this short question been put, which their duty ought first to have suggested, 'Is it for the interest of our employers?' they would not have hesitated one moment about it; but this criterion seems never once to have occurred.

"All barriers being thus broken down between the English and the country government, and every thing out of its proper channel, we are at a loss how to prescribe means to restore order from this confusion; and being deprived of that confidence which we hoped we might have placed in our servants, who appear to have been the actors in these strange scenes, we can only say, that we rely on the zeal and abilities of Lord Clive, and the gentlemen of the Select Committee, to remedy these evils. We hope they will restore our reputation among the country powers, and convince them of our abhorrence of oppression and rapaciousness."

In the general letter, under date the 19th February, 1766, recurring to the same subject, they write:—

"With respect to the treaty with Nudjum-ul-Dowla, it is proper here to insert, at length, the fifth article, which runs in these words:—'I do ratify and confirm to the English the privilege granted them by their firman, and several husbulhookums, of carrying on their trade, by means of their own dustucks, free from all duties, taxes, or impositions, in all parts of the country, except in the article of salt, on which the duty of two and a half per cent. is to be levied on the Rowana or Haughley market price.' This fifth article is totally repugnant to our own order, contained in our general letter, by the Kent and Lapwing, dated the 1st June, 1764; in which we not only expressed our abhorrence of an article in the treaty with Meer Jaffier, literally corresponding with the present fifth article, but in positive terms directed you, in concert with the Nabob, to form an equitable plan for carrying on the inland trade, and transmit the same to us, accompanied by such explanations and remarks as might enable us to give our sentiments and directions thereupon. We must remind you, too, that in our said general letter we expressly directed, that our orders, in our letter of the 8th February preceding, which were to put a final and effectual end to the inland trade in salt, betle-nut, and tobacco, and in all other articles produced and consumed in the country, should remain in force, until an equitable and satisfactory plan could be found and adopted. As, therefore, there is not the least latitude given you for concluding any treaty whatsoever respecting this inland trade, we must and do consider what you have done as an express breach and violation of our orders, and as a detrimental resolution to sacrifice the interest of the Company, and the peace of the country, to lucrative and selfish views.

"This unaccountable behaviour put an end to all confidence in those who made this treaty, and forces us to resolve on measures for the support of our authority, and the preservation of the Company. We do therefore pronounce, that every servant concerned in that trade stands guilty of a breach of his covenants with us and of our orders; and in consequence of this resolution, we positively direct, that if that treaty is now subsisting, you make a formal renunciation, by some solemn act to be entered on your records, of all right under the said treaty, or otherwise, to trade in salt, betle-nut, and tobacco; and that you transmit this renunciation of that part of the treaty, in form, to the Nabob, in the Persian language. Whatever government may be established, or whatever unforeseen occurrences may arise, it is our resolution to prohibit, and we do absolutely forbid, this trade of salt, betle-nut, and tobacco, and of all articles that are not for export and import, according to the spirit of the firman, which does not in the least give any latitude whatsoever for carrying on such an inland trade; and, moreover, we shall deem every European concerned therein, directly or indirectly, guilty of a breach of his covenants, and direct that he be forthwith sent to England, that we may proceed against him accordingly. And every native who shall avail himself of our protection to carry this trade on, without paying all the duties due to the government equally with the rest of the Nabob's subjects, shall forfeit that protection, and be banished the settlement; and we direct that these resolutions be signified publicly throughout the settlement."

These letters were meant to be in support of the measures Lord Clive was supposed to have adopted; but the opinions of the Court in regard to the salt trade differed essentially from those on which he had acted. This subject, however, will be noticed hereafter. In a subsequent letter, (May 17th, 1766,) after stating the earnest request they had made of Lord Clive to remain one more season in Bengal, and giving their sentiments on the importance of his services, they drew a strong and just contrast between the conduct of the Select Committee, of which he was president, and that of the Governor and Council, whose power it had superseded.

"The article in the treaty with Shuja Dowla, stipulating a trade duty-free, through his dominions, we direct to be confined solely to the Company's trade; and even in that sense of it, we mean only if his dominions produce any goods fit for the European markets, or if it can be made the means of extending our trade in the woollen manufactory, or any other European goods.

"We come now to consider the great and important affairs of the dewannee, on which we shall give our sentiments with every objection that occurs to us.

"When we consider that the barrier of the country government was entirely broken down, and every Englishman throughout the country armed with an authority that owned no superior, and exercising his power to the oppression of the helpless natives, who knew not whom to obey; at such a crisis, we cannot hesitate to approve your obtaining the dewannee for the Company.

"When we look back to the system that Lord Clive and the gentlemen of the Select Committee found established, it presents to us a subah disarmed, with a revenue of almost two millions sterling, (for so much seems to have been left, exclusive of our demands on him,) at the mercy of our servants, who had adopted an unheard-of ruinous principle, of an interest distinct from the Company. This principle showed itself in laying their hands upon every thing they did not deem the Company's property.

"In the province of Burdwan, the resident and his council took an annual stipend of near 80,000 rupees per annum from the Rajah, in addition to the Company's salary. This stands on the Burdwan accounts, and we fear was not the whole; for we apprehend it went further, and that they carried this pernicious principle even to the sharing with the Rajah of all he collected beyond the stipulated malguzary, or land revenue, overlooking the point of duty to the Company, to whom, properly, every thing belonged that was not necessary for the Rajah's support. It has been the principle, too, on which our servants have falsely endeavoured to gloss over the crime of their proceedings, on the accession of the present Subah; and we fear would have been soon extended to the grasping the greatest share of that part of the Nabob's revenues which was not allotted to the Company. In short, this principle was directly undermining the whole fabric; for whilst the Company were sinking under the burden of the war, our servants were enriching themselves from those very funds that ought to have supported the war. But to Lord Clive and our Select Committee we owe, that the Company are at last considered as principals in the advantages as well as dangers."

Clive had recommended, that the Governor of Bengal should have an adequate salary, and be restrained from trade. In one of his letters already quoted, he strongly urged that he should be vested with authority to take a resolution in cases of emergency entirely on himself. He subsequently not only pointed out the expediency of making Calcutta the chief seat of the government of India, but proposed, in any future arrangement, the nomination of a Governor-general, with the full powers he now enjoys. All these propositions have been adopted; but the most important were not carried into effect till thirty years of collision and confusion in the administration of the Indian Government, through the means of separate and independent presidencies, compelled the divided and jealous authorities in England to follow the wise counsel of one whose experience and foresight enabled him to predict the evils which must result from the weakness and distraction of their government abroad, and the necessity of forming one uniform system for the administration of our Indian territories, and placing them under one efficient general rule,—the individual at the head of which should be of a character that justified his being clothed with paramount power over the whole.

Such was the magnitude of the evils that now weighed down the government of Bengal. It was at this period of danger from external enemies aggravated by a system radically corrupt, and in the continuance of which the interests of almost the whole of the public servants, and of all the free traders, were involved, that Clive evinced all the energy of his extraordinary character. We trace that quality, however, more in his private than in his public letters; and some extracts from the former will exhibit, better than the most laboured detail, the nature of the obstacles he had to encounter, and the measures he took to surmount them, and to restore and fix, on a firmer foundation than ever, the interests of his country in India. He observes, in a letter to Mr. Palk, Governor of Madras, dated Calcutta, 4th May[261];—

> "I have little more to say than that I arrived here yesterday, and that all affairs, civil and military, are in a state of confusion beyond what I had even reason to expect. I can see no end to the troubles in these parts. Suja Dowla has been joined by the Rohillas and Mahrattas, and he is marching down with them to make another effort to recover his dominions, which, at present, are entirely in our possession. Their apprehension seems to be, that our principal object is to support the King, and establish him at Delhi; and if this is the case, we may expect all India will go to war with us. Such a continued scene of fighting as this seems to open, will not, however, suit with us; and, in a very short time, I believe I must march up to camp, in order to settle measures, if possible, upon a pacific plan. I beg you will send us as many small arms, as well as men, as your settlement can spare, out of the next and succeeding ships."[262] * * * * *

[261] 1765.

[262] At the time of Lord Clive's writing the letter quoted in the text, to Mr. Palk, the Governor of Madras, which was the day after his Lordship's arrival at Bengal, Suja Dowla was, as is mentioned in that letter, threatening to invade our provinces with a large army, joined by the Mahrattas and Rohillas. But he altered his tone very shortly after; since it appears, by a letter written by him to General Carnac, that he offered to make peace on any terms.

This letter, it appears from the public records mentioned in the Report of the Select Committee of 1772, was received by General Carnac on the 19th of May, 1765, and was probably written by Suja Dowla two days before; which allows for his having received intelligence of Lord Clive's arrival on the 3d of that month, and that it had the effect of his proposing to make peace with the English.

The letter is worth transcribing in this place. (3d Rep. of Select Comm. App. No. 84.)

Suja Dowla to General Carnac.

"It is known all over the world, that the illustrious chiefs of the English nation are constant and unchangeable in their friendship, which my heart is fully persuaded of. The late disturbances were contrary to my inclination; but it was so ordered by Providence. I now see things in a proper light, and have a strong desire to come to you; and am persuaded

In a letter to General Carnac, he describes the state of the Nabob of Moorshedabad and his ministers, and the recent events at that court, in the following terms[263]:—

> "I cannot yet write you particulars; however, matters seem drawing to a conclusion. The Nabob and Mahommed Reza Cawn are arrived. The Seets and Roydulub will be here to-morrow, and I am determined to give an impartial audience to all of them, who are ready enough to disclose every transaction, and will prove to demonstration, upon what grounds and principles the gentlemen have been actuated, thus precipitately to conclude a treaty before our arrival.
>
> "Although Nundcomar may not prove guilty of the crimes laid to his charge, yet, believe me, my dear General, he will do no honour, either to the Nabob or to the Company, in any great or eminent post, which he never was formed or designed for; and I can give you unanswerable reasons against his being the principal person about the Nabob, when I have the pleasure of seeing you. I am as fully averse to Reza Ali Cawn's remaining in the great post of Naib Subah. His being a Mussulman, acute, and clever, are reasons of themselves, if there were no others, against trusting that man with too much power; and yet the young man must have men about him capable of directing and governing him; for besides his youth, he is really very simple, and always receives his impressions from those who are last about him. It is really shocking to see what a set of miserable and mean wretches Nundcomar has placed about him, men that the other day were horsekeepers. I proposed that three or four of the principal families in Bengal shall assist him in his government; and make no doubt of obtain-

you will treat me in a manner befitting your own honour. You have shown great favours to others; when you become acquainted with me you will see with your own eyes, and be thoroughly sensible of my attachment, from which I will never depart while I have life. I am this day arrived at Belgram: please God, in a very short time I shall have the happiness of a meeting with you. As for other particulars, I refer you to Monyr-o-Dowla and Rajah Shitabroy."

(And with his own hand.)

"My Friend,—I regard not wealth nor the government of countries: your favour and friendship is all I desire. Please God, I will be with you very soon, when you will do for me what you think best."

The fame of Lord Clive having been so long established in India, it will not be thought extraordinary by those acquainted with that country, that the news of his return to it should have operated, as it did, so instantaneously with Suja Dowla, in the manner expressed in the above letter.

Lord Clive soon after concluded a treaty of peace with him, of which an account is given in the letter of the Select Committee at Calcutta, 30th September, 1765, in the same Report, App., No. 86.

[263] Calcutta, 20th May, 1765.

ing his own consent for adopting such a plan as may make him perfectly easy in his own mind, and do the English nation honour.

"I hope fifteen or twenty days will enable me to put affairs in such a channel, that the gentlemen may go on with the reformation during my absence; and upon my arrival we must heartily set about a peace: for the expense is now become so enormous, (no less than 10 lacs per mensem, civil and military,) that the Company must be inevitably undone, if the Mahrattas, or any other powers, should invade Bahar and Bengal; for it will then be impossible to raise money sufficient to continue the war. This is a very serious consideration with me, and will, I make no doubt, strike you in the same light."

Treating the same subject in a subsequent letter, Clive observes[264]:—

"Strange discoveries have been made, which prove your conjectures about revolutions to be true. The enclosed will give you an idea of what is intended. The more I see of the Nabob, the more I am convinced of his incapacity for business: whether it proceeds from want of natural abilities, or want of education, time will discover; certain it is, the most difficult task we have is to act in such a manner as not to put too great a restraint upon the Nabob's inclinations, and yet, at the same time, influence him to do what is for his own honour, and the good of the Company. There is no submitting to be dictated to by every plaguy fellow about him."

And again[265]:—

"There seems to me to have been a combination between the blacks and whites, to divide all the revenues of the Company between them, for the Nabob knows nothing about the matter. Large sums have been taken out of both treasuries, by Mahommed Reza Cawn at Muxadabad, and by Nundcomar at Calcutta. Every day convinces me, that so long as that man with his instruments continue about him we shall never have that influence which appears to me absolutely necessary, as well for his own reputation as to prevent the revenues being dissipated on a set of plaguy rascals."

The evidence which Clive about this time obtained from the officers of the Nabob, of the sums paid to the different public servants on the conclusion of the treaty, are stated in a letter to General Carnac[266], with some severe remarks on the conduct of those who, on that occasion, sacrificed the interest and honour of the public for venal objects. This subject would, in its details, lead us too far. Suffice it to say, that the strong measures which the discovery he made led him to adopt, particularly that of suspending several of the older civil officers from the service, added to the number of his enemies in a degree that made them more powerful

[264] General Carnac, 27th May, 1765.

[265] Ibid., 30th May, 1765.

[266] 8th June, 1765.

in England than in India, and was the chief cause of that parliamentary inquiry into his conduct which took place on his return to his native country. Meanwhile, however, the honest course of investigation which he pursued, though fatiguing and painful to his mind, and severe on his spirits, left him resolute and composed in his sense of duty. He had a great object in view, the salvation of an empire, through the repression of wrong, and the amendment of the public character and morals. "Let me but have health sufficient to go through with the reformation we intend," says he, in writing to his friend Carnac, "and I shall die with satisfaction and in peace." The same feeling, which seems at this period to have deeply penetrated his mind, he expresses to many of his friends.

Clive, it appears from several letters to other friends, had been, at this period, seriously hurt at the long, and, as he thought, the mysterious silence of General Carnac. He was at last relieved by a letter, which satisfactorily accounted for the apparent neglect of a friend for whom he cherished so sincere an esteem. The following extract from Clive's reply is singularly illustrative of his feelings, and of the principles on which he acted:—

> "The receipt of your letter[267], number eight, gave me as much pleasure as your long silence gave me real concern. Indeed, I had resolved to write no more, being convinced that, from some cause or other, the friendship which had so long subsisted between us was drawing towards a conclusion, since you had declined even giving me your sentiments upon a subject or subjects in which I conjectured we may have differed in opinion. But surely that could be no reason for not writing at all; neither ought a difference of opinion, where both are actuated by principles of honour and justice, in the least diminish that cordial affection which hitherto hath subsisted, and I trust will subsist to the day of our deaths.
>
> "I was not ignorant, when a general Court of Proprietors prevailed upon me to resume this government, what an odious as well as arduous task I had undertaken. Foreseeing, in a manner, every thing at the time which has since happened, I was determined, if possible, to answer the expectations of the Proprietors, who did me the honour to think me the only person who could, by my power and influence (and example, I hope,) put a stop to that universal corruption (some few instances excepted) which seems to have spread itself over all Bengal.
>
> "Although a reformation both in the civil and military department appears to me absolutely necessary, yet if there be any thing which can occasion you the least uneasiness, for God's sake let the whole weight fall upon my shoulders. I can go through every thing with pleasure, so long as I can, with truth, and without vanity, apply to myself these beautiful lines of Horace:—
>
> 'Justum et tenacem propositi virum,'" &c.

[267] Mootagyl, 8th July, 1765.

Clive, in the following letter to his friend Walsh, dated 30th September, 1765, gives full scope to his feelings, both as to public transactions, and those connected with them:—

"Our friendship and connection have been of so many years' standing, and I have always observed in you so much real warmth of heart and zeal for my interest and honour, that I think of these marks of your affection in this distant part of the globe with the greatest satisfaction.

"To you, and to you only, I shall communicate every transaction of consequence which has passed since our arrival, because I know you have judgment and discretion to make a proper use of them.

"It will be needless to expatiate on the very great things we have done for the Company, since the several papers which accompany this will make you a perfect master of the whole of our proceedings.

"I have referred many of my friends to you for information; but you will communicate to them what you think proper, Mr. Grenville excepted, to whom I have been very explicit, having inclosed him a copy of my letter to the Court of Directors, translation of the treaty of peace, and a map of Bengal, with some marginal explanations.

"You will therefore lay before him, without reserve, all papers of a public nature; such as relate to individuals, and are not made public, you may not think proper to reveal to any one. There is only one paper which I could not send you, viz. the letter from the Select Committee to the Court of Directors, being bound by oath not to make any of our proceedings public until laid before council, or communicated to the Court of Directors; neither of which being yet done, with respect to the committee's letter, is the reason I cannot send you a copy; but you will, undoubtedly, obtain a sight of it from Scrafton.

"Had I known Mr. Sumner as well as I do at present, I would never have consented to his being appointed my successor, let the consequences be what they would. I did, indeed, entertain hopes, that my example and instructions might furnish that gentleman with a plan of conduct and political knowledge, which would have enabled him to fill the chair with honour, and me to leave it with satisfaction to myself. But I am sorry to inform you, that I had been but a short time on board the Kent, before I discovered him to be a man no ways fit to be my successor. His ideas of government differ widely indeed from mine; add to this, his judgment is weak, timid, and unsound, and resolution he has none.

"Nor was my opinion of him changed on our arrival here; for

I was frequently mortified with instances of his conduct, which made me look forward with regret to the day on which he was to be intrusted with the government of Bengal.

"When affairs of the utmost consequence to the Company were transacting by me, at the distance of seven hundred miles from the presidency, Mr. Sumner, governor for the time being, would have yielded up some of the most material privileges of the committee to Mr. Leycester, Gray, and Burdett, the most factious among the counsellors; and, if I had not written to him very severely on the subject, and prevailed on Mr. Verelst to hasten down from Burdwan to remonstrate to him on the weakness of his conduct, I verily believe he would have joined with those gentlemen in endeavouring to abolish the power of the committee.

"Whether his behaviour arose merely from timidity of temper, or from a consideration that his actions formerly, in the Burdwan country, could not bear a scrutiny, if the resentment of those whom he had been obliged to join in condemning should prompt them to retaliate, I cannot say; but it is certain that his attention to those gentlemen, guilty as they had been of the most notorious acts of oppression, was mean and absurd. His conduct, upon the whole, convinces me, that had he been in council during the late transactions he would have stood next to Mr. Johnstone in the donation list, which I almost wish he had, since the Company and I should, by that means, have been freed from the apprehensions we now labour under, on account of his succeeding me in the government.

"Imagine not that I have exceeded the bounds of truth in this description. A due regard to my own honour, as well as to the advantage of the Company, obliges me to be thus plain; but it is not my intention to impress you with ideas so far to the disadvantage of Mr. Sumner, as that he may be set aside from the government. I think I cannot go such lengths without hurting my own reputation. I must make a point of his succeeding me according to his appointment; and I hope affairs will go on very well, as long as he has a good committee or council to watch him.

"If you can prevail upon the Court of Directors to empower me alone, or me in conjunction with the Select Committee, to regulate matters, I will be responsible for his good behavior: if not, I much fear things will fall into the old channel; and to the advantages arising from salt will be added every other that can be grasped at.

"Remember the oath and penalty bond mentioned in my public letter. If by increasing the Governor's salary, or ordering his proportion of salt to be greater, there was a particular oath for the Governor, whereby he should not be allowed the liberty of private trade at all, but obliged to attend to the affairs of the Company only, leaving trade to the second, &c., I think the plan of government would be much more perfect, as it would be less liable to abuses from the head.

"I have hinted to Dudley only my sentiments of Mr. Sumner, and he knows from me that I have explained myself to you. Consult, therefore, together about the matter; settle it, if possible, in such a manner that I may not be taxed with breach of promise to Mr. Sumner, and I may at the same time resign the government without apprehension for the consequences.

* * * * *

* * * * *

"It would be endless for me to send you the particulars of every act of extortion and corruption. I had prepared a great many, under the hands and seals of the several zemindars and phousdars, in order to make it impossible for such men to succeed in any of their future designs; but the total overthrow of Sulivan and his party makes such authentic proofs unnecessary, especially as we have sent home sufficient to convince every impartial Director of the general corruption and profligacy of their servants in Bengal.

"Among other papers, you will find a letter from the King to the Governor and Council, in favour of General Carnac. The 2 lacs of rupees he has given him is lodged in the public funds, until the pleasure of the Directors is known. I shall only say that Carnac has acted with such moderation and honour in the service of the Company, and with such good deference and attention towards his Majesty the Great Mogul, that the Directors must be the most ungrateful of men, if they do not, by the return of this ship, or the first conveyance, order him this money, with a due encomium upon his services, disinterestedness, and modesty. I am sure your interest will not be wanting to push this matter to the utmost, if it be possible that such an order from the Court should meet with the least resistance.

"I have determined to remain in this country until I receive an answer to our proceedings. No consideration on earth shall prevail upon me to stay beyond the month of December, 1766; and my friends may be assured, if no accident happens to me, of hearing of me from Europe in April or May, 1767. In the mean time I shall dedicate every day of my life to the service of the Company; a thorough reformation shall take place; every department, both civil and military, shall be examined, and regulated by a disinterested committee, upon oath; and the Directors will be surprised indeed at the extravagancy, inattention, and frauds of their servants, both civil and military, at the same time that they must be greatly pleased at the reduction of their exorbitant expenses.

"Can you believe me, that the civil and military charges at the time of my arrival, amounted to between 11 and 12 lacs per month?

"I have dropt all thoughts of what I mentioned to you from Rio Janeiro, concerning my jaghire, and am resolved to let it rest as it is.

"That you may assist with confidence the justice of my cause, I do declare, by that God who made me, it is my absolute determination to refuse every present of consequence, and that I will not return to England with one rupee more than what arises from my jaghire. My profits arising from salt shall be divided among those friends who have endangered their lives and constitutions in attending me; the congratulatory nuzzurs shall be set opposite to my extraordinary expenses, and, if aught remains, it shall go to Poplar or some other hospital."

Clive, the same day, wrote the following letter[268] to Mr. Grenville, with whom, throughout this period, he appears to have kept up a constant correspondence:—

"Give me leave to call to your remembrance some discourse we had together about the Company's affairs (in which the honour and interest of our nation was so much concerned), and to inform you, I have now the particular satisfaction of seeing the great object of my wishes nearly accomplished.

"The enclosed copy of my letter to the Court of Directors, and a map of Bengal, with some marginal explanations, will open to you a full view of the present great and flourishing condition of our East India Company, and show how near it was to destruction, from corruption, extortion, and luxury. If you have leisure and inclination to be further acquainted with our transactions, Mr. Walsh has orders from me to lay before you our proceedings. May what we are about, in times of distress and necessity, contribute towards lessening the debt of the nation. If you imagine the King can find amusement in perusing any of these papers, or some particular friends whom you can trust, I shall have no objection.

"I hope by this year's conveyance to send you a particular account of the revenues of these provinces, which, put under proper management, cannot fall far short of 4,000,000*l.* per annum.

"I return you many thanks for Mr. Strachey: I have found him in every respect deserving your good opinion; and I must not for-

[268] Dated Calcutta, 30th September, 1765.

get to express how thankful I am for the assistance you have given Mr. Nevil Maskelyne, to obtain the Regius professorship.

"My best wishes attend Mrs. Grenville and all your family."

Clive observes, in a letter to Lord Halifax, of the same date,—

"I will not attempt entering into a detail of affairs in this part of the world, especially as I have enabled Mr. Grenville to give your Lordship a very explicit account of the prosperous and flourishing condition of the East India Company: too prosperous, without they have better heads and hearts to manage such grand and extensive concerns than heretofore."

In the following letter[269] from Lord Clive to Sir Matthew Featherstonhaugh he states,—

"We have just concluded a very honourable and advantageous peace with Sujah-u-Dowlah. To convince him, as well as the Mogul empire, of our moderation, we have restored to him all his dominions, upon condition of paying to the Company 50 lacs of rupees, or 600,000*l.* (the half down, and security for the other half.) This he very readily consented to, and has exactly complied with his engagements; so that Bengal, by such a powerful alliance, will in all probability enjoy tranquillity and peace for some time.

"Was I to paint to you the anarchy and confusion which reigned in these rich provinces upon my arrival, you would be much surprised. Indeed, the Company's affairs were at their last gasp, not from our enemies, but from that universal licentiousness which had overrun the whole settlement of Calcutta. Extortion and corruption were practised openly and at noonday. The three kingdoms of Bengal, Bahar, and Orissa, whose revenues amount to 4,000,000*l.* sterling per annum, had been put up to sale, and the profits divided among the civil and military; the Company's interests have been most scandalously sacrificed; but on this subject let me refer you to Mr. Walsh, who will give you such proofs of the venality, corruption, and extortions of the Company's servants, as must give you great pain, from the consideration of the national honour being so much prostituted.

"We are making use of the power given the committee to check these great and growing evils, and have made great progress already. Our vigorous proceedings towards retrieving the national honour, and obtaining for the Company those great and glorious advantages, which they are so justly entitled to, will, I make no doubt, create us many enemies; however, conscious rectitude will enable us to go through our undertakings with pleasure. With regard to myself, I do declare, upon the word of a gentleman, and upon my honour, that, although history can scarce furnish an in-

[269] Dated Calcutta, 30th September, 1765.

stance of any subject who hath had such opportunities of acquiring an immense fortune, it is my determined resolution to return to my native country not one farthing richer than when I left it.

"The very great attention you have always paid to my interest, and the favourable opinion you have always entertained of my abilities and zeal for the Company, bind me to you by ties of the strongest gratitude.

"The Company, in consequence of a grant from the Great Mogul, and with the Nabob's approbation, are in possession of a clear revenue of 2,000,000*l.* sterling; and all our expenses, both civil and military, can never exceed the half of that sum in time of war, and in time of peace, not more than 600,000*l.* per annum: so that, at the worst of times, there will be a clear gain of 1,000,000*l.* sterling per annum to the Company. Neither are these revenues chimerical or precarious: the rents are regularly paid; and we have established such a force, that all the powers of Hindustan cannot deprive us of our possessions for many years. Let me refer you to Mr. Walsh for further particulars, who, I am persuaded, will explain these matters much to your satisfaction.

"Although I find I cannot, as formerly, struggle with the inclemency of this hot climate, yet I am determined to wait for an answer to our despatches by this ship: my duty to my family will not permit me to stay longer. I hope to kiss your hand in April or May, 1767.

"The Duke of Devonshire's death has given me inexpressible concern: the nation has lost a nobleman who was an honour to it, and we the best and sincerest of friends. I could with pleasure have attached myself to him for the remainder of my days."

The following letter[270] to his friend Scrafton exhibits a short view of the prosperous state of the finances, and closes with a postscript written on Clive's hearing of his friend's election to the office of Director:—

"You must not expect a long letter from me, because I know you will have many particulars from other friends, and because the public business will really not allow me time for that purpose.

"Revolution upon revolution, rapacity, extortion, and corruption, have at last reduced us to the necessity of doing the only thing which could be done, to save the whole fabric from being ruined. The King hath granted to the Company the dewannee of Bengal, Bahar, and Orissa, and expresses himself in this manner:—'In consideration of the great services rendered me by the English Company, and on the condition of their paying me the annual tribute of 26 lacs, and allowing sufficient for the support of the dignity of the Nizamut, whatever remains of the revenues

[270] Dated Calcutta, 25th September, 1765.

of Bengal, Bahar, and Orissa, I give to the English Company as a free gift, for ever and ever.'

"The Nabob's allowances are 53 lacs, which he signed and agreed to; so that there will remain little short of 200 lacs to the Company, clear of all expenses in collections. What think you of the stocks? We shall draw bills for about 16 lacs this year, and, in future, I believe, there will be an end to bills of exchange. Our investment this year will exceed 40 lacs, and we shall send 15 lacs to China. We have 24 lacs of restitution money to pay, and 30 lacs of bonds to discharge, or we should not have drawn at all, even this year.

"We have concluded a firm and lasting peace with Sujah-u-Dowlah, by giving him up all his country, for which he pays 50 lacs to the Company: 25 down, and security for the rest in twelve months. I have not leisure to entertain you with an account of our proceedings with regard to the gentlemen of council: the upshot is, as you have expressed yourself in one of your letters, 'There are not five men of principle in the whole settlement.' I believe this is the first instance of such a paper appearing upon record as we have sent home.

"There is an account in our committee and consultation proceedings, as large as a general return, with as many columns, specifying the sums of money received, and to be received, by whom, and to whom, and on whose houses drawn; in short, the Directors, when they first see these papers, will imagine it to be an account of increase of revenues. If you can get John Walsh into a humour of entertaining you upon these matters, he is qualified to do it better than any man in England. My time and paper grow short.

"I am, dear Scrafton,
"Yours, &c.
"Clive.

"May it please your Honour,

"I did not know at the time I wrote the above, that your Honour would have been one of my masters, as I might have saved myself the trouble of writing so much, or referring you to Walsh. Believe me, there is an absolute necessity of getting some of the Madras servants here, or we shall never bring about a reformation. The gentry here will do nothing with a good will.

"I am
"Your Honour's most obedient servant,
"Clive."

Clive, in answering a letter[271] from Mr. Fowke, a Director, observes,—

"I have received your letter of the 13th November, 1764, from the contents of which I can easily perceive our affairs in Leadenhall Street are not likely to be upon a solid foundation for some time: indeed, Rous, though a very honest man, is the most unfit of all men living to preside and govern a Court of Directors. I am now convinced, a man of lighter principles, with more abilities, and a certain degree of resolution, will manage both private and public concerns to more advantage than Mr. Rous. My only hopes are, that the next year's election will produce one or two men well versed in the politics of India, and then Mr. Sulivan may be entirely excluded.

"I am not at all surprised at your disappointment; nothing less could have been expected from such a divided and distracted Direction; nor should I be much surprised if something of a disagreeable nature, touching my powers, should find its way to India. If the Directors dare take such a step, woe be to them, for I am pursuing measures so manifestly to the nation's honour, and the Company's advantage, that envy and malice themselves will not dare to enter the lists against us.

"Was I to enter into a detail of all our transactions in these parts, volumes would not suffice. To Mr. Walsh, therefore, I refer you, who will be perfectly informed of the great and glorious things we have already done for this Company; too great, indeed, for such a Company. I shall only say, that such a scene of anarchy, confusion, bribery, corruption, and extortion was never seen or heard of in any country but Bengal; nor such and so many fortunes acquired in so unjust and rapacious a manner. The three provinces of Bengal, Bahar, and Orissa, producing a clear revenue of 3,000,000*l.* sterling, have been under the absolute management of the Company's servants, ever since Meer Jaffier's restoration to the subaship; and they have, both civil and military, exacted and levied contributions from every man of power and consequence, from the Nabob down to the lowest zemindar.

"The trade has been carried on by free merchants, acting as gomastahs to the Company's servants, who, under the sanction of their names, have committed actions which make the name of the English stink in the nostrils of a Gentoo or a Mussulman; and the Company's servants themselves have interfered with the revenues of the Nabob, turned out and put in the officers of the government at pleasure, and made every one pay for their preferment."

It may be questioned whether any of Clive's many and great achievements

[271] Dated 25th September, 1765.

called forth more of that active energy and calm firmness for which he was distinguished, than was evinced in effecting the reform of the civil service of Bengal. It created a host of enemies in India, several of whom were men of talent, and possessed both of wealth and reputation. These, when they returned to England, gave vent to their indignation against one whom they represented as an arbitrary tyrant, who, having made his own immense fortune in a rapid manner, now desired to obtain fame by depriving others of the same advantages. They found, among the Directors and the House of Commons, many who listened eagerly to their grievances, and to accusations against a man whose fame and fortune made him an object of envy and of calumny; and who, besides the numbers he had rendered his enemies, by detecting and exposing their nefarious conduct, had deeply offended others, of whose character and principles he had a better opinion, by his impatience at their weak or undecided conduct. Born, it may be said, to command, clear in his views of what was right, and devoted to the public service, he was not only uncompromising, but impatient of check or hinderance in the pursuit of objects he deemed essential for the good name or interests of his country. This impatience led him too often to evince indignation or contempt of those who opposed him, or whose minds could not keep pace with his own, but whose conduct and character merited more justice and consideration.

But we must close this chapter, the events detailed in which occurred within a twelvemonth of Clive's arrival in Bengal. The second year afforded him a still greater opportunity of displaying his wisdom and courage.

END OF THE SECOND VOLUME.

Printed by Libri Plureos GmbH in Hamburg,
Germany